BY TANK

D to VE Days

BY TANK

D to VE Days

Ken Tout

ROBERT HALE · LONDON

This edition is an edited and abridged version of Tank!, Tanks, Advance! *and*
To Hell with Tanks! *published in 1985, 1987 and 1992 respectively*

ISBN 978 0 7090 8148 7

Robert Hale Limited
Clerkenwell House
Clerkenwell Green
London EC1R 0HT

A catalogue record for this book is available from the British Library

2 4 6 8 10 9 7 5 3 1

Typeset in 10/13pt Sabon
Printed in Great Britain by
Biddles Limited, King's Lynn, Norfolk

To those who went with us on D-Day but did not return

Contents

1 Up from the Sea

6 JUNE 1944:

D-Day, or so the BBC said. We were tank crews. Spearhead troops. Elite in our own eyes. But General Montgomery hadn't bothered to inform *us*!

Allied troops were landing on the Normandy sands. It was clear that on those beaches there was not room for all the million of us who now queued for many miles back from the south coast ports. So I, in my fast, light Honey tank, and my regiment, 1st Northamptonshire Yeomanry, mainly in the towering 30-ton Sherman tanks, joined the queue. Waiting for our ship to come in.

13 JUNE 1944:

Still edging forward. In Southampton it is raining. Even on D + 7 people wave us on towards the Normandy shores. But the warmth of human emotion does little to banish the greyness. Grey streets, grey rain, grey skies, grey tanks, grey fatigued faces, grey denim overalls, grey guns.

Beyond the grey houses and grey warehouses, the grey sea is alive with grey ships. The ships wriggle and bobble and swerve and interlink, like grey mealworms in a fisherman's tin. At the end of our quay a cobbled ramp runs down to the sea. A huge American ship has now nuzzled into the quay. An iron ramp, which is the front of the ship, has been lowered to meet the cobbled ramp of the quay. A little grey spume froths and bubbles about the join.

'Driver, start up!' I say into my microphone. 'Advance!' Our tank crunches down the cobbles as driver Johnny Taylor unleashes his impatience. We gather speed. Johnny drives up the ship's ramp like a hill-climber at Shelsley Walsh. 'Yippee!' yells Gunner Wilf Mylan. Frantic American sailors leap for a quick exit route. We brake and settle into a vast iron cavern. Grey. More grey than the skies and the seas. Sullen, war grey.

15 JUNE 1944:

The entire front of the ship falls forward, outwards. From the huge auditorium in which we sit waiting in darkness, we see slowly revealed the great sunlit stage of the Normandy beach. A stretch of foaming surf, a slope of holiday sand, anonymous wreckage, a few shattered houses, an occasional puff of black smoke, and, away to our right, a low cliff which must be the hill above Arromanches. This is the first time that any of us has seen what poets term 'some foreign strand'.

All through my young life my hopes had simmered slowly up to this boiling, spilling delight of foreign adventure. The schooling, and training, and drilling, and stamping of steel-rimmed boots on bare parade-grounds, and slapping of rifle butts, and bruising of shoulders upon gun recoils, and waterproofing of tanks – all for this moment of truth. These beaches, the grimy sunshine, the gun-metal surf, the chill of imminent battle, the pageant of massing vehicles: Normandy!

We are the first tank to roll off the ship, but in front of us a single truck must disembark. An American sailor in black, glistening thigh-boots ambles down the ship's ramp. Walks cautiously into the sea. Anti-climax! The surge of tiny breakers hardly reaches his knees. He waves the lorry to descend. The three-tonner quickly gathers speed down the steep ramp, hits the water with an explosion of spray, runs on a few yards. And disappears!

We gape at the swirling waters where the three-tonner was. The American seaman still stands, up to only his shins in water which has swallowed a large truck. Two frightened faces appear in the water at his feet and start swimming for life. The American hauls them out and they too stand shin deep in the rippling waters. 'There's a deep crater,' thigh-boots yells to me. 'Tide is turning. No time to back the ship out and come in again. Have to try it. Carefully. It's your skin.'

Our engine is still running, throwing up blue fumes in the faces of the tanks and seamen behind and around us. I explain over the intercom to Johnny. 'Bloody hell!' he exclaims. 'We didn't waterproof for fifty feet of water. Can I get out and walk, mate?' And now Johnny, the fastest and most reckless of drivers, eases the gear and steering sticks with the tenderness of a surgeon assisting a complicated birth.

We begin to roll. Faster. Still faster. Too fast. Far too fast. 'Hold it, Johnny! Hold it! Right hand down! NOW! Hard!'

We hit the water crab-wise. Tilt and skid. Swinging right. Not quickly enough. Tilting over and swinging. Tilting more and swinging harder. The American seaman backs away frantically. Then we are heading right, away from the deep hole, driving through the surf for the beach. In front of us a chain of impatient marshals ('beach marshals, not field marshals,' I think frivolously) waving us on. 'Don't stop! Hurry! Keep moving! Get off the beach!' Their mouthed words are unheard but the intention is clear.

As we cross the little promenade of Le Hamel we see our lieutenant and our other two Shermans waiting on a patch of grass at the roadside. They had embarked on an earlier frugal Free Polish ship, as we afterwards learned when sharing our tins of chicken and golden peaches donated by our affluent American shipmates. We line up, my eager Honey leading, and follow the road which arrows straight from the beach towards Bayeux.

And romance and glory await us at the first bend. An old French farmer stands at a gateway, his arms full of roses. And his dark-haired daughter flings a rose to each vehicle as it passes by. She laughs and throws a rose. I laugh and catch the rose. Then a belching, battering gusher of stones, earth, metal, smoke, flame blows up out of the road in front, hovers like an evil genie over our heads, and comes showering down to fill turret, mouth, eyes, shirt, nostrils with foul-smelling particles of filth. In fact, the explosion, a large-calibre shell-burst, was some yards ahead of us but Johnny had been accelerating, taking us into the vortex of mess as it disintegrated. In a moment we rumble through into green fields.

'Hullo, Roger 4.' (We are all Rogers today, as dictated by the daily variations of call signs, the lieutenant using the call sign of *my* tank, the lower-ranking station.) 'Are you fit? Roger 4 over.'

'Hullo, Roger 4. Fit and heavier by one rose and a ton of rubbish. Over.'

'Hullo, Roger 4. Well, the padre did warn you that the French girls were rather explosive ...'

'Funny for some!' comments gunner Wilf within the private world of our I/C (intercom) circuit. 'He isn't chewing on minced cobblestones.'

16 JUNE 1944:

We roll downhill to a tiny river running through lush orchards. A water-tanker is piping water out of the stream. (They will dose the water with thick chlorine and the taste of it will sully our palates for months on end.)

On up the opposite bank to a church, a crossroads, an *estaminet*: Castillon. Down again to a wide field on the left. Woods on the right and in front. A narrow road leading half right through the woods. We turn into the field. And are at rest. The lieutenant calls a conference of everybody.

'This is where we are, lads,' he says, tapping the map, 'and this is where we will stay in reserve until the regiment calls us up. No room for everybody to fight at once. We are on the divide between the American and British armies. About a mile as the crow flies behind the lines. So we may get strafed. Dig in under your tanks. Remove all the waterproofing. Clean the guns. Two guards on the gate and a prowler guard. Keep alert at all times. The Germans are just over ...' – he looks across the woods and calculates carefully – '... there!'

Our defence preparations are simple. The four tanks are parked with their guns facing the four compass points. Under our four-man tank we then dig a deep T-shaped trench. There is room for two of us to sleep in the top of the T and two in the downstroke. Wilf verbalizes our thoughts: 'If they blow us to hell, this trench is just the right depth. All they need to do is fill it in.'

17 JUNE 1944:

Where is the army? Where are the fighting millions? We are not yet used to the strange vacuum which can occur on a thronged battlefield. We walk up the hill to the *estaminet*, a word much more evocative than 'caf'.

Before I can air my schoolboy French, Wilf triumphantly enunciates his entire French vocabulary, 'Van blong, MAD-m. Seal voo plate.' The stout Frenchwoman with babe in arms looks uncomprehending. She pours *vin blanc* anyway. We sit and stare at the French. The French sit and stare at us. A peasant says, '*Boche! Kaput!*' patting his elbow mysteriously but meaningfully. We reply, 'Yeah, *oui oui, Boche kaput.*' Only we know that the wily, tough *Boche* is nowhere near *kaput* yet, and we shall have to seek him out, through the woods, over the hills and far away.

We ramble back to our field within the hour allowed us by the lieutenant. The sentry at the gate shouts 'Halt! Who goes there?' Johnny shouts back, 'Use your bloody eyes.'

A little later, squatting on the grass and sucking our fingers after another helping of corned beef hash, we see a singular sight. It is as though, far across the vast field, a giant is beneath the ground throwing up scuttles full of coaldust. A noise slams at us, like the clatter of salesmen beating their empty tea-chests in Hereford market. That and nothing else. We sit. And stare. And think.

'Jerry shells!' yelps Johnny. 'Bugger me!'

'They nearly did,' growls Wilf. 'Another 300 yards!'

22 JUNE 1944:

We have been sitting here since the 16th. It is frustrating to play at picnics in a field in France whilst the 7th Armoured Division and the 50th Division tear themselves to pieces around Villers-Bocage and Tilly-sur-Seulles.

True, we have had some adventures. One day the clip-clop of a horse's hooves stirred the lazy interest of the guard at the gate. Down through the woods came a small dairy cart drawn by a horse. And in the dairy cart were two Germans in full uniform. They reined in in astonishment right under the guns (unmanned) of one of our Shermans. At that, our guard roused from *his* astonishment sufficiently to shout 'Halt! Who goes there?' The totally disorientated Germans raised their hands and called '*Kamerad*.' At which the still astounded guard, prompted only by years of training, called back, 'Advance, friend, and be recognized.'

Fortunately, at that moment the little lieutenant appeared, waving a revolver, and concluded that particular armistice, requisitioning the horse and cart to convey the Germans to higher authority. This did not encourage our faith in whatever British or American fortifications might be erected along that road through the woods.

Given permission now and again, we wandered in those woods and, failing to find rabbits or partridges, fired our pistols and my tommy-gun (donated by our American shipmates) at gateposts and fallen trees. Then we caught the full force of the smell which had been with us since landing. A putrid, sickly sweet smell, leaving a loathsome aftertaste on the palate, like the taint of a rotting orange. The smell of death. There were, in the woods, horizontal shapes which were not fallen tree trunks. We stalked closer but not too close. There were several Germans in uniform. Dead. Dead for some time by the smell. At the *estaminet* we asked about the bodies but suddenly they could not understand my French. One word muttered could have been '*Resistance*' and another '*merde*'.

For days it has rained as though the heavens have turned all their water cannons upon the rioting populace down earth. We heard that supplies had been held up as ships were unable to come in to the beaches. Battles postponed in the swamps. The rain drove us to cower under our great tarpaulin tank sheet which we had rigged as a low tent slung from the Honey's tracks.

So much for six days of the flashing spurs and blaring trumpets and fluttering pennants of cavalry tradition. One of our spare corporals has gone home with chicken pox. Notoriety indeed.

23 JUNE 1944:

A motor bike skids to a halt outside the field. The rider confers with the lieutenant. Salutes. Rides bumpily away. The lieutenant calls me.

'Load up. Mount up. Start up. You are wanted at HQ Squadron. Here is the map reference. As soon as you are ready, move out.'

Wilf observes over my shoulder, 'Can't go very far wrong on an eight-figure map reference. Piece of cake! Here, look! Through Balleroy and on to that patch of wood.' We mount up, the heroes of the hour.

Balleroy is a dead place, its main street wide and empty, leading up to the gates of the great chateau park. The rattle of our tracks echoes back from tiny shops and cottages. Then we are among country hedges again. Johnny presses the accelerator and we boom down the hill towards our eight-figure map reference. Down the hill, over a brook, round a corner, says the map.

A green figure leaps from a hedge, like Robin Hood accosting a travelling bishop, and waves us to stop. He is American, garbed in a camouflage smock with baggy trousers tucked into sagging gaiters. A latter-day Davy Crockett, brandishing a carbine. Johnny halts and I climb down the front of the tank. The American, face unshaven, scarred and aged by combat strain, looks me up and down with a grimace of surprise. 'Where are you-all headed at, son?' he asks in what must be a Southern or Western drawl, slow and intensely musical and not indigenous to front-line battle posts.

I place my map on the sloping tank front and point at my eight-figure reference. A neat red cross near a patch of wood. 'Our HQ Squadron,' I explain.

He looks into the distance and philosophizes, 'If'n you-all wanna git to thet cross, wanna 'ave yer guns ready to fight a few 'underd wild A-pachees disguised as German Panzer Grenadeeries.'

'But we're well behind the front line,' I argue.

Our front-line Socrates sighs. 'Son, this yer man talkin' at you's Abraham Lee-roy of the United States Army. And in this neck of the woods, Abraham Leroy *is* the front line.'

An American 'lootenant' clambers through the hedge. 'What's the trouble?' he asks in a deliberately casual voice. 'Can I see your map reference? ... Looks like you are right but your HQ is wrong. As Abraham here says, he is the front-line. Round that bend are the enemy. That wood where you're headed is probably filled with Tiger tanks.'

We study the map. I see the light. 'Change the last number but one and that puts HQ Squadron right there in that other wood.' Johnny reverses at my instructions (he has no rear vision). The young officer leaps back into the hedge. Abraham Leroy ambles back to his lodgement in the bushes. We clatter backwards into Balleroy and use the ducal park to turn round in.

The brigadier, 'Black Harry' Scott, needs my new, sleek, sweet-running Honey for his own use. He needs the driver, Johnny. He needs Wilf in the turret. He does not need me. A brigadier can command as efficiently as a temporary lance-corporal. Nobody waves me goodbye. Nobody apologizes for the wrong map reference. I head back to Castillon, 'unhorsed', in cavalry language, and no longer a 'lance Jack' as I have no tank to command.

26 JUNE 1944 (D + 20):

The post corporal called and brought us pulsating news. C Squadron is going into action. My squadron. Today. The post corporal had no details about time or location or plan of battle. We listen for echoes of that battle.

27 JUNE 1944:

The lieutenant tells us that we are to rendezvous with the squadron at Jerusalem crossroads. I resist the temptation to ask whether that is on the Calvary side of Jerusalem. It could be too flippant. Or it could be terribly relevant.

There is nothing sensational about the winding lane leading from Foliott to Jerusalem. There are a thousand orchards in my Herefordshire which are almost identical to this orchard in France. An old orchard where the trees are spaced by the vagaries of nature, gnarled, ancient, prolific trees. Not the sheared, regimented, crowded young trees of the modern orchard. This is a place for chickens to peck and pigs to chunter and horses to champ. What makes it different are the huge, turreted Sherman tanks standing between the trees. And the crowd of tired, ashen-faced men in oily overalls who work on the tanks or converse mechanically in the orchard or sit dejected on the grassy bank which runs along the edge of the trees.

Nobody pays attention to us at first, so we accost the first person we see, Michael Hunt, a driver in 4 Troop, and ask the inevitable question, 'What was it like, Mike, at La Taille?'

'Bloody awful,' blurts Mike. I am disappointed. I wanted to hear heroic words. I wanted to know that C Squadron had conquered. I wanted to shake hands with victors. 'We got clobbered. It's the *bocage*, you see. The fields are so small. You go through one great hedge into a field and within fifty yards you have to cross through another hedge even thicker. And the orchards. And farm buildings. Ideal places for Jerry tanks to hide. And hide they did. Waiting for us.'

'Did we lose any tanks? Did we knock any out?'

'Of course we lost some. Tanks popping up at fifty yards range. But we got some of them too. Harry Graham knocked out a Panther at fifty yards with his first shot.'

'Great! Good old Harry! Knocking out the Panthers.'

'Who cares? What's more important: Frank Hickson is dead ...' Oh no, not Frank, that big, hearty smiling fellow whom everybody liked. A corporal, commander of a Sherman. Never raised his voice to give an order. Gone! 'And Tommy Madelaine's had it ...' No, not Tommy. Tell us it's not true! Tommy, young, slim, upright, intelligent, popular. Gone! 'And George Valentine ...' The gods have been unkind to the squadron. George, Tommy, Frank. A trio to liven up an evening in a pub or in a dull NAAFI canteen. Gone! 'And three of Frank's crew. Brewed up. Didn't have a chance.' Gone! 'And Len Wright with a wound in his skull, and tanks going up on mines, and Jerry tanks with their great guns waiting behind the hedges ...'

Mike's story winds down like an old-fashioned gramophone needing winding. The squadron sergeant-major (SSM) comes looking for his reinforcements. SSM Sidney Turton, a dapper, humorous but sometimes supercilious little man. I sometimes crewed on his tank in England as a reserve.

'Right, lad. You're back in the big league. Glad to be home? Not nice malingering about in the reserve, you know. Here we are. Gunner on the troop corporal's tank. Corporal Snowdon just made up to commander. Look after yourself, lad.'

I report to Ken Snowdon, 'Snowie', who had the grisly experience of evacuating a very badly wounded commander yesterday. Tommy Tucker, a great character, will share the turret with me. He eats enormous amounts of food but is the thinnest man in the squadron. The front compartment of our Sherman is shared by the driver, Stan Hicken, who looks a mere schoolboy and is of a very sunny, easygoing disposition; and the co-driver, Rex Jackson, who wears glasses, chubbier than 'Hickie', a very quiet, thoughtful chap.

Looking at the four twenty-year-olds who will be my companions in battle and at rest, I am again impressed by the level of intelligence in most tank crews – as also, I suppose, in air crews – for the tank, in addition to being immense in dimensions, is a complex machine, and its battle equipment requires most delicate control.

I toss my bedding roll up onto the engine covers of my new home, one of the four Shermans of 3 Troop, C Squadron, 1st Northamptonshire Yeomanry. There is a troop leader (Lieutenant Bobby McColl), a troop sergeant (Chris Wilkins), a troop corporal (our tank), each commanding a five-man Sherman mounting the normal 75mm gun. Another sergeant (Jack Ginns) commands our fourth tank, which is the four-man Firefly, a Sherman with an immense seventeen-pounder gun. In England each tank was given a Northamptonshire name (Bobby McColl's being 'Helmdon' and ours 'Hellidon') but in action we shall be known by our wireless code, '3 Baker'.

The flaps covering the engine and forming the slightly sloping rear deck are on a level with my eyes. I have to clamber up there before I can continue my climb into the domed turret of this tallest of tanks. My gunner's seat is a cramped little niche on the right of the turret, hunched up between the great, shining gun breech and the rough, curving armoured steel wall.

As I stand by the turret I catch an overpowering dose of the battlefield stench as the breeze swings from west towards south. This testimony of decomposition has come to us faintly in the remote fields of Castillon but here at Jerusalem it is more potent and persistent. It is the familiar odour of open latrines spiced with lilies and rotting oranges. Sweet but abominably putrid. We have encountered it in destroyed gun-emplacements near the beaches and we have savoured it along the Norman lanes. But then it was from dead Germans, aliens from a field-grey culture. And from the swelling, sun-bloated carcases of cows and horses. Now the treacherous breeze blows from fields where our own mates still lie, dead hostages to the enemy guns behind them. And either the nose or the mind descries a hint of charred human flesh, from the tanks which burned out yesterday.

I seek the company of my living comrades, crouching around a primus stove.

Today those of the squadron who bore the brunt of yesterday's horrors have been sleeping for long periods. Some of them drowning in the deepest reaches of unconsciousness. Others half-waking and fighting yesterday's battles, suffering their comrades' wounds, all over again. A number bed down after eating supper. Some bring out the inevitable pack of cards. Others scribble on field postcards which have ready-printed messages such as 'I am in hospital' or 'I am coming on leave.'

A few of us amble down the gentle orchard slope to the road. There being no dens of vice locally to which we can gravitate, Tommy begs my ration of cigarettes and we go door-to-door bartering in the tiny hamlet. At one house we swop four English cigarettes for half a dozen eggs and a hunk of some dark sawdusty bread (we have only hard ration 'dog' biscuits). And next door we are invited in by an elderly Frenchman who has a bottle of wine to share with the liberators.

Yesterday our mates won back 500 yards of France. At the price of Frank, the other Tommy, George, so many: all dead. A blood price. Tonight the old Frenchman regaled us with the blood of the French vine. We are heroes to him.

30 JUNE 1944:

Remote flashes illumine our faces under the apple trees. Down in the valley, beyond our immediate darkness, the battle is like one of those long-exposure photographs taken of a busy road junction at night, with intricate patterns of headlights and sidelights and rearlights and neon signs and traffic signals, all frozen into a kind of tartan woven of coloured streaks and patches of light. The battle is like that, except that it is a flaming tartan pattern fed into a giant kaleidoscope and then run through a high-speed cine camera. The effect is of all the firework displays that ever happened, laid one over the other and interspersing, frantically changing, blooming and disappearing.

Up here it is fascinating, awe-inspiring, hypnotic. Down there scared infantrymen are clawing their way through the roots of the hedges. Machine-gunners and artillerymen and air bombers of both sides hurl flaming packages of pain and destruction over the heads of the chosen few who close up to the enemy in actual mortal combat. Us? We are pretending not to be fearful.

5 JULY 1944:

Almost a month gone by since D-Day. And what have we done? Except for La Taille, we have sat in counter-attack positions, fired at invisible enemies in shrouded woods. Called by higher authority, we have dashed off across one of the wide, dusty tank lanes now criss-crossing the Normandy countryside. We have arrived at a map reference. We have sat. Eaten. Slept. Been called away in another dash, to position ourselves, sit, wait, fire, eat, sleep.

'Don't worry, lads,' says Harry Graham, one of our wits and a La Taille hero, lying naked except for a pair of shorts, and sunbathing on the rear engine covers. 'We are menacing the enemy. We are scaring the balls off Rommel. We have got silly old Hitler guessing. We're winning the war, boys. Pass me the sun-tan oil.'

'Well, at least we can almost see Caen now,' Tommy Tucker comments. 'And we were supposed to have captured Caen on D-Day. Why is Caen so important? I reckon it's just like any other town: houses, railway station, churches and schools, butcher's shops and brothels. Why should Jerry get so excited over it? I bloody well wouldn't if I lived as far away as Berlin.'

'Ah,' intervenes one of the sergeants who, by dint of his three stripes, considers himself an expert in the Grand Strategy of War. 'A front line is like a door. There's the bit that is the hinge. And there's the bit by the knob that swings in when you push it. But if the swinging bit is locked and bolted then the best bet is to bash in the hinges. And Caen is the hinge. So Monty says.'

'Ignorant sods, these generals,' answers Tommy. 'Me, I'd go in by the window. At night!'

We are now at Fontaine-Henry, strung out along a hedge on a rising slope which rolls up behind us to a stretch of woods. In front, a wide panorama is closed off by the Lebisey Woods on the outskirts of Caen. We wait to advance on these pleasant slopes, their natural scents of clover and mint and dung faintly desecrated by the encroaching stench of battlefields.

It was only curiosity which induced us to explore the burned-out German tank near Creully. We did not expect to intrude on the privacy of the crew still seated inside, charred to the size of wizened monkeys and to the consistency of burned sausages. The roasting of human flesh and the combustion of ammunition and the defecation of a million voracious flies created an aura of such sense-assaulting horror that we recoiled. We retreated even before our minds could aspire to the pity and loathing which would, in any case, have sent us hurrying from the presence of those incinerated mummies.

Then there was our encounter with a dead German near that same place. We had smelled the presence of death. And we had found him sleeping undisturbed from some previous battle. Bobby McColl had ordered us to bury him where he lay. We were used to digging slit trenches for our own shelter and, in the soft Norman earth, it was no great toil to dig an enduring shelter for this alien in a strange uniform. We dug deep, not out of respect for the dead but because we must continue to eat and sleep nearby. With some reluctance, but hurried on by our own revulsion, we grabbed his limbs to swing him into the trench. The arm which I seized disintegrated under my fingers, and the clumsy body slumped to the grass again. We vomited into the handkerchiefs which we had tied over our noses. Then, taking our spades, we unceremoniously shovelled the decomposing pieces of human residuum into the deep pit.

7 JULY 1944:

Rumour has it that we are about to advance on Caen. The exhausted D-Day troops are requiring the infusion of fresh attacking blood which we represent. And Caen is still the sore thumb sticking in Montgomery's eye.

It is a surprise, however, when the bombers begin to arrive. At first just a distant droning, then a louder booming, a noise which should indicate great bombers right above our heads. But no planes are yet visible. The noise increases until the sound of planes reverberates inside our skulls, the very bones of our heads setting up fresh echoes to torment us, until we become scared that we are hearing ghost planes, the ghosts of all the dead planes since the war began, for the sky above our heads is clear of both planes and clouds.

At first in the distance a few specks above the horizon hardly justify the ferocity of noise. The specks accumulate and spread and advance and accelerate. The noise becomes, unbelievably, even greater. The planes come near enough to quantify as flights and squadrons and wings and groups and even higher massed formations. They are near enough to identify – the wide wings, the four engines, the smooth lines, the gun turrets, the RAF roundels, as Lancasters. They are overhead, high but linked to us by the noise which laps about us as an invisible ocean. We are counting them, losing count, scanning back through the formations to spot the tail of the armada. But they extend back to the farthest horizon as out of the far mists more and more specks appear in continuing squadrons. Dozens. Scores. Hundreds. Thousands (we think) of planes.

Down the slopes from Fontaine-Henry, behind the trees of Lebisey, in front of Caen, we now witness an extraordinary sight. It is as though someone in the sky were drawing up from earth a wide latticed curtain reaching almost into heaven. Or rather one of those curtains consisting of vertical strings of beads. But these beads are sparks of tracer and series of anti-aircraft shells merging into an impregnable blazing wall against which the air armada must dash itself to pieces in its hundreds and thousands.

The first Lancasters drone majestically over Caen, maintaining height and formation and speed. From leading planes soundless flares descend, like warning messages to the people beneath. We line the hedgerows and cheer. This is the real war, at last. Massed movement and united valour and overwhelming noise and ourselves lining the touchlines ready to assist. From the succeeding Lancasters we see, or imagine we see, clusters of tiny black bombs detaching and winging, rather than falling, diagonally towards the target area. We hear their first concussion and in a moment we feel the shock waves. We cheer again. 'Give'm hell, boys!'

The endless succession of heavy bombers rolls on. The anger of their bomb-flashes surges above the trees like a swelling, fiery sea. The impregnable curtain of anti-aircraft fire begins to waver, to droop in places, to thin, to descend, to splutter, to disappear. The anti-aircraft response has ended. The marker flares have merged into dense smoke. The distant concussions continue to pummel our faces like the punches of a lightweight boxer. And finally the inevitable smell, compounded of cordite and burning buildings and disembowelled streets and singeing flesh.

Later we bed down in a darkness painted over with a red scumble of flame from the inferno beyond Lebisey Woods. We can see the troop leaders' conference taking place behind the squadron leader's tank. Major David 'Hank' Bevan, as imperturbable as ever, sitting upright on a camp stool; the others leaning on the tank or squatting on the grass. After a while they break up and Bobby McColl comes back to our group of four tanks. Snowie and Troop Sergeant Wilkins move to meet him. They huddle around their maps and make careful marks on the perspex covers, lines and arrows and circles and code-names. Our corporal detaches from the group and ambles back to us as we sit in our blankets.

'Operation Charnwood. That means capture Caen. At last. We go in with the Shropshires, 3rd Division. Reveille not until 06.00 hours to move off 10.00 hours at the earliest. Leading wave will try to take those woods. It'll be the second wave, that's us, who actually liberate Caen.'

Tommy guffaws. 'That's it, then. All the other buggers in the British and Canadian armies have had a go. Now it's the NY that has to liberate Caen.'

Pulling up his blankets, Hickie says, 'Hope the Jerries have gone home before we get there.'

Our commander's face, as he stands looking down at us, is flushed the colour of damson wine in the reflection of the fires still burning through the night.

8 JULY 1944:

It is late morning before we trundle down the lanes and across the main Caen-to-coast road and on towards Lebisey Woods. Here I see for the first time a scene reminiscent of a Great War photograph of troops massing for a 'big push'. 'Big push' is not of this war's terminology. The Germans have implanted the word *blitz* on all vocabularies. The *blitzkrieg*: the 'lightning war'. But today's scene is more like the opening day of the Somme big push in 1916. A couple of thousand infantry, an entire brigade, assembled in open order across a wide parkland on the safe side of the woods – platoons and companies and battalions of men in khaki, all loaded with equipment for the advance. In open ranks they stand, waiting attentively.

Except for one man. A motor cyclist. He hangs sideways against a tall hedge as though crucified there. His motor cycle has been flung up even higher, into the top branches of the hedge, by some high explosive blast. Today's first sacrifice. If I could get out of my tank and touch him, his body would still be warm. But dead. Discarded. Evacuated by his spirit in search of safer realms. The searing blast wrenched the very life force out of his body but left no visible mark.

And the others leave him hanging there, with less compunction than a herd of deer abandoning a wounded stag and with less interest than the soldiers guarding the crucified Christ. In a more civilized setting, how different it would have been. The priest mumbling holy prayers, the women keening and sobbing, the children peeping scared through a crack in the door, an elder placing a sprig of evergreen in a jar of holy water between flickering candles. But here, their backs turned, the men stand about, laughing and smoking and cursing the delay. The officers study their maps one final time, checking anxiously on landmarks. The women and children, if they exist, hide in cellars.

Untouched by his puny sacrifice, we roll immensely on, my tiny periscope scanning distant views of marching companies and close-ups of bored, sullen light infantrymen. The motor cyclist totally forgotten, as though he had never existed. Maybe in some eternal Records Office they have inscribed his name. And, in a day or two, in a small terraced house in Shrewsbury or a farm cottage by Clun, a yellow telegraph envelope will drop softly onto the mat ...

'Operator, load 75 with AP [armour piercing shot]', snaps the commander's voice as we pass between woods, and the infantry open out into single files on either side.

At my feet are two buttons. If I now tread on the right-hand button, the 75mm gun will belch and bellow into flame, leaping back on its spring haunches inside the turret and flinging from its barrel at thousands of feet per second a spinning shot of iron, weighing 6 pounds or more, primed to rip through armour plate, exploding the armour plate as steel splinters into the interior of an enemy tank. If I tread on the other button, the Browning .300 machine-gun, linked up to the 75mm cannon, will chatter out a stream of tracer bullets from Tommy's side of the cannon. Tommy sits invisible on the other side of the guns, ready to reload and tap my leg as a signal to fire again.

We continue to advance, not so much the galloping glamour of yester-year yeomanry as a country tour aboard a steamroller. The woods fall behind us and we have a view over a wide valley to our left. A huge factory down there.

'Hullo, all stations, Yoke.' – that is Hank's voice speaking on the 'A' set frequency but audible on our internal I/C set. 'All stations Yoke. There are undesirable elements somewhere among those chimneys. See if you can knock them down. Range about two thousand yards. Open fire as you are ready. Stations Yoke, over.'

I nestle down into my seat, my left shoulder brushing the gun shield, my right shoulder scraping the hard turret wall, my forehead rammed into the rubber shield on the front wall, my eye to the telescope, my right hand subtly touching the twist grip which sends the turret hissing around to left or right, my left hand delicately raising the gun so that the hairlines meet the target chimney, my back aware that the commander's knees are pressing into it.

'Operator, reload with HE.' High-explosive shells now to wreak damage on bricks and mortar and possibly human bodies. 'Gunner, a shot or two. Get the range. Then in your own time.'

My own time. My own gun. My own decision. My own war.

I tread hard, firmly, once! The entire tank shudders. A winter's ration of blazing fire burns from the muzzle of the gun. A thunderstorm rolls back up the barrel, out of the automatically opening breech, and through the tiny cracks in the telescope and periscope mountings. A thunderstorm wrapped in black clouds of stinking, blinding smoke which, outside my telescope, for a moment blind me to the flight of my shot. Then, as smoke and flame clear, I identify my own tiny spark of tracer racing away from me, straight at the chimney, but dipping, dying away, falling into dead ground somewhere near the unseen river.

'Short! Up two hundred,' I hear.

I ignore the traverse grip and touch the elevating controls. Up 200 on the graded marks. Tommy slaps, I tread, the 75 crashes, the smoke clears, and out of the ground just down the slope a fountain of mess, laced with raging flame, flings a roaring challenge back at me. A dud, I think. My shell was a dud. But in the distance *my* shell is still speeding. It sparks low on the chimney. Other fountains of flame and noise leap at us, along the slope left and right of our own tank's tracks. Then I realise that it was no dud. It was a real live enemy shell, from Colombelles or thereabouts. The unholy gun music swells.

Ron West's tank on our left stops firing. Misfire? Ron's commander has ordered him to cease fire. Gunner Ron queries the command. 'I'm declaring peace!' declares the commander over the open wireless net. 'I don't believe in all this war and slaughter.' In a moment the medical half-track slides between our two tanks. The medical officer (MO) and the regimental sergeant-major (RSM) board the tank. The sergeant is whisked away to destinations unknown. Ron's head appears out of the turret assuming command of his tank. But the firing is dying down. The massive chimneys remain erect. The 75mm shells bounce off those reinforced layers of brickwork. A steady cloud of smoke, mobilizing the evanescent goblins of single shell smoke, begins to form over the factory.

'All stations, Yoke. Hold your fire. Watch for movement. Fire at your own discretion ...' We relax one twist on the ratchet of intensity.

It is rapidly becoming dark when the commander taps me on the shoulder. 'Come up, Ken, and keep watch. There is a commanders' conference. Call me if you need me.'

I nod and haul myself up from the gunner's seat and the comradely reek of human sweat and urine. I inhale the pure air, as I think, then recoil violently, for the air outside is more polluted than our hot, rank iron den inside. The wind is now blowing from Caen and bringing an overpowering version of the stench to which we think ourselves accustomed. After that tremendous bomber raid last night there must be thousands of bodies down in the outskirts of Caen, having lain unburied all through this hot July day.

In ten minutes or so Snowie is back. 'We're going into Caen,' he says, 'to probe through the ruins left by the bombing. Our tank will lead the way. The Canadians are still fighting their way in across the airfield from the west. Against the SS. So we are going in from the north. In the dark.'

8/9 JULY 1944:

We move off in the darkness, easing away from the protective grouping of the squadron. Somewhere in the distance westwards another battle is continuing. The flashes from that battle are our guiding light but a very fickle light at that. Like the light from a flickering coal fire seen whilst blinking one's eyes rapidly. An irritating view of the world in a succession of snapshots.

We recognize the outskirts of Caen not by the houses but by the ruins. At one moment we are running through grassy open slopes, the next moment the slopes have become uneven and mounded with rubble. Our progress changes into a series of thuds and crashes and tumbles as we climb over fallen houses and descend into interlinked craters. 'For what it's worth,' comes the commander's voice, 'we are now in Caen.'

The wireless clicks and the atmospherics die away as he switches to transmit on 'A' set. 'Hallo, Yoke 3 Baker. Code sign Ranter now. 3 Baker, over.' (Tonight our code signs for objectives are the names of John Peel's dogs. 'John Peel' is our regimental song.)

'Hullo, Yoke 3 Baker.' (Troop leader replying; the higher authority always using the lower station's call sign.) 'Am in sight of you. Off.'

As we have swung down the hill, the street gap between the houses has become rapidly more distorted by piled rubble until now it has disappeared. There is no more street. There are no more houses. There is no more Caen. Only a towering wilderness of indescribable ruins pervaded by the worst stench we have yet encountered. There is no escape from it. I tie a handkerchief over my nose, but the foul, almost tangible odour desecrates my sinuses. The weird flashing battle reflections turn this ruined world into a bogeyland fit for hobgoblins and fiends and ogres. Surely no German soldier would remain in this uncharted chaos. Yet a wonderful site for ambushes! Behind any mound may be a panzer grenadier waiting to pounce. The ruins have no form, no symmetry, no recognizable architectural traits to enable us to discern a foreign shape. The place may well be haunted not by hobgoblins but by human werewolves.

Now we are grinding up Everests of pounded rubble. And sliding and rocking down Wookey Holes of RAF excavation. I cling to my gun handles and jam my head firmly into the rubber pad in order to keep my eye close to the telescope of a gun whose sights I cannot distinguish in this light. The continual shocks jar my forehead, whiplash effect rips at my neck, my nostrils are soured but not anaesthetized by the reek of death, my eyes are alternately dazzled and blinded by the fluctuations of light, and my heart is squeezed by fear of what may be lurking out there. And an inner voice whispers through it all. 'You wanted the glory, boyo, and this is it. The first tank into Caen. Reeking, stinking Caen. Glory, Hallelujah, and tell it to your grandchildren, if you come out of this lot at all.'

I put my feelings into a message through the mike. 'Commander, I cannot see to aim the gun. Visibility is nil down here.'

'That's OK. It's just as bad up here. If we need to, just blast away regardless with the 75 and hope it scares them more than they scare us.'

'Whoa!' shouts driver Hickie. 'Hey up! Hold tight! Can't hold her!'

We have topped another peak of rubble, and before us lies a black void, blacker even than the momentary pauses of blackness that are the night. And, even with the tracks braked and halted, the Sherman is toppling and sliding down into what seems an underground cavern. Hickie plays the brakes and gears off against the slope and we crash down safely but with bone-shaking violence to the floor of the ultimate pit in a system of intertwined craters. This must have been the very epicentre of the earthquake unloaded by the RAF last night. There is silence for a moment. The engine has stalled. The only sound is Tommy singing faintly from 'The Grand Old Duke of York', the refrain:

> And when they were up, they were up;
> And when they were down they were …

'Oh, shut up, Tommy, you ass,' growls Snowie through the headphones.

'My view is absolutely blocked down here,' I report, 'but gun seems to be working OK – for what that's worth.' Hickie chimes in, 'It's dead stop ahead.' Rex adds 'Just a blank wall, like a blinking quarry.'

'For your information it's no better up here. Come up a minute, Ken, and keep watch. I'll see if I can find the Ulsters and Bobby.'

As the commander's feet, thighs and stomach – my own visible impression of him – ease up through the turret hatch, I follow him up, expecting to find a whole world outside. As he said, it's no better up here. The incessant repetition of thousand-pounder bombs falling over an area half the size of a football pitch has hollowed out a massive abyss with its own high and irregular parapet of rubble. I stand on the turret of the Sherman, my feet 9 feet above the ground, but the parapet of rubble is still higher than my eyes. I see no world.

Corporal Snowdon is a tall blob of black detaching himself from the side of the tank and intermittently flicking alight into a ruddy apparition as the Canadian guns continue to grumble not so far away. Another tall blob, too tall for Bobby McColl, materializes – almost certainly an Ulster officer. A smaller blob-apparition-blob is our own troop leader scrambling down through the glacis of mess behind us, like a mountaineer losing his footing on a steep scree in Bobby's own Highlands. The three indistinct figures consult and move slowly around our roofless dungeon. I watch the dim skyline between our premature grave and the less dark living world. No further figures, enemy or friendly, appear.

Our corporal blob attaches itself to the tank again and climbs up to the turret. 'No way forward. Bobby agrees. Ulsters say no use staying here. We came. We saw. We conquered. And a fat lot of use it was.'

Back down in the turret I clip my headphones over my beret in time to hear Bobby calling: 'Hullo, Yoke 3. Total, I repeat, total devastation here. No street visible. Craters bigger than biggest hornet. Our little friends agreed we do no good here. Propose we pull back. Yoke 3, over.'

Hank's voice, cool and fresh as at midday, responds immediately: 'Yoke 3. Permission granted. Come back to Ruby. Over.' 'Ruby' is our start point. (Tommy: 'I'll come back to Ruby any day.')

The Sherman engine roars into life. Hickie reverses. Fast! We run level for a moment. Then the Sherman tail lifts like a plane taking off backwards. Lifts until we feel we are falling forwards. Lifts and topples ... backwards! Crashes down onto what is comparatively solid earth. We scrunch around in the ruins of people's lives and homes and follow back the way we came.

We do not dig a trench. We throw our groundsheets down and collapse. At some time in the night a big German panzer grenadier in his coal-scuttle tin hat raises his head above a lip in the ground down the slope and sees me lying, rolled up in my blankets on the open grass. He raises himself slowly out of his trench and equally slowly and cautiously begins to crawl up the slope. I watch in horror. He is crawling directly towards me and I am lodged the farthest away from our tank. He comes nearer, crawling carefully, body pressed to the ground, no weapons in his hands. Huge hands. Staring eyes. Hate personified.

I try to move but have wound myself so tightly in my cocoon of blankets that I cannot even loosen my arms. I try to shout but my dry throat emits no sound. He is near. I can hear his breathing. I can smell his breath. I can feel the warmth of his nostrils on my face. He extends his hands to throttle me as I feverishly wriggle. 'Where are the prowler guards?'

His hands clutch my throat and begin to squeeze. Those huge hands. That rancid breath. Those hateful eyes. The steel fingers give a last squeeze. I kick and struggle and fight with the hands. And my pal, the prowler guard, holds on to my hands and says 'It's all right, mate. It's not Jerry. It's yer old mate Jim. Settle down. Get some kip. Soon be dawn.'

'No, mate. It's young Ken there … bin dreaming … bin down in Caen … bin doing a bit o' conquering, like …'

9 JULY 1944:

They let us sleep on this morning. Later still Hank came strolling along, nonchalant as ever, commiserating, 'Sorry it was impossible for you to get through last night. At least you can tell your grandchildren you were the first tank into Caen.' Tommy, never cowed by authority, replied, 'I haven't got any grandchildren, sir.' Hank smiled, 'Knowing you, Tucker, you'll probably have 500 one day.' We credit Hank with one winner on that remark.

12 JULY 1944:

Being located only a few miles from the sea, a truckload of 'other ranks', selected by lot, went down to the beach at Luc-sur-Mer, but bathing was inhibited by the presence of dangerous underwater obstacles.

14 JULY 1944:

We are parked in the idyllic grounds of the Chateau d'Audrieu. It is very much like a scout camp in the high summer sun. Maintenance done, Rex and I sit swinging our legs on the back of the tank with not a care in the world. At this moment a plane hops over the trees, dips towards us, comes racing at us emitting a ripping noise and, before we can even gasp or gulp, zooms away over the chateau roof. Gone!

'That was a Jerry!' I gurgle at last.

'And the beggar was firing at us,' says Rex. 'Don't nod your head too hard. It may fall off.' We dive off the tank, grab spades and begin to deepen our half-dug shelter trench. The plane does not return.

16 JULY 1944:

First light: our troop is lined up in a lonely stretch of a French lane, totally anonymous – no houses, no signposts, no animals, no people. And no outlook. Both sides of the lane are obscured by hedges higher than our tank. Hedges, for what we can see, wider and deeper than our tank. All about us the fury of an artillery barrage crashes and whistles and flashes. But none of it touches us. We are in a tiny, leafy asylum for psychotic youths who leave their ploughing and baking and clerking to go hunting men as though beasts of the jungle.

Corporal Snowdon passes on orders to Hickie: 'Start up. When I say, come right and go over the hedge. Slowly. There's a damn' high bank under that hedge ... Advance!'

The Sherman climbs up the bank. I get a view of the tree-tops above the hedge. We level off and stay perched on the bank. This is the evil moment when the Sherman shows its thinly plated bottom to any gunner or bazooka man sitting out in the field beyond. It is a naked, unprotected feeling. Hickie revs the engine a little, we begin to topple, a giant hand seems to rip the hedge aside, we crash down to earth, and are through.

We come looking for guns, for flame, for smoke, for the frantic sudden movement of mechanical monsters behind hedges. Or the solitary field-grey hero nursing a bazooka and challenging us to move our big gun more swiftly than his modest iron tube. But this is an empty field. A tiny field. Not big enough to kick a football in. Certainly not the space for cricket. A tiny grazing area defended by high ramparts of hedgerow. And nothing to see. Another tiny private world of our own. Conquered by us. And nobody the wiser.

Behind us the infantry (South Staffords) will be moving up and peeping through the horrendous hole we have just made in a farmer's hedge. Across the field we nuzzle into the next hedge and the gun prods through. 'Can you see yet, gunner?' The leaves fall away from the periscope and I can see. Germans! By the next hedge. But dead. Lying in a group face downwards as though thrown there by some mighty blast.

As we begin to cross this further field, Rex, down in front, calls, 'Those Jerries aren't dead!' I swing the guns, see the Germans, leaping to their feet, hands held high and empty; mouths expressing the desperate words, 'Kamerad! Kamerad!' and trembling into incontinence as my great gun almost grazes their faces in its onward swing. By dint of much waving and kameradly grinning, Snowie manages to persuade our petrified enemies to work their nether limbs back towards our Staffordshire cousins behind us.

Again we probe through a hedge. This time the opposite hedge is penetrated by a wide gateway. A German hops across the gate space like a scared rabbit. I am too astonished to react. Another German runs across the space, left to right. I douse the right-hand hedge with machine-gun bullets. A third German takes the leap. Again I press the floor button and tracer spits into the hedge on the right of the gate. I am waiting for the fourth German, with his basin-shaped helmet, his wide neat tunic, his sloppy, baggy trousers, his carbine in hand. As he sprints across the gate I fire into the hedge, his destination. He keeps running. I am totally perplexed.

'Gunner, there's obviously a trench behind that hedge! Or a deep ditch to give them cover. Operator, reload with HE. Gunner, three rounds of HE in your own time!'

Obvious! But not to me. Tommy slaps my leg, I tread hard. The flame at the gun and the flame at the hedge are almost simultaneous. The hedge is so near that the tempestuous concussion against the hedge rebounds and slams the turret whilst the gun is still recoiling from its own discharge. For a moment we have the sensation of a small ship hitting a big rock in stormy seas. A hurricane of noise, flame, smoke, sods, leaves, burning air, wraps us round. The gate space is twice the size it was. Tommy slaps. I tread. Another tornado. Slap. Tread. Blast. The hedge, what is left of it, begins to burn.

No more Germans leap the gap.

Until now my main fear has been the elephantine shape of a heavy German tank suddenly appearing downwind of us, its all-destroying 88mm gun pointing at us and its armour plate impervious to our 75mm shot. Now a new peril is evident. A single German infantryman may be crawling through the hedges alongside us, carrying the notorious *panzerfaust*, a simple, throwaway, anti-tank bomb-projector, looking something like an outsize bassoon, but one which, at 50 yards, can blow our turret to smithereens. The cosy little fields darken into a tight, ugly death-trap.

Beyond the gateway is a small black-and-white farm. A South Staffs captain stands with two or three soldiers and lights up a cigarette. He notices us watching him and deliberately gives us a thumbs up signal. Objective gained! Another 500 yards of France liberated. And Noyers village. (More than 100 enemy have surrendered: the largest surrender in Normandy yet.)

17 JULY 1944:

Instead of sitting behind a hedge we are arrayed in a long line in front of a hedge. At dawn we advanced along another lane and turned right into an endless field whose far side is bounded by the main Caen–Villers road. Nobody can use that road without being blasted away by our guns.

All in the afternoon, hot and drowsy, in the world of droning bees and shimmering squadrons of gnats, a black object, like the head of a seal in the water, scythes through the tops of the corn across our front. One rending howl, like a dog in pain, rushes past our left shoulders. A noise like a huge door slamming comes from across the main road.

'SP [self-propelled gun]!' shouts Snowie. 'Gunner, traverse left and fire. Fire! Fire!'

Another black object scythes the corn again, screaming, howling – instinctively I duck – to our right. They don't miss twice. That one did. He won't miss the third time. I drive the turret round harder. As my hairline sights meet smoke in the hedge, a new flame lashes up out of the greenery – but it is one of *our* shots landing. I tread button. Tracer shoots for the hedge. Other tracers arrow in. Hedge becomes a blazing beacon. Whatever was lodged there, crewed by suicidal idiots or inveterate heroes, has been blasted to Valhalla. Above the hedge there writhes a grotesque shape of smoke like a human being suffering *in extremis*.

'Hallo, all stations Queen.' (Queen is B Squadron.) 'Air reports of thirty repeat thirty Tigers heading this way at two thousand yards ...' Hank's voice now, 'All stations Fox, did you hear? Thirty Tigers ...'

And, a few days ago, one single Tiger knocked out twenty-five British tanks in less than twenty-five minutes, super-heavyweights against middleweights.

I duck abruptly as something screams. But this scream goes on and on. Over the enemy hedge, beyond the road, above the trees, a slim, winged shape comes hurtling earthwards. Fizzing flame shoots from its wings. The plane swoops upward and is chased by an immense cauldron of fire and smoke bubbling up from its target area.

'Rockets!' yells Tommy. 'Bloody hooray! Typhoons with rockets!'

A second Typhoon dives and scatters fire beneath it. A third, fourth, fifth. The boiling concussions sweep across our field like a veritable China Sea typhoon and rock our tank back on it springs. 'Pity the poor sods under that lot. Jerries or not!' gulps Rex.

Nothing ventures along the road. There are no roars from hidden Tigers.

19 JULY 1944:

Back from our field at nightfall to replenish and maintain, we switch the wireless to BBC wavelength. The armoured divisions have smashed out from Caen. The German line has broken. The way to Paris is open.

20 JULY 1944:

Major Hank Bevan has told Captain Bill Fox, who has told Lieutenant Bobby McColl, who has told Corporal Ken Snowdon, who has told us in strict confidence (Hitler might hear!), that the break-out from Caen has been another 'bloody balls-up' (undoubtedly Bill Fox's paraphrase of Hank's more technical description). The armoured divisions did *not* break out, the Germans did *not* break up; in fact *nothing* broke except an exaggerated press story. The Germans are still holed up, behind lines of 88mm guns, on some ridge called Bourguebus, still overlooking Caen and still able to annihilate anything that creeps on all those slopes. And our Second Regiment has lost God-knows-how-many men dead, dozens of tanks and a whole squadron disappeared.

So much for the trumpets and banners of military pomp. Some A and B Squadron lads are staying behind when we leave Noyers. The only flag they will get will be on their coffins when they are reburied after the war.

21 JULY 1944:

At Fontenay-le-Pesnel, a hard name for English tongues. Fontenay-le-Pisshole is a popular rendering. Tommy has even more vulgar versions. At night German bombers unloaded showers of propaganda leaflets, telling us how the traitor Churchill had hoodwinked us into fighting the good Nazis. Normally we would have laughed. Today we only growled.

26 JULY 1944:

Demouville, and notices saying 'Dust costs lives,' 'Dust brings shells'. Demouville, a flat plain of dust. A boot scraped in the ground caused a small hover of dust. Lorries crawled slowly along raising young cyclones of dust. A tank turning in its own length threw up a veritable cumulus of dust. Shells and 'Moaning Minnie' mortar bombs came crashing down. One of A Squadron's sergeants was killed and several crew wounded.

But the menace of the guns soon diminished in comparison with the Demouville mosquitoes. The breed took sadistic delight in sinking teeth into skin, veins, cheeks, ears, arms, ankles, out of sheer rabid animosity towards mankind. Someone suggested a wood fire to keep the mosquitoes at bay. That immediately brought a sustained stonk from those other predators in field grey. Within hours faces became unrecognizable and limbs began to swell with an affliction like an itching, bloating dropsy.

'Hullo,' says Hickie to Tommy. 'Who are you?'

'Bloody funny,' snarls Tommy. 'Your own face is like a football. Lie down and I'll kick a goal.'

'First time any part of Tommy as ever been fat,' laughs Rex.

'You look like you've got scarlet fever, mumps, smallpox and flaming shingles, all in one,' retorts Tommy.

All is not lost. The MO provides a repellent ointment. We smear ourselves and look as though we have bathed in motor grease. The mosquitoes settle on us in droves, armies, myriads.

'Jumping Jehosaphat,' groans Tommy. 'They're effing-well eating the ruddy stuff. It's mosquito bait. I can't stand it. I'm going to throw myself in front of a low-flying Moaning Minnie.'

28 JULY 1944:

Corporals McKenzie and Stanley manage to extract a few moments of grim humour from Demouville dust. They discover two German SS uniforms, dress up and come strutting past the camouflaged tanks lined across our front, giving the Nazi salute and bawling fantastic German like *'Donner und blitzen'* or *'Sie müssen mein Backside kissen.'* They climb onto the backs of several tanks, cause consternation and, they say, more than one instant surrender. Almost everybody enjoys the joke until the sergeant-major hears and reads the riot act. SSM Turton has reason to be harassed by the idea of mistaken identities. We have not yet heard what he knows.

We had heard on the wireless that one of our corporals out on the flank was astonished to see a Tiger tank making a charge at him from the German lines. He gave the order to fire. Reporting in, he revised his assessment to 'an unknown enemy SP'. The gunner hit the stranger first shot, but the SP kept coming. A second shot hit the SP before the bigger gun could fire back. The corporal wirelessed 'They must be fanatical heroes in that tank. They are still firing, even after being hit.' Then both vehicles went up in flames. The Sherman crew escaped but the corporal died in the last flurry of shots. The SP also was reduced to burning wreckage.

We had listened in horror. What the sergeant-major now knew was that the SP was in fact British. It was a new type of SP (M10) which none of us had ever seen before. It had got lost and was, or so its commander thought, colliding with the enemy when our corporal's well-hidden and disguised tank opened up. The two heroic Britishers thereupon fought their duel to the death. It is called 'friendly fire'!

4–6 AUGUST 1944:

For two days and nights they have been teaching us to march in columns of four – not on foot but in tanks. 'Flipping drill – in the front line,' comments Hickie, 'worse than being in the Guards.'

When they sent us advancing bunched up in fours, we thought of the marvellous target we would make for the German gunners. As the practice continued into night we began to worry about how we might defend ourselves in the dark. Our gun-sights are useless at night. But there were no answers to our questions. The entire regiment simply drilled up and down the gentle slopes near Gazelle (Tommy humming, 'The Grand Old Duke' again).

Now we have crossed the River Orne and gone into 'harbour' at a place called Cormelles, suburb of Caen. Above us are the infamous slopes of the Bourguebus Ridge (instantly christened 'Bugger's Bus Ridge' by Tommy). All this is the scene of slaughter of the armoured divisions a week or so ago. From here the slopes look unimpressive, just a gentle upward roll of the cornfields. But the contour lines tell us that everything that happens along those slopes will be visible to the enemy gunners at the top.

However, here outside Cormelles, there is a final dip in the slopes which gives cover from observation, and here the entire regiment is harboured, spread out across the grass at the city's edge like the vehicles of a circus before the grand marquee is raised. Quite what *our* circus is to be we have not yet been told, but it is to be performed in columns of four at night.

And a skirl of bagpipes tells us that our infantry colleagues will be from the 51st Highland Division, the Scots known in the last war as 'the Ladies from Hell'. Rex says glumly, 'Elite infantry equals bloody battles to come.'

2 Dark Omens

7 AUGUST 1944:

08.00 hours: Bank Holiday Monday, the traditional day of seaside and country picnics in Britain. Most of us still find a holiday element in this life, touring through quaint French villages, sleeping out in the verdant countryside and listening to the strange foreign sounds when the guns are silent. In those idle moments there is laughter and jollity, for many of us have only lately left school. Were it not for the war, some of us would still be in the sixth form or continuing at college, striving for nothing more arduous than a 1st XI cricket cap.

Today there is a session of breakfast hate from the enemy. Amid the sustained roar of our own guns, ebbing and flowing, there is a sudden crump-crump-crump sound. High, thick splashes of dirt leap up among the tanks of A Squadron a couple of hundred yards away. German shells! Lads in A Squadron dive for cover. We continue dressing, cooking, eating. There is a tin of bacon for breakfast, yielding a decent rasher each, fried in rancid French butter and accompanied by a French egg each. These have been obtained by bartering with local peasants, paying with ration chocolate. A thick, hard, issue 'dog biscuit' serves instead of bread. To drink we add boiling water, stinking with chlorination, to a few teaspoonsful of Compo tea, a mixture of tea leaves, powdered milk and grey sugar.

09.00 hours: Squadron leader David Bevan has been to see the brigadier with the colonel and has now called a brief meeting of troop leaders. We sit and watch the quiet group as Major Bevan chats to them. A few sentences only. Mr McColl turns away with the other lieutenants and heads back to us. Hickie hazards a bet. 'Short conference! Six to four on we don't do anything today.'

Bobby McColl stops by his own tank. He says a couple of sentences. His crew cheer, wave, jump down from the tank and start rushing furiously around. Tommy says quickly, 'I'll take you up on that bet, Stan. Five francs at six to four on, and I say we *do* make a move today.'

Bobby McColl is near enough to hear. He grins at Hickie, 'Well, how much did you lose on that bet, Hicken? We *do* move, but not until late evening. Full briefing this afternoon. Meantime fill up, check everything and be ready for action by 18.00 hours.'

There was no need for detailed commands from Ken Snowdon at this point. We all knew our functions on the tank and set about them with minimal comment. Our 34-ton Sherman M4 tank is a huge and complicated machine: 27 feet 7 inches long – as long as the house I used to live in; 8 feet 9 inches wide – as wide as the street I used to live in; and 9 feet high – as high as I was when leaning out of my bedroom window at home. The Sherman is equipped with a 500-bhp engine, big enough to power a small plane up into the sky. It carries a 75mm gun so heavy that all five of us together cannot lift its barrel. There are also two Browning .300 machine-guns, a four-channel wireless set and large stocks of ammunition of various types and sizes.

Snowie and Rex climb onto the flat back of the Sherman behind the domed turret and help Stan to lift the large armoured flaps covering the engine. Then, whilst driver Stan peers down into the huge engine compartment and begins checking oil and fluid levels, commander and co-driver vault down to the grass and start examining tracks and driving wheels. Tank tracks have a peculiar habit of spooling up anything which is lying loose on the ground. On one occasion we spooled up a mile of telephone wire from the side of the road before anyone noticed.

For me the 75 gun is a good friend but a hard master. It needs endless cleaning, servicing, checking, pampering. To clean the barrel there is a stiff brush with an extremely long handle, like those used by old-time chimney-sweeps to clean narrow chimneys. Two of us together can summon up enough strength to force the tight-fitting brush up the seemingly endless barrel. Rifle grooves inside the barrel cause the brush to spin, making it difficult to control. But once the barrel has been thoroughly scoured and polished from without, the breech can be tackled from within.

A voice calls 'Are you coming today, Stan? Scobbie has butchered a cow and there's steak for everybody.' Scobbie is a butcher in civilian life. Now he drives a tank in 2 Troop while a former Post Office van-driver cuts up the meat in the squadron cookhouse. Here in the field there is no cookhouse and every tank cooks its own food, Stan being our best cook.

Stan shouts back, 'I hope the cow was dead before he butchered it. I don't want Scobbie's bad butchering spoiling my cooking, like the last time he provided steak.'

'You need to hope the cow *wasn't* dead,' chimes in Rex. 'Any dead cow around here is likely to have been lying around for a week or two.' The fields of Normandy, green and fertile, have been tragic with dead and dying cattle and horses, caught in the cross-fire of battle. A familiar sight is a dead cow, lying on its back with all four legs pointing rigidly towards the sky like a battery of anti-aircraft guns. Frequently the cow is bloated to twice its normal size. Sometimes only the skin is left where the scavengers have been busy. Sometimes only the white skeleton.

'I hate this stupid war when I see dead cows,' says countryman Rex. 'I hate it even more when I see half-dead cows.'

12 midday: As Tommy and I haul ourselves up out of the turret, we suddenly have the feeling of a huge aeroplane crashing on top of us. There is a noise of indescribable violence, a lashing of eye-searing flame, a breath of angry, incinerating heat. At this moment every British gun has started firing. It seems that the entire Royal Artillery has lined up 20 yards behind our tank. The main barrage has commenced.

At our backs huge flames leap from the muzzle of every gun, increasing the summer midday heat to baking point. I have been working bare-chested in the sweating turret. Now I hastily pull my overall top around me to shut out the burning heat. Overhead each departing shell seems deadly close and sluggardly, like an aeroplane taking off with insufficient power, screaming and whining as it tears into its patch of sky. After some seconds the initial ferocity of thunder upon thunder slackens sufficiently for a shouting voice to be heard. Tommy, as usual, shouts loudest and soonest.

'Don't stand up too straight on the turret in this lot, lads. If there's one dud shell, we've had it, stuck here. Why in God's name do they always put us right in front of the guns and not behind them? Hey though, stick our steak on forks and stand a bit nearer that crowd and the steak'll be grilled in no time.'

'So will you,' I shout, ducking back into the comparative quiet of the turret and pumping my eardrums with my middle fingers. My last task is to check the gun sights. Crawling under the gun and into the loader's perch, I exert all my 11-stone 10-pound force on the breech lever and swing open the breech block. I can now peer up the brilliant, silver-blue steel barrel to the bright cobalt-blue sky beyond. Oh, yes, August Holiday Monday at home today! I crawl back under the open gun, stretch up, hook fingers over the turret hatch and haul myself onto the flat dome of the turret; then slide down the steep front of the turret, down the lesser angle of the front of the driving compartment, onto the ground.

I pull two hairs from the abundant growth on my head. The muzzle end of the big gun has tiny slits in cross shape and, with a little grease, I fix the hairs to form a cross at the end of the orifice. Back up the steep tank front, in through the turret hatch, down and under the gun. Wedged in the loader's seat, I look up the barrel again and see the cross hairs outlined against the sky. Under the gun again and squirm into the even tighter gunner's seat. Jam my eyes against the telescope fixed to the gun. Fine lines on the telescope indicate exactly where the gun is, or should be pointing. Now all I have to do is check that the hair cross seen through the gun barrel is also dead on the same spot. If not I adjust the telescope sight to correspond to the actual aim of the gun as indicated by my two surrendered hairs, freely given up for king and country.

'If you do that often enough, you'll end up bald, not to mention blind from doing the other thing too often,' says Tommy. 'Jobs done, I bags first wash!'

14.00 hours: 'Let's go for the rations,' Ken Snowdon calls to Stan and me. A ration truck has dumped some boxes in the middle of our troop of four tanks. Someone has opened the boxes and spread the contents out like a grocery store on the grass. Typically the army is not able to supply rations for the normal five-man tank crew, nor the four-tank troop. The army appears to cater only for seven men who eat six rashers of bacon between them every two days, or who in the same time consume seven and three-quarters hard biscuits each. So representatives of the four crews sit on the grass and barter for the odd ends which are not divisible by four.

As we carry the rations to our tank, spurts of dirt and smoke shoot up between the parked tanks a hundred yards away. Troopers over there dive and hug the ground. We continue our stroll, ducking slightly and instinctively, hurrying the pace just a little, watching each other's reactions, all waiting for one to dive. Nobody dives so nobody dives. Panic and un-panic are very similar in their causes, if not in their effects. The enemy violence stays far enough away. Except for one piece of shrapnel, a freak piece of jagged steel which buzzes frantically like a toy aeroplane or like a wasp's attacking signal magnified a thousand times. The buzzing traces wild, skewing patterns across the field, over our heads, and finally fizzles out 50 yards beyond. Somewhere someone calls 'Stretcher!'

An elderly corporal, prematurely bald, comes round the back of the tank, approaches our operator, Tommy, slips a piece of paper into his hand and says, 'Netting at four o'clock.'

'Watch that,' crows Hickie. 'There might be a copper about. Passing betting slips is against the law of the land, Corporal Bolton.' Tommy opens the slip of paper and reads the row of numbers on it. At four o'clock he will switch on his wireless set, tune to the frequency indicated on the slip of paper and dial in to a fine tuning on a test signal sent by Corporal Bolton for the whole squadron.

16.00 hours: Tommy is in the turret at his task of netting the wireless on two optional frequencies. Little Bobby McColl happens by. He is not wearing his beret and we do not leap up and salute him. The four tanks of 3 Troop are a tight family unit and Bobby has been somewhere in the vicinity all day, so we take no notice of him unless he requires our attention.

'Stand up there! Stand still! What d'you think you're doing, bloody well sitting down when an h'officer is talking to you?' The gruff roar of RSM Jelley's voice sends us jumping to our feet. We turn round to face the wrath to come. And meet only loud laughter. RSM Jelley's voice was the work of Harry Graham, the star impersonator of our squadron concert party. I should have spotted the impersonation. The give-away is simple. The imitation RSM throws in the occasional 'bloody'. The real RSM never swears at a trooper. He was a young soldier himself in the Great War and treats this war's youngsters with respect.

'All right! Take it easy, lads,' Graham continues in the RSM's voice. 'There's a very important person coming to see you-u-u-u!' The VIP turns out to be an official war photographer who has chosen to photograph our tank because the angle is good for covering the panorama of a hundred vehicles parked along the slope. He speaks to Ken Snowdon, obviously discussing a good pose for a photo.

'What about cleaning the gun barrel!' I suggest.

We get out the barrel brush and screw it on to its long, jointed handle. Tommy and I push the brush into the barrel, strike a heroic pose and wait to be photographed for posterity. 'I think it would look better with more men pushing the brush,' comments the photographer, squinting through his view-finder.

'Two of us is all it needs,' states Tommy, but the photographer retorts 'I am talking about what the photo needs. The handle looks bare with only two people holding it in front of a huge tank.'

'Come on, you'se guys,' bawls Harry Graham, still in George Jelley's voice but using his own Scouse twang, 'You heard what the man with the camera has said. Get on parade to scrub out gun barrels. Left, right, left, right, left!' and he leads a rush of lads from other tanks all anxious to get into the picture, straining at the brush handle like a tug-of-war team.

'That's great! That's great!' cries the photographer, clicking away. 'That's the spirit that wins the war. Push!' Then he hands out cigarettes.

We were photographed also at Noyers. Later a photo appeared in a daily paper. White patches had been painted over our silver horse badges on our black berets. Presumably some German spy in England might send a report 'Soldiers wearing a silver horse badge are reported to be on the Western Front.' By devious routes via Lisbon, Vichy and Berlin, couriers might speed to report to Hitler's bunker. Adolf himself would stroke his moustache and say *'Hoch, hoch, mein Gott!'* Allied strategy might be imperilled. Thrones might fall. So the censor in Britain draws white patches over our badges. Yet any German soldier at the top of this slope, using his Zeiss binoculars, could spot our badge on the beret of each commander looking out of his turret, for we never remove our badges. And the Black Watch with their red hackles on their bonnets, are even easier to identify. Who was the censor fooling? Certainly not Rommel or von Rundstedt!

17.00 hours: For an hour the little clique of officers has squatted close together in a clearing amid the vehicles. David Bevan on a camp stool. The rest on the grass. Now they are standing up. They salute. Hank Bevan taps his cap with his riding crop. The lieutenants move back to their troops. Ken Snowdon picks up his map case and, whistling under his breath, goes to meet the troop leader, who has our destiny marked in red and green lines on the perspex map cover under his arm.

17.30 hours: Ken Snowdon strolls slowly back towards us, studying his notes. Now we can stop surmising. Now we must each write down the vital details of our task. Crew members must be ready to interchange if casualties occur.

'We go in at 22.45 hours, just after dark.'

In his precise schoolteacher voice, Ken teaches us the lessons we must learn. Successive daylight attacks up these slopes have failed, with horrible casualty lists to show for their efforts. Now we go up the slopes in the dark. We have to cross four miles of open country dominated by the German 88s, possibly one of the strongest defensive screens known in warfare. But we shall drive right through their front line and end up at dawn sitting in their rear. They will wake up (having slept through all the noise) and will panic when they find an entire army behind them. Simple!

Our objective is St-Aignan-de-Cramesnil at the top of the hill. The Germans have fortified the small villages between here and St-Aignan but we do not stay to attack them. We keep on rolling whatever happens. On our right will be another, similar column with 144 RAC, keeping close to the Falaise road. On their right, beyond the road, two more columns of Canadians. On our left, nobody. Behind us, nobody.

German infantry are in position in the villages but it is thought that an

SS panzer division may be moving across the rear. (God! The SS and the Gestapo, the mainstay of Hitler's power and terror. The SS, hand-picked, fanatical, physically superb cream of the Nazi army, conforming to no normal code of military behaviour, hated by the ordinary German soldier. Cruel, arrogant, unbridled, lethal, professional killers.)

Note down the various code-names: start line ... Another military mystery: when the Germans see us coming through Bourguebus and hear us on the wireless claiming conquest of 'Dragon', they will learn that 'Dragon' is none other than Bourguebus, whereas if we refer to Bourguebus by name, they will know that we really are where they can see us to be! Someone is playing at war games again.

'Let's synchronize watches! It's precisely 17.55 and coming up to 30 seconds ... now!' I stand and look out over the tanks and the slopes of corn and the factories of Cormelles. It all looks so ordinary. The crowds of men gathered about their tanks on the greensward could be farmers gathered to inspect farm machinery at the Three Counties Show on the race course at Hereford. The sky is not ominous with the colours of blood; there are no clouds shaping themselves into prophetic formations; no skylark soars suddenly as a symbol of hope. So I stand looking at the dull, stationary machines and the indolent men in drab overalls, and I poke around in the mind for a great thought before battle. And sense only an occasional icy prickle tingling up the spine.

Yet shall I remember for ever more that, at this moment, a group of lads from other tanks rambles towards us? Ray Ager mysteriously mouths the information that secret equipment has been installed on his tank, commanded by Captain Tom Boardman, so that it can be radio controlled like an aeroplane. We do not know whether to believe him.

There's also Corporal Jimmy Stanley, who sports a Hitler moustache and parts his hair Hitler fashion, his own tiny gesture of derision towards the great dictator. Trooper 'Sonny' Wellbelove is a little lad, younger than me, and in khaki uniform he looks like a boy scout. Trooper 173 Judge, on the other hand, is reputed to be the ugliest bloke in the regiment. Yet it was he who wooed the gorgeous country girl who serves in the canteen on Salisbury Plain. They are now engaged to be married.

'Do you think the Germans will really stay asleep with all this lot chugging around the countryside in the dark?' asks Sonny. 'And in low, gear,' adds Stanley.

'Trooper Judge will turn his gorgon stare on the Jerries and freeze them in their slit trenches,' comments Stan.

Trooper Judge, whose Christian name appears to be non-existent and who responds only to '173 Judge', enquires 'What the hell are gorgons?'

'They're a Highland regiment, you twirp,' blurts out Tommy in all inno-
cence. Gusts of laughter wash around the uncomprehending faces of Tommy
and 173 Judge. Then flames, lightning, blizzards of fire, skull-shattering
noise, earth, stones, smoke, Devil's laughter! By a freak of coincidence the
German and British artillery open up at the same instant and a huge shell,
apparently one of our own duds, erupts among our squadron lines. We stop
laughing, dive, grovel in dirt. Sackcloth and ashes in the face of fate! Scores
of shells howl overhead, travelling in both directions.

'Silly bleeding sods!' shouts Corporal Stanley at the distant artillery, his
fright slowly changing to humour. 'Pull the effing cork out before you fire
next time. You *schwein*, I vill 'af you for *mein* frankfurter meat next time
you vill at your *Fuehrer schutten*.' And he waggles his little Hitler moustache at the distant dots of artillerymen.

Bobby McColl approaches. He is wearing his beret. We stand up and
commander Ken gives him a salute. 'Business this time, lads. For real.
Orders are simple. Keep rolling. Keep moving. Keep in sight of the tail light
of the tank in front. And if ye get lost and end up in a village, ye will be in
the wrong place. All the villages have been fortified by the Hun. Any questions?'

Rex responds first. 'If we lose Corporal Snowdon, sir, how do we know
which way to go in the darkness, especially if we lose the tank in front, too?'

'Good question, Jackson. There will be Bofors guns firing green tracer
overhead, aiming at the objective. Keep beneath the Bofors tracer. If ye're
going uphill, ye're going in the general direction. Go right rather than left.
We are the far left-hand column and the RAF will be making a big raid on
the woods nearby, where there are thought to be German tanks hiding'.

He turns as another procession heads our way. The slim, immaculate 6-
foot figure of David Bevan. And the ambling squadron second-in-command,
Bill Fox, ex-jockey, cowboy, cavalry trooper, son of a baronet, and looking
like a country farmer going to a gymkhana. The staid colonel, Doug Forster,
once a midshipman, now commanding a land squadron, physically resembling a very large teddy bear but a fierce rider to hounds. Burly RSM George
Jelley, 1916 boy soldier and most vocal of soccer referees. SSM Sid Turton,
perky as a sparrow, neat as a blackbird, wounding as a hawk.

'Gather round, 3 Troop,' the SSM shouts. 'Wakey! Wakey! Pick the
whites out of your eyes, but put them back later. Jerry's going to need them
to shoot at.'

The colonel fumbles in his mouth for the words of his little speech. It is
an open secret that he doesn't like sending mere lads out to die. 'The
Germans are now almost surrounded. We are being asked to slam the door
on their retreat. When we advance tonight I shall be just in front of you.

Keep closed up. Keep moving. We are due at code-name "fly by night" at 03.00 hours. Nobody really expects us to do it. But I shall be there waiting for you.' He taps his cap badge, surrounded by a silver oval and set on a bright blue background. 'Our little silver horse does not look very savage. But he can gallop across country. Good luck! Carry on, please.'

The officers drift away over the grass, chatting unhurriedly and tapping their rears with their riding crops in some kind of atavistic throw-back to the days when they would have ridden horses down the slopes to inspect us before battle.

The SSM pauses and looks us up and down, then stares fixedly at our assorted footwear. 'Stone a bleeding crow! What a shower! Roll on the day when we can get back to proper soldiering. Shining brasses, polished boots, mess tins used for seeing your faces in, not for eating bleeding porridge out of ...' He gives an exaggerated shudder. Then follows the colonel, grinning broadly.

19.00 hours: We strike camp. Roll our bedding bundles inside ground-sheets, tie them tightly, lash them to the flat rear deck. Put spare kit in storage bins. It looks like a hot night, so we opt to travel in our one-piece denim overalls with only a pair of pants or shorts underneath. In theory we should wear battledress, thick, suffocating, under the denims. Stan and Rex wear PT pumps, giving good purchase on the armour plate but quite illegal. Tommy is in regulation boots. I wear a strong pair of brown shoes from Stead & Simpson. Snowie has a pair of jaunty black civilian leather boots. (Sergeant Randy Ginns in our Firefly dons a liberated pair of German jack-boots.) We are all in our black berets as the special tanker's basin-shaped steel helmet is unwieldy inside the tank. We are ready, dressed for action – not quite like the Buckingham Palace Guards, and yet not complete ruffians. And hoping that Jerry is putting on his pyjamas or nightshirt at the top of the hill. At 19.30 hours he must feel it is a little late for an attack today. And today is still a Bank Holiday.

20.00 hours: Time for our Last Supper. We eat slices of bully beef on thick 'dog biscuits'. (The Americans came ashore with bakeries and white bread.) We feel snared in a net of indecision, knowing that zero hour is remorse-lessly approaching and wanting to delay it, yet, because it must eventually come, wanting to hurry the time along and get moving. While we eat and wait, we muse on the higher strategic implications of these very slopes. Rex begins it: 'They say that hundreds of our 2nd line [the 2nd Northamptonshire Yeomanry] "got theirs", trying to get up this hill.'

Stan continues: 'It's logical, isn't it? If there are rows and rows of 88s lining the ridge, the best gun that's ever been invented, what vehicle could get up there in daylight? Certainly not flaming Shermans, nor infantry carriers.'

'Flaming Shermans is an appropriate term,' I say to myself.

'So what? We're the BLA, ain't we? The ferking British Liberation Army,' comments Tommy, looking round to see if there is anything else to eat.

Behind the frivolity and the 'micky-taking' and the 'shooting the line' there is a real awareness that enemy launch sites are sending V2 rockets over London from just up the coast. Our advance means quietness and safety for Stepney, Camden and Camberwell Green. Meanwhile we scrape the last globules from the corned beef tins.

A great cheer sounds from the next tank. The SSM and squadron quartermaster-sergeant (SQMS) appear round the back of the tank, carrying a stone jar. 'Come on. Look lively. Rum ration up. Get lubricated,' chirps the SSM. We empty the horrid chlorinated tea from our battered tin mugs. I don't drink but my mates enjoy the extra quarter-tot each from my mug.

'Go on,' laughs Stan. 'Have a sip. Jesus won't see.'

'No thanks. They say the SQMS thins it down with battery acid.'

21.00 hours: I look at my watch for the hundredth time this evening. With an entrenching tool I have dug a small hole and thrown into it two corned beef tins, a biscuit packet and some other bits of rubbish, keeping a landscape clean which is littered for miles around with putrefying bodies and scrap iron in every shape and size. This is one of the niceties of discipline that our squadron insists on. We fold our mess tins one into the other and put them into our small packs. We grab projecting pieces of the tank and haul ourselves up to the deck. Tommy and I pull ourselves up another stage onto the turret top. For a moment we stand there, tall, high above the ground, watching the busy panorama. Glancing southwards up the ridge through the cornfields the way that we must go.

Saying farewell to the sky.

Then Tommy first, I following, we drop through the turret hatch into our tight little den and wait for Snowie to follow us in, stopping up our only escape. We have suddenly become subterranean. Death beetles inside a steel wall. Mobile troglodytes. The commander's boots, legs, stomach appear over our heads. Jam the exit. Douse the daylight.

21.15 hours: 'Driver, start up!' I reach for my headset, two earphones joined by a thin, curved piece of metal which fits down over my black beret. From now on we shall be able to talk to each other only through the microphones and earphones. Behind my head the huge engine kicks into life and drowns the reverberating barrage of the guns.

I am now wedged in tightly, but fairly comfortably, and shall remain in this position indefinitely. It is something like the physical pose of a mountain climber ascending a chimney in the rocks and wedging himself firmly to avoid falling. Or, perhaps to carry the simile of chimneys a thought further, like a Victorian boy sweep jammed inside a dark, tight flue. This position has even something foetal about it, a sealed-off, wrapped-about, doubled-up feeling. The thought might be extended even to the other extreme with elements of both the womb and the shroud, for it reminds me of those ancient people who buried their dead doubled-up in ceremonial urns. For some of us the latter reference may become all too relevant.

On the other side of the great 75mm breech and the machine-gun sits Tommy, with rather more room than I have. I do not need to move. He does. At any moment he may need to swing away from his wireless set, pick up a 75mm shell – an armful indeed – and slam it into the breech of the gun. Down in front of us, through the revolving turret cage, Stan and Rex sit side by side. Stan has two brake levers, large sticks rather like the old-fashioned levers used in railway signal boxes. There is also a gear lever. Rex has another Browning machine-gun which protrudes through its own small mantle below the turret ring. He both loads and fires that gun. This means we can fire in two directions at once. Rex can fire over the front area even though the turret has been swung to one side and is firing at another target. But the time for firing is not yet.

21.30 hours: 'Driver, advance. Come left and follow the Firefly.' Stan throws the heavy gears into motion and 3 Baker moves forward, noisily but gently. The Sherman is the Rolls-Royce of tanks. A good driver can set a Sherman in motion without spilling a full mug of tea standing on the turret floor. We roll forward across the grass with a slightly swaying motion, more like a boat than a land vehicle.

We follow the Firefly, a Sherman which carries a huge seventeen-pounder gun. It is something of a secret weapon. Our 75mm Sherman is reputedly unable to destroy the German Tiger tank with its immensely thick armour plating. So one tank in every troop of four is the Firefly Sherman which we hope will scare away Tigers.

We have a clear run for about 100 yards. Then we halt. Wait. This seems to be the very essence of war. Halting. Waiting. Advancing a few yards. Halting. Waiting.

22.00 hours: At this moment we are too bored to be scared. We could be sitting in an English field. There is no exultation. We simply wait, patient and unmoving as a cinema queue waiting to see a poor film.

22.15 hours: 'Driver, follow the tank in front. The squadron will be falling in with the regiment now.' The landscape has darkened into that state of gloaming where the colours only remain as a faint tinge on the blacks and greys. The tank 10 yards in front of us is merely a stronger splash of grey on a greying background.

I swing my wide-vision periscope, into which the telescopic sights are also fixed, to get a view of the darkling procession. In front there are rows of familiar Shermans breasting the slope with their distinctive turrets like flattened domes. Behind us we now have a close-up view of turretless tanks, hastily converted to serve as infantry carriers. Sitting about on top of the carriers, not knowing quite what to do on their unfamiliar steeds, are officers and sergeants of the 1st Black Watch, wearing their highland bonnets rather than the tin hat. Very cheerful and reassuring people to have at one's back.

We sit and wait. The darkness deepens. The barrage slackens a little. When other helpers fail ... I see the colonel sitting on his tank turret ahead, perhaps thinking that he might have been commanding a battleship instead of a tank. Hank Bevan sitting tight-lipped, apparently impassive, but glad to be out of the Stock Exchange routine. Captain Bill Fox sitting restlessly, cussing under his breath. Captain Tom Boardman in the lead tank, checking his compass for the last time. Jerry, up the hill, frying his frankfurters and laying bets on whether the barrage signifies a dawn attack. All waiting for darkness to close in. Each in his own way ...

22.40 hours: Ken Snowdon taps me on the back. 'Come up and look,' he shouts in my ear. He points directly upwards. 'That's what we steer on.' A quick-firing Bofors gun is directing green tracer shells from behind us, over our heads and away up the slope. Into his mike he commands, 'Driver, tail lights only, tail lights on!' And in my ear 'Get down and check tail lights, will you? Be quick. Move off in four minutes.'

I vault down and bump into little Ernie Wellbelove from the tank in front, on a similar mission. He runs to me, cups his hands at my ear and yells 'Just like August Bank Holiday in Blighty. Getting the charabanc back home at the end of the day, eating fish and chips, picking the sand out of your toes.' I reply with the well-worn, all-purpose platitude, 'If only our mothers could see us now!' My mother will be kneeling by the bed praying at this hour. Ernie's mother too.

A monstrous force lashes out and knocks me off balance against the tank. Blast from hundreds of our big guns a few yards back which have stepped up into full unison. I lip-read Ernie's shout of 'Christ Almighty! It's a war!', as he runs back to his own tank. I check the tail light and give Ken the thumbs-up signal. Ernie, a dance band drummer, is still behind his own tank, making drum-roll motions and indicating to me that it is he who is causing all this thundering percussion of noise. I give him the traditional 'screw loose' sign, screwing my finger into my temple. He gives me the 'fancy salute', a pukka salute but with the hand trembling back and forward dramatically. We both grin and climb back onto our tanks after our psychiatric session.

A green Very light shoots up from our front and soars back over our head. 'One for ready. Two for go. Get in,' yells Snowie, pulling his goggles down over his eyes. I squirm down past him into my little armoured den again.

22.45 hours: 'Driver, advance, ten yards behind your leader in front. Gunner, keep your guns straight ahead until we are through our front line. Off we go!'

I press my mike switch: 'How shall I recognize our front line?'

'You won't. I will tell you when we get there ... IF I recognize it myself.'

In spite of the mounting barrage and the protecting earpads of our headsets, we hear our engine gun fiercely, our tracks shriek and scream. Roger 3 Baker (tonight the squadron is 'Roger' and we are as always '3 Baker') jolts back on its haunches, then lurches forward pointing slightly upward like an aircraft taking off. After a moment the hull levels off on the springs, rocking gently along the smooth slope.

Roger 2 Baker ahead is already running into dust from vehicles further ahead and throwing up its own detritus to thicken the grey-dun clouds. Its tail lights glow a sad pink on a heavier mass of grey within the moving clouds. A light wind blows from left to right, bringing more dust from the three files of tanks on our left.

'Steer straight, you drunken bugger,' shouts Stan into his mike (which does not, of course, transmit the insults to Old Daddy Jenks driving 2 Baker ahead). 'Can't you call him, corp, and tell him to drive straight?'

We are now driving up the slope beyond Cormelles, a gentle rise of cornfields. Darkness would be absolute but for the Bofors tracer passing overhead and greening our faces like ghosts. Suddenly the entire world seems to light up one degree more, as though somebody in Heaven has flicked a switch. It is an awesome, eerie, inexplicable light seen through the periscope, something like the prelude to the appearance of angels over Bethlehem fields on the first Christmas. I shudder a little and press the mike switch. Tommy's voice beats me to the statement: 'The whole ruddy world's lit up. What is it?'

'That ... is artificial moonlight,' explains Snowie. 'Searchlights shining on the clouds. It should help a little.'

'Much better to send along a load of dustmen to clear up all that muck ahead,' complains Stan, who is having to concentrate hard to pick out Daddy Jenks' bobbing tail light in the swirling dust storm which we ourselves are helping to create.

3 Night Moonscape

7/8 AUGUST 1944:

Midnight: Our engine plays a kind of fearsome tuba concerto with a whole orchestra of more distant engines maintaining the rhythm. If they can use real guns in the *1812 Overture*, then they should also experiment with tank engines in *The Sorcerer's Apprentice*. Farther away now, the unceasing reverberations of our guns are like sea breakers on a pebble beach, rising and falling and blending a myriad individual shocks into one continuous pounding. Overhead the traffic of shells sounds like huge express trains riding on rusty wheels.

But at this moment a new and even more powerful sound drives through the rest and rushes in on our noise-hypnotized minds. A new and more lurid light blazes into the distorted world beyond our periscopes. The new sound is a series of separate, deep, crunching concussions, each like a hundred of the biggest guns going off together. The new light penetrates the dust clouds around our tanks, and every mote of dust turns into a spark of flame so that the dust clouds becomes galaxies of fire.

Ken taps my back, beckons. I swing up beside him. He shouts in my ear. Ragged shreds of words sieve through the din. 'Called you ... I/C ... hear me ... up ... can't see ... can't fire ... stay ... look out.' I yell vainly, 'You mean you want me to stay up and help you keep watch, help you keep watch ... HELP ... YOU ... WATCH?' He nods and points. The tanks in front have two ghostly ruddy heads peering out of each turret. One man's eyes are not enough in this dazzling kaleidoscope of obscurity and light. He points to the left '... AF ... WOODS!' 'What?' '... F raid ... RAF ... believe tanks ...'

Now I understand: in Caen 3 Baker had plunged into the depths of vast caverns delved by the bombs falling from hundreds of planes. Tonight we are to ride along beneath those same opening bomb doors. David Bevan had been overheard telling Bill Fox that even 'Bomber' Harris, the RAF bombing supremo, had wanted to veto the raid as being too dangerous to the tank crews riding ½ a mile away. But the master bombers had set up a trial raid last night and proved they could aim accurately enough. And what cost would be a mere Sherman or two blasted by friendly fire?

We two Kens give up the impossible struggle to communicate. There is just room for two people to squeeze together in the turret top so I jam myself into the tiny space beside my slim commander and stare into the wastes. To our right there is a thin shimmering curtain of haze, compounded of dust, mist, smoke and reflected flickering light – and, beyond it, a phantom countryside, a mutilated and murdered countryside coming back to haunt us. Above us the searchlights' artificial moonlight and the green Bofors tracer constantly change colour in mad variations on the theme of fire. In front of us the blurred outlines of the four juddering, swaying Shermans are hardly discernible in the shifting patterns of haze.

Over on the left the holocaust swells. Over on the left the other three tanks of our troop are misshapen black beetles swimming in a cauldron of fire. Beyond them the sky and land have become brilliantly clear. It is as though the laws of perspective have been reversed. Images close at hand are indistinct of form and lacking in colour. Distant features assault the eye in clarity of shape and vividness of colour.

Great spouts of flame illuminate a long vista of forest. Some of the fire spouts are brief, momentary. Others rise and fall. Others poise erect and permanent. The main source of light, seen through thick woods, stencils each tree, each branch, each leaf individually, although a thousand yards away. In a hurricane of blast the tops of the trees dance against a sky of incandescent orange. The explosions, starting as vermilion pinpricks, bulge into leaping rainbows of light.

A massive square object rises lazily above the trees, turns slowly over and over, then drops back into the writhing forest. '... man tank!' yells Snowie, through the bomb detonations, each blast a brief, individual sensation like a thunderclap highly compressed, packing more intensity into less time. The blasts go on and on and on and on, so appalling that the high decibel drone of hundreds of planes, great four-engined bombers passing overhead, is hardly audible.

The physical sensation here on our turret is that of standing on a beach during a cyclonic storm. Warm, evil-smelling air rushes and rips about us, lashing us in the face and tearing at our collars. A spray blows in our eyes, not the clean salt spray of the ocean but a dead, burning spray of dust and filth. And we are still a 1,000 yards distant from the nearest bombers.

We cruise along on our rough, obscure tide of darkness and, as we pass by, stare like astonished mariners at this wooded island of light with its ever-springing volcanoes and geysers of fire. We are mesmerized by the immensity, the ferocity of flame. We cannot resist its attraction. The sight is so utterly removed from anything we have ever known and imagined that we possess no emotions to match it. Not fear. Not horror. Not terror. Only awe.

I tell myself that there are human beings in those woods, bodies shredded by blast and grilled by flame, minds paralysed or deranged by demoniacal torture. But my emotions and thoughts refuse to respond to the information. It is all too unreal. The ultimate nightmare, confined to a desolate island of somebody else's experiences. Us? We are only drifting past on an endless ocean of night. Drifting past and watching from the bridges of our little, rocking, wallowing ships.

A new thought jars me. If I can see our three fellow tanks as black beetles swimming on a lake of fire, an unseen enemy behind me can see US just as clearly. I swing from the light to the darkness out right. That shattered terrain, devastated by earlier bombings, now reflects the distant wildfire, so like a re-enactment of its own travail. And, as I shudder and close my eyelids for a moment, fearful oranges and reds and yellows have seared their complementary colours into my weary retinas: green, blue and purple splashes and flickers have been branded onto my vision.

I open my eyes again. In the gloom I see a Sherman tank. I ask myself why that tank is out of line. Then I realize it is a casualty of earlier attempts to mount this ridge, this infamous Bourguebus Ridge. The Sherman is a lonely, empty, iron monster, a high point of a former tide of enthusiasm and heroism, a roosting place for rats and shadows. I would like to go across and see if its crew is still sitting there, like some we have seen, grilled into wizened little black monkey shapes, each shrunken and hard like a beef joint roasted in too hot an oven. But there is no time to stop and sympathize. As we move slowly onward, the abandoned Sherman seems to be swimming away into a lost twilight, a gruesome parody on *Swan Lake*. The haze curtains close behind us and I return to scanning old shell holes. We pass a large crater filled with water. The present fires cause it to glimmer and glow like a torch with fading batteries.

8 AUGUST 1944 (Operation Totalize):

00.15 hours: A thick mist has risen around us, adding to the density of the night. Mist that creeps into the turret and brings a chill damp which does nothing to relieve the sweaty dankness of our metal cell. Ahead, 2 Baker is now a wraith of grey, dappled with white mist – a kind of piebald tank – enveloped in a moving grey-brown cloud. On our flanks we can see only the uneven ground, rucked and pitted by shell-fire. Ghosts of mist drift in the wind across this dark haunting ground and now and again a denser ghost shows where our Charlie tank keeps level with us 15 yards away. Look! This mounded shape here is a shattered farm cottage, dead, still, amputated. That square shape there is a destroyed British tank, its gun hanging loose like a broken limb, the mist smoking from it like a visible echo of its final agony.

Stan: 'How far do you reckon we have gone now, corp?'

Commander: 'About a mile and a half.'

Tommy: 'In forty-five minutes? I could walk it quicker.'

Commander: 'Would you like to get out and try?'

Me: 'At least he would be able to see. I can't see a thing through my firing sights. How am I expected to fire?'

Commander: 'If we need to fire, we'll just have to point the gun in the general direction of the enemy and then continue by trial and error.'

Rex: '*Hoch, hoch, mein Gott*, what a bloody fine lot … !'

00.30 hours: The column's pace and steadiness improve and we pick up speed to a fast walking pace, a trot, a canter. Excitement begins to simmer and ferment. An intensity communicates itself through the tank. Everyone adjusting themselves to the movement. Settling into seats, carefully scanning the outside world through periscopes. Even Stan will be more relaxed now, sitting with his hands loosely on the sticks, letting the tank ride – as it will do without the constant control needed by a steering wheel.

Perhaps the growing excitement is a reflection also of the growing wireless activity impinging on our consciousness. There are no messages yet for our regimental code-signs, but others are not observing wireless silence with the same discipline. Way out on the ether more distant voices are active, their messages indistinguishable amid the constant static. It is like approaching a new and unknown planet whose signals are obviously rational but incomprehensible. Tommy has been listening to it as well. I hear his mike click.

'Do you hear that? Morse! That's the first time I've heard Morse code being sent in action. Think of all the ruddy time we wasted at training regiment. Day after day. Week after week. Walking around in our sleep saying "Di-dah, Dah-di-di-dit, Dah-di-dah-dit" and all through the alpha-ferking-bet. All for nothing. Never use it.'

Our tank sways, stumbles, bucks and lunges forward again across a rough sunken track. We have topped the protecting slopes above Cormelles-le-Royal, and are out on the desolate, pitted lunar landscape of the 'Goodwood' battles, the ridge of Bourguebus, already rechristened by Tommy and others as 'Bugger's Bus'. Country fought over and destroyed like the Somme or Passchendaele battlefields of the Great War (and having suffered an even heavier weight of artillery shells and aerial bombs). Pocked with shell holes. Scarred with slit trenches. Littered with shattered vehicles and instruments of war. Studded with shredded trees and crumbled houses. Sullied above all by the stench of unburied dead, animal and human. The stench creeps in through the periscope fittings like a live, breathing fog.

Moonscape, wilderness, desolation, ruin, catastrophe, chaos, obscenity, devastation: I have plenty of time to think of the words as we rumble on. Each word has its own distinctive connotations and all of them are present here. Perhaps the most apposite word is 'waste'. (Tommy: 'Somebody's been muck-spreading the fields.' Rex: 'Jerry, with his guns!' Tommy: 'What? I don't get it.' Stan: 'Don't try explaining, Rex. It's too complicated.' Tommy: 'It stinks anyway.' Stan: 'Dear mother …')

Turning my periscope to the right, I see a small green light drift past, like a distant lightship in the fog upon a troubled sea. A few minutes later another tiny green light set against a piece of tin with numerals on it. I flick mike: 'Forgive ignorance. Route markers? Those green lights?'

Commander: 'Yes, we have those as far as the front line and then a bit into no man's land. Also white tape where there are minefields.'

Stan: 'I hope Jerry has the decency to lay white tapes on his side. I can't see any white lines or green lights. I can hardly see Daddy Jenks for dust. Corp, can I open up for a while?'

Snowie gives permission. Until now Stan has been driving on periscope vision (as per battle orders), not the easiest task even in broad daylight. Now he will be opening his own heavy hatch cover down in front of the turret, raising his seat, putting on his goggles and looking out directly into the night. If I have to fire, he will have to duck quick or risk being blinded and deafened by the muzzle flash of the 75. So, at little more than walking speed, Stan trails Daddy Jenks, who is following someone else, around the edge of larger craters. For me war at this moment is the sight of a small oblong of dust cloud, penetrated by a feeble tail light. The inescapable reek of sweet, horrid decay. The filthy breath of a million million maggots. The all-penetrating noise, unidentifiable as to its constituent parts.

And we halt. And we wait. And we move again.

00.40 hours: Tanks in front are slowing, halting, becoming erratic in their advance. We ourselves halt. I look out across a meaningless moonscape, whilst behind us and to the left and up above, the incredible pandemonium goes on, trailing streamers of scintillating colours.

Stan asks, 'What's up, corp? Total traffic block. Why have we stopped?'

Tommy interjects: 'It's probably a level crossing. They've closed the gates and we're waiting until the train goes by. Signalman doesn't know there's a war on.'

Patient, tolerant Corporal Ken explains, 'Truly, there is a railway line around here somewhere on an embankment. The delay might also be caused by a sunken road.'

In front, 2 Baker rolls forward again. His tail light disappears in the murk. Stan bangs 3 Baker's engine into gear, revs up, jolts forward and almost crashes into 2 Baker, which has stopped again. As soon as we have slithered to a stop, 2 Baker charges off into oblivion again. We give chase. Some British-made tanks would stall under such treatment. The Sherman keeps booming along. They are excellent vehicles, adequate to live in, but susceptible to several methods of instant destruction. The most feared and frequent event is a shot into the engine, which inevitably produces an instantaneous inferno. This has given rise to the nickname applied to the Sherman by the crewmen themselves, of 'Ronson' – after the Ronson cigarette lighter: just a flick and you get the flame – and the equally graphic description given to it by the Germans, the 'Tommy cooker'.

Very funny, unless you're the Tommy who is about to get cooked!

00.45 hours: Rumbling, jerking. We are shunting again. Stan says that we should train for tank warfare in a railway freight shunting yard. The column has slowed to a halt, engines still booming. The dust falls away. Dim shapes of tanks moving in disarray, breaking up the neat formation of fours. A Sherman 'Crab', a tank with a massive mine-sweeping boom attached, is lying jammed diagonally in a gap in a hedge, a vast square shape in a wreath of dark bushes. A recovery vehicle (ARV) has linked on a tow-rope already and is struggling to drag the Crab free. An officer standing on the back of another tank waves vigorously, directing us to look for another way past the obstruction. We do not recognize the dark profile of the officer in the multihued darkness but we know that he is an officer because he is waving a riding crop. So riding crops do have a purpose in modern war!

Ken Snowdon taps my shoulder, 'Ken, get down and find a way through to the left. Rex, get out and help him. Tommy, have you got a cigarette? Light it for Ken?'

Tommy objects, 'Ken doesn't smoke.'

'I know that, you idiot. He needs a lighted cigarette to guide us in the dark. No brighter lights allowed. Otherwise how are we going to see him guiding us?' There is a drill for guiding tanks by using cigarette glow signals.

I jump off the tank onto rough ground, holding the cigarette carefully away from me. I see somebody lying on the ground. In the darkness I bend down to give him a lift up. He doesn't need it. He is an 'it' left over from a former battle. The air seems to have gone as ice-cold as the flesh of his hand, briefly touched.

Thirty-ton tanks loom on all side like impatient elephants. A few pedestrians like Rex and me emphatically wave fag-ends to keep the monsters away from crushing flesh and blood. We are not at ease out here on our feet, treading the dangerous earth. We are not infantrymen. We inhabit a different element, as different as sea and air. Or perhaps a more pertinent comparison would be the difference between mariner and submariner.

A large hedge looms over us, deepest grey on black. Rex and I walk along it, farther to the left. I wave the cigarette and 3 Baker trundles obediently at my heels, trailing two or three other tanks behind it. I walk on tiptoe, not to avoid scaring the enemy but in the mistaken hope that if I tread on a mine the fact of my weight being transmitted through tiptoe may prevent the mine blowing my feet off! A large gap appears in the hedge. Rex and I yell at each other, cupping one's hands at the other's ear. 'No bloody engineer blew that one ... must have been made by a tank ... too wide for a Sherman by far ... probably a Tiger then ... hope the bugger's not waiting the other side ... Let's go see ...'

We climb the bank about 2 feet high. In the darkness the great Normandy hedge towers above us. God! These vast Normandy hedges! We slide down into a narrow lane. There is a similar gap in the far hedge. I return and wave the cigarette in a 'left hand down' sign. Stan swings the tank left and comes towards me, trailing a cohort of other tanks. 3 Baker lunges across the lane and bulldozes the opposite bank. Rex is waiting beyond the far hedge, unharmed by Tigers.

We plod into the field beyond. A tiny trail of light leaps from the darkness and hisses past our heads. Sounds like rats' claws scratching at the side of 3 Baker send us diving for the ditch as we hear the unmistakable ripping noise of a Spandau machine-gun, so much faster-firing than our weapons. We cower in the deep ditch by the hedge. Another burst of Spandau swings farther and farther away. 'Firing on spec,' I shout at Rex. 'Let's move!'

But there is a sudden, shattering scream of vertical sound. It could be great lorries driving down out of the sky, slamming on their brakes, skidding noisily on that vertical road, smashing through brick walls, crashing down on us. That is the noise! And the light is like whirling cauldrons of blistering flame as shell after shell explodes. Ours or theirs? Heat, noise, filth, poison gases around us, above us. And the force lifting us up and flinging us back into the ditch from which we have just emerged.

'Bloody get down!' screams Rex.

'I'm underneath you,' yelling back.

The night seems to have become white-hot with the breath of the explosions, the very curtains of blackness roaring into flame from the constant ignitions of blast. It is like sitting under a descending mass of molten steel pouring from a blazing furnace. We try to crush ourselves as flat as cardboard cut-outs. The ditch stinks with the comforting reminder of natural decay.

Still 3 Baker stands in the gap in the hedge. A shell explodes inches in front of it. Another hits the front of the tank and rages upward in fiery frustration. Smoke wrestles with the darkness. Shrapnel screams over our ditch. A red-hot lump of something hits my hand a glancing blow. In a split second I visualize all the ways in which a human body can be ripped apart, butchered, squashed, spattered, spread-eagled, grilled, racked with a million agonies.

Lord, let me be a tree standing guard on a Normandy hedge-row, asking no more than to befriend rooks, bees and squirrels, my greatest act cross-pollination with some distant sibling. But then war destroys trees too, smashing some and leaving others to die, their barks stripped, in unimagined agonies. Then let me be a mole or a grass snake, able to squirm into the safe recesses of the earth, far deeper than this exposed ditch. But then war delves under the earth itself, flinging inanimate sods and living creatures alike up into the flaming horror of human-invented destruction.

Someone turns a tap far away, and the shower of shells stops. Stops! Stopped!! The tank lurches forward from the gap in the hedge. Slowly, painfully, fearfully, suspiciously, we begin to slither out of the ditch and, flat on our stomachs, crawl ...

'Have you Yeomen had your legs shot off? Or got them caught in a game trap out poaching? Or got boozed up on Calvados?' drawls a voice high behind us. A dark figure in a beret stands on the top of the bank at the gap in the hedge.

'You can get shot up if you effing want, Sergeant blimming Prentice,' says Rex heatedly. 'Me, I don't mind filthying my belly as long as my backside is safe.'

'Now, now, that's not a nice way to speak to sergeants, Trooper flaming Jackson,' chortles Ted Prentice, he of the handlebar moustache. 'Here, Ken, lend me that cigarette, will you? I've got my entire troop waiting to come through.'

'This is our hole. You go find your own sodding gap in the hedge,' retorts the unrepentant Rex, heading for home in his safe co-driver seat.

I flick the still glowing cigarette to Ted, run after my own tank, swing myself up onto the back deck, gingerly avoiding the flailing, skidding tracks. Ahead in the darkness there is a vibrance and a yellowish-brown tinge. Then a faint red light shows through the eternal eddies of dust. Fresh bright fire streaks out ahead, away from us. Lines of fire interspersed with odd flashes.

On tank top I shout, 'Ken, do you realize we are now on the left of the march since we came through that hedge?'

Yells back, 'Yes, I know. But we're all out of formation anyway. We'll just keep moving. Get back in and traverse left.' (Then into his mike) 'Driver, close down again.'

I hit my seat, grab earphones to hear Stan sing, 'OK, corp, going down. Ground floor – perfumes, toiletries, ladies' knickers. Basement – restaurant and bogs. Closed down now, corp.'

And before Snowie can utter, an A Squadron station breaks in: 'Hullo, Oboe 3 Able. Nasty people in holes. Over.'

'3 Able. Keep moving unless they interfere. Over.'

'3 Able. OK. Off.'

Slotted into my hard narrow seat I feel more secure behind solid steel walls. In my own element again. My right hand closes over the metal grip, twists to the left; the turret spins swiftly left. Through the periscope, with no dust-churning tanks to my left, I can see the burning woods clearly, with the ground in between fitfully lit. I look through the gun sight telescope. Individual trees stand starkly in the glare of the raging fires. Exposed to an invisible enemy on our left, our tank rolls over the bumpy terrain and I travel sideways, looking out on my own private oblong of blazing world.

01.10 hours: Stan's next question is 'how far now, corp?' and Ken calculates, 'About two and a half miles, I reckon. We must have crossed our own front line near Bourguebus. ('Bugger's Bus', echoes Tommy.) The green markers have ended.'

'But it isn't like a real front line, is it?' says Rex. 'When my dad used to tell me stories about the Great War, there was always this huge trench, deep and wide and barricaded with barbed wire. There was no way to get across it. Only down into it. Here there are only bits of holes dotted across the countryside and odd thickets of barbed wire between.'

Snowie adds, 'Yes, but with hundreds of land mines hidden in between. Lucky there are flail tanks up ahead!'

'Whacking the ground with those big, rusty chains fixed to that bloody great spinning drum on the nose of the tank.' (Tommy)

'Ugly but beautiful!' (me)

'Yeah. Tommy's going to buy one of those after the war to beat his wife with.' (Stan)

'When I beat my wife, when I've got one, I won't need the British Army to help me!' (Tommy)

The distance comes alight with quick splashes of red fire, closely bunched. Each flash is a momentary brilliant blotch of flame surrounded by a wig of curling grey smoke. But just as quickly the black night snaps shut on each flash with the efficiency of a camera shutter. The hazy mist swirls about the darkness again. A louder crash sounds, once, twice, thrice. A fan of fire shoots high into the sky, silhouetting a distant Sherman tank. Tiny figures of crewmen come squirming from its turret like maggots out of an over-ripe Camembert cheese. A new puff of fire lifts the turret into the air. Then there is only a Roman candle of flame spurting the usual fireworks. There is no recognizable shape of a Sherman left. There is a silence amid the continuing cacophony.

The column shunts forward again, sending up clouds of dust to snuff out that horrendous Roman candle. Rex's microphone clicks, 'God, that dust! When my dad told his stories of the 1914–18 lot, it was always deep in mud, and water slopping in the trenches. People falling off duckboards and getting drowned. They must have had some dusty days, some Junes and Augusts. But he never told of those.'

Stan's mike answers, 'With my pop they were always marching back, just a few survivors behind a brass band, and the French girls saying how they looked young and old all at the same time. "That was glory!" he used to say, "that was glory!" But he could never get around to saying where or what they were coming back from.'

I press my microphone switch. 'My father's greatest moment was making a new pair of riding boots for the Prince of Wales in France. He was a saddler. Joined up in his trade.'

Stan clicks, 'Who? The Prince of Wales?'

'Hullo, Oboe 2 Baker. Firing on right. Over.'

'Hullo, Oboe 2 Baker. Those are our other friends. Don't interfere. Over.'

'Oboe 2 Baker, OK. Off.'

Stan's voice again chuckles through the earphones. 'God! They've got some long ferking miles in France.'

'Well, I reckon we should be just about on the German front line,' calculates Ken above us. 'But no trenches like my old pop used to march back from after capturing them,' says Stan.

We have breached the enemy front line? This is so different from our fathers' leap into that endless trench, stretching from the Vosges Mountains to the North Sea coast, packed with enemy. We do not struggle with him, bayonet against bayonet. But we have, since landing, invaded his shelters and his dug-outs after he has retreated. We have picked up his letters and tried to decipher the strange Gothic script. We have seen him surrender in his baggy, field-grey uniform and his easily recognizable coal-scuttle helmet. We have heard his guttural language and smelled his strange, animal smell, a foul odour acquired from chemically treated clothing (we also carry a similar smell on our khaki), constant proximity to putrefying flesh and consumption of rancid food.

We have not yet had opportunities to converse with our prisoners. We have simply waved at them, frightened, grey-faced men, frequently much older or younger than any of us, often shocked into incontinence, indoctrinated with a fear of being shot on surrender. We have waved at them in a rather sympathetic manner and have pointed them back towards less sympathetic echelon wallahs in the rear.

Now we are moving through their front line. Yet all that is happening to me is that I am sitting at a periscope, as though in front of a tiny television set, watching a slow war film, and travelling sideways-on sedately in the wake of known comrades: Tom Boardman, Colonel Forster, Daddy Jenks, Ernie Wellbelove, Trooper Judge, Old Uncle John Peel and all! Old Uncle John Peel and all!

01.20 hours: New flame ahead and on right! Too much like splashes of luminescent blood on the night! 'Oboe 2 to all stations. Nasties right front … Wow! Got one! 2, off.' Fire mushrooms up from our right front. A slow spread of fire. Too slow to be a Sherman brew-up.

'Oboe 2 Able. Two nasties at two o'clock. I've been hit. Engage! Off.' Slamming guns. Vicious, aimed, intended death. Not like the more patient grumble of the artillery, fired from afar. Another slow, slow fire-mushroom. '2 Able. That's another nasty gone. Are you all right, Sunray? Over.' '2 Able. Hit but still aboard. Keep shooting. Off.'

BANG-SLAM! BANG-SLAM! A fast fire. Roman candle! 'Ronson!' God! That's a Sherman gone up. 'Somebody in 2 Troop, A Squadron,' comments Snowie. More fires linking into a chain of brilliance against which our tanks move as black blotches surrounded by haloes of crimson, shimmering silk, their own haloes of dust catching the firelight.

'Hullo, Oboe 2 Able. Oboe 2 has bailed out. Have brewed another hornet. 2 Able to 2 Baker, 2 Charlie, look out right! Off.'

More vicious close explosions, gunfire and burst together, against the continuing background of barrage and tank engines. Flashes upon flashes upon firelight upon the more distant flickering battle glow. We come to a halt behind another Sherman, known only by its tail light and humped turret. We wait. Thinking. Almost able to hear each other think in the close proximity of sweating bodies within the darkened tank.

Stan: 'That makes … three of ours … for three of theirs.'

Rex: '2 Baker and 2 Charlie of A have bought it. That's Sergeant Ryan and somebody. Not bad though, three of them for three Shermans. They usually say three Shermans down for every one of them.'

Snowie: 'Three Shermans for every *Tiger*. Not three to *any* nasty. Three to a Tiger.'

Streaks of light shoot out of the ground on our left. The Sherman in front starts to traverse left. I twist the pistol-grip, spin the turret, eye to telescope, crosswires swinging and dipping at the source of the firing. Snowie orders 'Gunner, fire! Reload HE. Driver, swing left. Co-driver, fire when on.'

I stamp on the firing button of the 75mm, then on the co-ax button. The huge breech of the 75mm leaps back into the turret, jams against its springs, slides forward again into place. It thunderclaps in my left ear. The automatically opened breech coughs stifling cordite fumes. In my telescope the mighty muzzle flash of the 75mm obscures and blinds momentarily as a tracer spark leaps across the brief space and slams into the ground by the German machine-gun. Our tank rocks back on its haunches under the power of the 75 recoil. Streaks of smaller tracer from our co-axial Browning follow the same trajectory as the larger shot, sparking around a hardly visible dug-out. The tank in front also bangs off a 75mm shot.

All this within a second, without breathing, without thought. Our 75 had been loaded with AP, not necessarily effective against men in a hole in the ground but a very discouraging package to receive, travelling at 2,000 feet per second with force sufficient to split open any tank but a Tiger. Now Tommy is ramming a high-explosive shell into the breech. He slaps my leg, signing 'loaded', even while I think, 'Those must be SS fanatics in that slit trench.' A touch on the traversing grip, stamp on the button, blaze, blast, shock, then leaping tracer hitting target. Explosion, massive, sudden, vivid, brief. A flame of sunset condensed a thousand times, mixed with a thousand thunderheads, compressed into an area in, and above, and around the dug-out. Expired in a split second. But even in that brief flare I see a whirling mass of sandbags, a shattered machine-gun, metal objects, equipment, boxes, helmets, pieces of human bodies, all clear, distinct, in Technicolor, quickly dying.

The tank in front of me fires half a second after me, and the shell exploding seems to catch the descending vision of Hell created by our shell and throws it up even higher, more brilliant, more rapidly disintegrating. Leaving a silence, dumb and stunning. And the darkness, double black darkness blooming with purple and green flashes. Which allows me to go green myself, unashamedly, and swallow the bile rising in my mouth.

Tommy groans, 'Got to shit!' In his private world beyond the big gun he will be retrieving an empty machine-gun ammunition box and surrendering to the inexorable demands of nature. Several of us have already had to urinate in empty brass shell cases ideally shaped. We have tried to avoid the grosser bowel function, which residuum has to be left in the ammo box on the floor until we can get out. A nauseating whisper of the additional odour reaches me already.

Snowie, in relatively fresh air aloft, comments, 'Good shooting! But keep your eyes peeled. And Tommy cover that damned mess up.'

Good shooting? Artillerymen fling their mightier shells but are not sitting a few yards away from the victims, watching their fate. The infantry move closer to the enemy. But they do not wield a flesh-threshing weapon like the 75mm, HE. RAF bombers and fighters hurl their own types of devastation at the earth, but they swoop past at 300 mph and are gone before the explosion erupts. The navy uses immense shells, but fires them at an enemy beyond the horizon. We sit here, within the yards of the enemy, as though sitting in our, or their, own kitchens and parlours, press a button and then watch a human being shredded to death. And cheer. All right, he was a Nazi. All right, it was 'him or us'. All right, we did it under orders.

Good shooting! I suppress the desire to ask if any evil thing can ever be good. But then that would only be reviving the old, old questions. Questions which I had answered the day I registered to wear the king's uniform. The day my friend told me that he was going to register as a conscientious objector. And I had said, probably quite arrogantly at the time, 'And I'm a conscientious objector to swastikas!'

01.35 hours: 'Hullo, William Able, [Captain Tom Boardman in the lead tank].' 'Guy Fawkes exhausted. Permission to collect more from William Baker? Over.'

'Hullo, Able,' (the colonel replying). 'Is Guy Fawkes essential? Over.'

(Tommy, on I/C 'Who the hell is Guy Fawkes?')

'William Able, friends say Guy Fawkes essential. Only fifty yards walk. Over.'

'William Able, be it on your own head. Report back. Off.'

Rex on I/C queries 'Didn't you ever let off fireworks on Guy Fawkes night, Tommy?' Tommy responds, 'Course I did. But that's in November. Not now.' Snowie explains, 'Guy Fawkes is code for Very signal lights. Captain Boardman has obviously used up his entire supply and is walking back to the second navigator, Captain Todd, to obtain more flares.'

I comment, 'I wouldn't want to be walking back in all that lot, dark, mines, Jerries in slits, bombs.'

Snowie's response carries a smile, 'You and Rex have already done that.'

'Hullo, William Able. Guy Fawkes now hale and hearty again. Pleasant stroll. Going good to soft. Pushing on. Over.'

'Able. Leave your shoes outside the door for cleaning. Off.'

01.50 hours: So we travel on through a night within a night within a night.

The outermost night which has descended on the Normandy fields will last from about 22.45 hours on 7 August 1944 to about 03.45 hours on 8 August 1944. This darkness will cover an action termed 'a turning point of the war' – only one of a hundred such 'turning points' but each one vital enough to cause a major change of fortunes for the contesting armies.

But, within the calendar night, another more gruesome darkness is being created – darkness of smoke and dust, permeated by the smell of hot oil, urine and death, intensified by a noise as of a hundred tempests. Machines, invented by human beings, roll through Nature's darkness, casting up clouds of nauseating filth. Each tank creates its own night within the night, tracks milling the earth to fine tilth at the front and throwing up that powder as dense clouds behind. And the entire column rumbles on in a series of insulated, self-perpetuating palls of confused obscurity.

The incredible din obliterates every human sound and reduces logical thought to imbecilic imaginings. And so, within the double darkness, we ourselves retreat into an even deeper darkness. For this is world's end, the final precipice of chance. Ahead, along the crest of the unseen hill, death lies ready to leap on us, on the chosen ones among us. So each of us digs a little dug-out among the rubbish of our adolescent beliefs and ambitions. And burrows for comfort into the most secret places of the soul's own darkness to avoid the outer realities.

We have reason to be fearful. We are packed inside a tank as inside a blind, tight, odorous, moving sewer. In a moment our mobile home can be transformed into a self-igniting crematorium … a self-sealing mausoleum … or a self-detonating bomb, its own walls shattering into lethal shards of sharp steel projected in wild ricochets, back and forth through the confined space. At best it is simply a cramped, bruising caravan, alternating between arctic cold and equatorial heat.

But, most of the time, nothing happens. The truest literary representation of a typical hour of war might well be fifty pages left completely blank, which the reader is compelled to read through at the same speed as if they were printed pages. During that time nothing happens. Nothing at all except noise and dirt and smoke and glaring confusion.

02.02 hours: I sit bolt upright in my seat. Glance at my watch. I must have been dozing. The constant sway of the Sherman on its springs, the incessant, unchanging drumming of the barrage, the interminable roar of our engine, the steady hiss of the wireless in the headphones, the repeated sequences of flashes and darkness, flashes and darkness, flashes and darkness through the periscope, the stuffy atmosphere permeated by sweat, body waste and cordite, the lateness of the hour – all these induce sleep. This is one of the great problems for the turret crew.

I blink furiously for several seconds. Reach for my water-bottle. Take a swig of the ghastly chlorinated liquid with a formula hardly approximating to H_2O. I try to breathe more deeply, but the foul, oxygen-starved air gives me no boost towards wakefulness. I rub my eyes vigorously. Bounce up and down on my confined seat. I reach for my water-bottle. Cannot find it. Eventually encounter it lying on my knees. Take another mouthful. It has not improved with keeping. Normandy vintage 1944. Not nice *eau*. I find myself dozing again. Crime of crimes: asleep on watch. Sleep is one of the worst problems ...

It is dangerous! Dangerous for me to sleep when at any moment I may need to swing the guns blazing towards a target capable of destroying me within seconds. It is even more perilous for the driver down in his little compartment. If he and his co-driver doze off, nobody need know. Once he has set the Sherman moving in gear and taken his hands away from the levers, the tank will go on and on for ever if he falls asleep. On and on past fortified villages, past St-Aignan and past Falaise, on and on throughout France with the crew fast asleep and nobody able to stop the tank. Crewed by the Sleeping Beauty and the Flying Dutchman and Rip van ... sleep is the ... sleep is ... great problem ...

I rouse, ask, 'Stan, are you awake? STAN!' And Stan: 'Of course, I'm awake. Who d'you think is driving the ruddy tank? And who—' Tommy: 'Speed you're going, we would move faster if we all got out and pushed the ferkin'—' Stan: 'Get out and push whoever's ahead, old Daddy Jenks or—' Snowie: 'We lost Daddy Jenks ages ago. Don't know who is in front or who—' Rex: 'The Ancient flooding Mariner.' And the conversation bumbles on between a dream and a nightmare.

Stan suddenly begins to tell a yarn, saves our souls, lights a tiny candle of cheer in the grim pit of our terrors.

'Remember Weston-super-Mare? And camping on the golf course? Remember the latrine was a big pit? And just a long pole over it to sit on? And on the Saturday night old Preece W. had been out on the booze and had come staggering in and was sitting over the pit. He says he fell asleep. But really he was dead pissed. Whatever it was, he suddenly sways backwards and forwards like one of those toy clowns on a stick. And his legs go up in the bleeding air and he does a perfect high dive into the pit, head first! Oh boy, poor stinking Preece W., up to his neck in the proverbial – the wrong way up.'

The sufferings of Preece W. down in the miry pit carry us another 50 yards on the route to a sterner Hell, laughing fit to bust. We must look like a Hogarth caricature, or an illustration for *Pilgrim's Progress*, of sinners carousing on their way to damnation.

Rex continues, 'And then he crawls up out of the pit, does Preece W., and looks over the edge like Chad looking over his wall, and somebody shouts "Wot! No rhubarb?"'

Stan again, 'And somebody else, "Doesn't your mother use Persil?" And Jim Stanley yells, "Don't go down the mine, Daddy, there's plenty of manure in the midden!" And we all grab him and carry him down to the shore and drop him in the sea. And he would still be there now if we hadn't scrubbed him in sea water and carried him back to his tent.'

We sit staring into the dust haze of the treacherous night, chortling at the blessed memory of Preece W. Our headsets are silent: the guns grumble into our consciousness again. Stabs of uncertainty, of dawning fear, throb through us as we view the unfamiliar, yet so similar landscape of enemy territory (although this is Allied France, under the horror of enemy occupation, the sinister domination of an enemy's will). But the tragedy of this night is interrupted again and again by little explosions of mirth from those apostles of Preece W. who had been destined to be there to witness his transfiguration in the pit. Saving visions of Preece W. crawling out of the hole vie with images of Tiger tanks lurking beyond the haze. My favourite Preece W. wisecrack came from our learned clerk-corporal who said that Preece W. evidently had ambitions towards 'Ordurely Corporal'.

02.15 hours: Once again we have fallen into the pattern of stopping and starting, crawling forward slowly over the shattered fields. The famous formation of fours has now completely broken up. We push on in random groups. The barrage still continues overhead but there is an increasing network of blazing tracer bullets criss-crossing our front, coming mainly from our flanks. Much of it seems aimless, and partly spent. Rumours from other battles. Fairly harmless while we stay inside the tank.

'Hullo, all stations William.' (That's the colonel's voice and code-sign.) 'Hullo, all stations William. Our friends on right have been held up. Message from Supreme Sunray asking us to keep moving at all costs. I'm relying on you all to keep moving, keep pushing on, whatever happens. All stations William, off.'

Tommy: 'And who the hell is Supreme Sunray?' ('Sunray' is the tanker's name for commander.)

Snowie: 'That must be Montgomery himself.'

Stan: 'Sunray? I like that. Supreme bloody Thundercloud, that's Monty.'

Tommy: 'Monty at this time of night? He must be having a bad dream.'
('Aren't we all?' I think.)

Stan, sharply: 'Commander! People left, ten o'clock, slit trench ...' Me,
shouting, 'I see them. Can't depress the gun enough. Too near. No go!
Too ...' Commander, 'Hold it! I'll try a grenade.'

I feel behind my head for the little satchel containing Mills bombs.
Before Ken can act, the tank commander in front and someone in the slit
trench have thrown grenades at each other simultaneously. Twin flashes
light slit trench and tank turret. Commander's head disappears. Ken grunts,
lobbing a grenade. Commander in front pops up, flings another bomb. Two
flashes. Both down by the slit trench. No more movement down there.

Commander in front, unrecognized, points energetically down right. I
traverse swiftly. Through periscope see another slit trench. Eye to telescope,
depress gun fully, cannot see trench. Back to wider periscope. In the trench,
10 feet away, wearing familiar coal-scuttle helmet ... a German, pale face
turned upwards toward us, a kid, staring in frozen, paralysed horror. He
does not move. Neither do I. Our tank rumbles past, almost shaving his
grey chin. I realize what we look like to him: thirty tons of crushing steel,
50 feet of churning iron track, swaying towards him like a diabolic mincing
machine. And our great gun, yawning steel-black, probing down, straight
at his head.

Had I fired the gun, our shell would have screamed over his head. But
the flame and concussion would have killed him. Already the memory of
that pale, paralysed face is imprinted for ever on my mind's eye. I shall take
him, nameless and for ever unmoving, with me wherever I go. And I want
to go back and tell him that it is only Stan and Rex and I and the others
who were passing by. Just ordinary, inoffensive youths like himself.

02.30 hours: Sporadic bursts of tracer still spurt in and out of the eternal
clouds of dust around us, their freakish light making the tanks seem even
more insubstantial and ghostly. Tracer bullets speed back and forth in every
conceivable direction, at all angles to the horizontal, and in all stages of
ellipse, as the muzzle velocity dies and the bullet goes cold. There is a naked
feeling about advancing through a jungle of shadows and false lights, with
our left flank wide open, behind the enemy lines. In front, on the right,
behind, the massed column trundles on in perpetual bottom gear, flinging
up its conveyor belts of muck. But on the left we are alone, unprotected,
menaced. Enemy troops are out there, and some of them belong to the SS,
the name we have been brought up to dread.

Our myopic periscopes reveal only a few yards of rising land. And then
the darkness, constantly splashed by flashes which paint alien faces and

enemy tanks and hostile guns on the black canvas of a lost night. Now and then something taps or scratches in ghostly seance on the outer walls of the tank. But we are safe if we stay inside, safe from the unmentionable hordes that people the darkness, safe ... until a mine explodes underneath us or an 88mm erupts in sudden anger out of the darkness and smashes through the turret wall, lighting the instant cremation pyre.

Overhead the Bofors gun still flings its fiery green shells amid a confusion of contending flashes. But we here seem to be marooned on an island of stippled darkness. We move from one anonymous, unidentified spot to another. The lack of definition contributes to a continuing sense of unreality and non-event which blunts the scalpel-edge of fear. But fear hovers, a miasma around us, nearer than the close, hard turret walls, ready to spring back into our minds at the slightest variation in the pattern of flashes across the night.

02.38 hours: The constant inane crackle of 'A' set atmospherics clicks into a more subdued and expectant hum as someone nearby presses a microphone switch and his 'A' set begins to transmit.

'Hullo, William Able ...' (Tom Boardman in the lead tank.) 'Hullo, William Able. Code-name "Fly by Night now!" On target, on time. All clear. Halted. Over.'

'William Able,' (the colonel) 'Jolly good show! All stations William press on to "Fly by Night". Off.'

Stan: 'The lead tank is there then? That's the objective, isn't it?'

Tommy: 'Gawd, that was an easy battle!'

Snowie: 'It isn't finished yet. You could say it isn't even started yet. It depends how Jerry reacts now that we are behind him.'

Rex: 'I know how I would react with a Hun armoured division behind *me*!'

The tremendous percussion of the barrage seems to have been left behind, back with the burning tanks and blazing woods. The erratic crossfire of machine-guns is also falling away behind us. The ground is noticeably more even every minute, less pitted by the fury of former battles. We are now coasting along comfortably within our own private dust cocoon. The night has become much darker as the fires have died away. I am still riding sideways, traversed left. There is only blank blackness to be seen. Nothing moves, nothing looms on that side.

02.55 hours: The haze has taken on a much more silvery sheen. It cannot yet be dawn, can it? I wonder about the strange radiance on our left. At the same time I am struggling against sleep again in our squalid, reeking, stifling closet as we meander slowly through the abandoned country. I wonder whether I have dozed momentarily as I become aware of a continuing conversation. Stan is saying 'That means that Hank has arrived already? We can't be more than a few yards behind.' And Snowie replying, 'Don't forget ... mixed up ... sunken road ... special look out ... not run down any pedestrians ...'

Pedestrians? I reach for my haversack and find my half-eaten bar of chocolate. It is Duncan's blended chocolate and comes up as part of the rations. (The Yanks get ice-cream and fresh bread.) Duncan's blended has a mauve wrapper. Duncan's are an Edinburgh firm of which I had never heard before I joined up. I wonder whether Duncan's have a monopoly of supply, because we never see any other type. I carefully break off two squares of Duncan's blended. Keep-awake tactics! At this moment all eternity and the entire universe are embodied within my two squares of chocolate.

The atmosphere in the tank is now fetid and enervating. All of us have difficulty in holding our water for long periods under extreme stress. We relieve ourselves into shell cases. Tommy had even more severe internal problems, using the ammo box which still stands under the gun contributing to the polluted atmosphere. Normally in less perilous situations we would empty these containers out of the turret top. Tonight we do not emerge from behind our armour for such trivial pursuits.

After a brief canter across open fields, the shadowy group of tanks ahead is slowing to a stop. We shunt forward. Stop. I doze. Shunt forward. I chew the chocolate which I find still in my mouth. Stop. Doze. Shunt ... trees close left. Perspiration from my forehead and eyebrows has smeared into my periscope. Take out handkerchief. Wipe the lens. Polish it. Really I am polishing my consciousness. Polishing away the sleep.

One last lurch forward. Halt! The silver radiance continues to increase. More Bethlehem angels? Or angels of Mons?

03.00 hours: It is like ringing up the curtain on the first act of a play, the darkened theatre giving way to the vivid detail on stage. Or perhaps watching a grey photograph in the developer gradually clearing into black and white.

The column has halted. The dust cloud has subsided and the new breeze moves the mists away – rather like the falling of the seven veils. A brilliant full moon appears. In the moonlight the fields are a dull, flat pewter. The details of trees, branches, leaves are etched in fine black detail on the dull silver background. Scores of armoured vehicles are square, solid, black shapes near at hand. A vast long, shadowy hedge runs across our front. This must be the objective code-named 'Fly by Night'. The entire regiment is strung out in bunches of tanks and single vehicles along the line of the hedge. Behind the tanks are low, flat personnel carriers moving up, each emerging from its own private shroud of dust.

Reluctantly, on command, I traverse the gun away from the confused but fascinating pageant of the regiment sorting itself out. My view to the left is restricted by another high hedge or small wood. I am alone on the edge of a strange uninhabited world where man has never trodden. I know that tonight we have successfully achieved one of the most unusual and imaginative feats of arms in modern war. We have used the tank to the utmost of its ability, taking up station well to the enemy's rear. But it is all unreal and has no more substance than a small rectangular photograph of a moonlit field and a dark hedgerow. So I sit in my little monk's cell all alone, wearing the contemplative habit of khaki denim, and I study my little world, and think ...

First I try to stop myself thinking, for thinking is dangerous. Within my skull lurk horrific hordes of murderous SS fanatics and thugs, who, when I open the door of my mind, rush forward and occupy and terrorize my entire being. And those 54-ton Tiger tanks, with their high-velocity guns and impenetrable armour, smash down the walls of the mind and set my Sherman blazing on the instant. So stop thinking! But, if I stop thinking, what am I become? An automatic extension of the tank gun and the wireless set, a more subtle, adaptable and considerably cheaper version of a solenoid, a mechanical joint in a mechanical system? The replaceable fuse that sparks the electric current? A piece of fire-lighter material in the chain of Tommy cremation?

So I try to feed on mental images, benign memories, so that there is no room for the Hunnish invaders: even the harsh discomforts of my army life are kinder than those mental insurgents. Remember then a December day on the golf course at Aberdeen when, clothed only in vests and shorts, we watched an immense black blizzard sweep in on us from the North Sea so that we huddled together for warmth, for very life, in a bunker on the golf course. Marching over the Scottish hills, 15 miles at a stretch, in driving sleet, but seeing Highland cattle for the first time. Waking, at day break on Thetford Heath, and finding my eyelashes frozen together. The drill sergeant's profane insults ('You lot waddle like pregnant ducks' – they all said it). The training instructor's command to wade a deep rushing river, fully dressed ('Never f-ing mind if your mother did tell you to keep your f-ing feet dry'). Lining up for a six-seater latrine, back of an old jute works, watching the lucky six defecating, then the next six, then yourself sitting to be stared at whilst your meagre genitals are graphically commented upon. Fun, comparatively.

Moments of rare exhilaration and fascinating surprises amid the endless deserts of meaningless functions and idle repetitions and needless obscenities and odious environments. All, in some way, kindly preparing us for this moment in Normandy.

This Normandy: an oblong silver field and black hedgerow. The clarity and utter stillness of the scene have a Wagnerian effect of grandeur and inhumanity. Why is it (thinking again) that the human mind can escape to fly free through many worlds whilst the body remains clamped within an immobile physical trap, as cramped and solid and material as a halted tank?

Not halted! We are rolling again, moving into a line of tanks much more spaced and regulated than when I last looked in that direction. Infantrymen crouch by the hedge, staring through the roots and beyond it. Others set up mortars and move equipment. We swing right and left again, and come into a gap between two Shermans of our own troop. The well-known aquiline profile of Bobby McColl looks down from one of the tanks. He leaps across the gap onto our tank as we roll into line.

'Driver, halt,' (Ken's voice). 'Switch off. Gun front. Crew, rest.' Bobby McColl's voice takes over. 'We did it. We reached "Fly by Night" on the dot and within fifty yards. A little mixed up in the ranks but all sorted out. Good work, all of you. Any problems?'

In the new silence, Stan is able to shout from the driver's seat, 'Did we lose anybody, sir?'

'Only one tank of C Squadron missing. Sergeant Duff. No sign of him. Nobody saw him hit or in trouble. Probably down a bomb crater somewhere. Right, ye can get out for a while, one at a time. Empty bladders. Have a smoke. But keep close. Don't wander off. We don't know about mines under foot. And things might get sticky at first light. I'll keep ye genned up.'

His boyish face disappears from my view as I sit looking up out of the turret. Snowey's moustache and bushy eyebrows interpose. He shouts down past me. 'All right, Stan. You stretch those driver's legs first. Five minutes.'

Stan grumbles, 'About time. My arse has as many corns as a postman's feet.'

'And Tommy, empty that stinking tin of yours. No, don't pass it to me. Carry it out yourself. Well away from the tank, even if you have to tread on a land-mine.'

03.15 hours: I take my five minutes' breather. Climb stiffly out of the turret. Drop gingerly to the ground. Pins and needles shoot up through my cramped ankles and calves. I trot vigorously on the spot for a few moments. After the clammy heat of the turret it seems cold here outside, with wisps of damp mist rising from the fields. I move to the back of the tank where the engine outlets are still hot from the night trek. I lean against the warm armour and sniff the peculiar homely odour of hot rubber, sweating iron and grease.

A weather-beaten Black Watch corporal strolls up and leans beside me. 'Cigarette, Jock?'

'No thanks, I don't smoke.'

'Good lad. Keep it up. Me, I smoke forty a day. If can get. They started me on it when I was a boy soldier. Now I can't break the filthy, sodding habit. Hard on yese when the ration's only seven a day.'

'We share out the fags and boiled sweets on our tank between smokers and non-smokers.'

'Don't have any non-smokers in our lot, selfish buggers!'

A group of tank officers stands near us, talking to the Black Watch colonel. The officers look as though they are dressed for a fancy dress ball. One has a leather jerkin. Another is wearing denim overalls. One has a cricket sweater on. Others are in battledress. One or two are in shirtsleeves. Trousers range from sloppy corduroys to neatly pressed serge. The Black Watch colonel has a red hackle in his bonnet. Our colonel is there and David Bevan and Tom Boardman. Several carry the habitual riding crops which serve for nothing more lethal than to decapitate inoffensive dandelions. My Black Watch corporal comments, 'Cooking up some more nice, enjoyable warfare for us.'

I agree, 'Looks like it. What was it like for you, riding in those new carriers?'

'Hell. Shattering, shaking Hell, boy. Better than walking. But I wouldna be a tank man for a general's pay. Only advantage yese have got is wearing shoes.'

'At least we don't risk treading on anti-personnel mines.'

'Very small beer, Mac, compared to these 88s yon Jerry throws at tanks. Me, I've walked all the way from Alamein and s'w'elp me God, I'll walk all the rest o' the way tae Berlin and back again, so's I can keep away from ye'r kipper-smoking furnaces, yon Shermans.'

We stand there moon-gazing for a few moments in one of those frequent casual encounters thrown up by the ceaseless permutations of war. The Black Watch corporal carefully pinches out his cigarette half-smoked and equally carefully puts it away in a packet. Will he ever smoke the other half?

'My time's up,' I say. 'Must get back in now and let somebody else get a breath of air.'

'Guid luck, t'yese, lad. See yese in Berlin or Glasgae. Won't catch me getting in one of those buggers. Nice safe holes in the ground, that's me. Who wants tae sit up there waiting for Jerry tae blow his f-ing head off?'

Ken Snowdon takes his stroll, whilst I keep turret watch – and he makes a rather self-conscious pause behind the tank, hurriedly 'doing himself up' as another Black Watch Jock accosts him. I sit on the turret top and study the line of sixty tanks, nosed up behind the endless rampart of hedge, nameless until christened 'Fly by Night' by some witty Canadian staff captain. Away in the distance, back towards Caen, sound of machine-guns and heavier explosions. Behind us and to our right rear the moonlit night is ruddy with flashes. But here all is doom quiet, silver frosted. Is it possible that the Germans have not realized that we are here?

4 Dawn Attack

03.30 hours: The colonel ordered Lieutenant Des Coakley, enthusiastic footballer and popular troop leader, to take his tank through an ominous hole in the rampart of hedge, a hole probably made by a large armoured vehicle, and check for Tigers in the jungle beyond. With only his eyes and forehead showing above the turret rim, Coakley commanded his Sherman through the gap. Moments later, his operator and fellow footballer, Jack Pentelow, reported in broken tones, 'Sunray OOA [commander out of action].' An enemy sniper had shot the lieutenant precisely between the eyes at 500 yards range. Ominous indeed.

Snowie's voice: 'Driver, start up!' The great engine roars into life again. We grab our headsets and pull them on over our berets. 'Driver, advance. Come right. There's a hole in the hedge about twenty yards along. Loader, load with HE. Gunner, keep your guns pointed through the hedge and ready to fire co-ax.'

Stan drives the Sherman through a gap too large for it. Obviously Tigers have passed this way. Other tanks are moving ahead of us. As we pass through the hedge, we fan out on the other side. Hedge 'Fly by Night', like most Normandy hedges, is sky-high and forest-thick. Now, passing through it, we can see, 300 or 400 yards away, the jumbled outline of a small village with woods or orchards at each end. ('All the villages have been fortified,' said Bobby.) Mist still obscures the distant cottages, but nearer at hand the bright moonlight turns a large expanse of corn stubble into the semblance of a snowfield.

'Hullo, all stations William. Fire in your own time. Now! All stations William, off.'

Snowie: 'Gunner, take the edge of the village straight ahead and douse it with co-ax. Co-driver, same target. Fire in your own time.'

I make a small adjustment of height and direction, a touch on the traverse grip to the right, a push on the elevating wheel forward and downward. Stamp briefly on the co-ax button. The familiar dotted lines of fire leap across the space as the Browning thuds for a moment. The tip of my tracer hits what might be the roof of a house in the huddle of shapes. I depress the guns fractionally. Through the telescope I can see our artillery shells bursting along the target. I can hear their explosions coming with the rhythm and frequency of a dog barking excitedly. I touch the floor button again with my foot, feeling the metal disc clearly through my illegal thin-soled shoe. Heavily-nailed War Office issue boots do not make for efficient firing. Tracer streaks again, right on turret. I put my foot down and keep it down, at the same time twisting the traverse grip in my right hand. Tracer hoses the distant village edge as the Browning thuds solidly away.

Down in the front compartment Rex is also firing his Browning, which he controls directly by hand (which I cannot do because my Browning is invisible and inaccessible to me on Tommy's side of the big gun). My tracer overlaps and merges with the tracer from other tanks. Alien tracer, probably enemy, crosses our front from the right. The multiple lines of fire criss-cross and interconnect like the warp and woof of a brightly coloured oriental carpet.

I keep the Browning firing until the entire belt of 250 bullets is exhausted. A dull click. Tommy whips the old box away, pushes in a new box, threads the metal end of the new belt under the flat cover of the machine-gun and out through the other side. Cocks the gun manually. Slaps my thigh. Loaded! Again I tread the button. Traverse back and forward along the front edge of the village. More large shell flashes mingle with the sparkle of our tracer. This is like a tremendous firework display. Correction: this *is* a tremendous firework display. Great fun. There is no response from the enemy. There is no feeling of wounding or killing men. We are simply directing pretty jets of fiery sparks into the mists and half-seen huddled buildings, just as we did on the Stanford battle area in East Anglia.

The sight and sound of thousands of bullets per minute coughing from our sleek black barrels, and fifty jets of brilliant red dots from our other tanks playing at patterns over the field, the sense of power under my hands and feet, the telepathic unity of so many pals who, with me, have dared to ride right through the invincible defences around Bourguebus – all these sensations add up to exhilaration and excitement. Fear, death and blood-shed do not obtrude into our thinking at this moment. Actual enemy bodies and machines are nowhere to be seen. So the symphony of disciplined noise, and the tapestry of flaming colours, and the ballet of moving vehicles and men create a kind of glory. And the misty village walls add an element of mystery and intrigue to the splendid pageant.

As I traverse left and right at will, I catch glimpses of the entire scene. All the tanks of at least two squadrons – and that will be nearly forty – are strung out in a straggling line 100 yards or so in front of hedge 'Fly by Night'. The moon continues to silver the wide field and to throw up the tanks as huge, bleak, vulnerable masses of black. At the far side of the vast field, hedges and trees merge with the mist and smoke into an incomprehensible medley of shapes, writhing and changing. Among the jagged, leafy contours of nature about a dozen houses show as squared, lighter grey blotches, dancing wildly in the swirling smoke and haze. Shell flashes appear like brief, fiery grins – red mouths momentarily opening and closing amid the greys and blacks. Into this lunatic scene quick, random machine-gun bursts frisk in dotted arrows of flame, now quite distinct from the long, continuous dotted lines of earlier firing. Where tracer strikes against a solid wall, a tiny sprinkle of sparks radiates upwards and as quickly falls away. The noise of the bursting barrage slams back at us, still with the irregular barking dog rhythm – whoof-whoof; whoof-whoof-whoof; whoof-whoof; whoof; whoof-whoof-whoooof!

The only perceivable reaction to our pandemonium consists of a few unidentified curls of tracer flighting straight across our bows, the overspill from another battle on our right. Then, to left and right, the low headless tanks – the infantry carriers, crawl slowly, cautiously forward across the wide field. Surely someone will contest the progress of the infantry carriers? As I think that thought, six small but angry red flashes merge into six puffs of acrid black smoke along the moonlit ground near one of the carriers.

Stan: 'Jerry Minnies on left.'

Snowie: 'Yes, I see.'

These are the German multi-barrelled mortars which drop shells in neat batches, causing consternation, if not fatal injury, to the person who happens to be sitting in the centre of the bursts. Infantry and dismounted tankmen hate the 'Moaning Minnies'. You hear them coming as a chorus of distant howls, but when they start to drop there is no time for dodging, simply a swift swishing noise before the six drum-roll explosions occur. Inside a tank one is normally fairly safe, but here again the tankmen have a vivid idea of what will happen the day a Minnie drops vertically straight down inside the turret.

A world-rending flash between two cottages! An earthquake rages out of the flash! I swing the turret. Stamp. Watch. Other tracers join mine in pursuing the author of the earthquake between the cottages. Flash, flash, flash as our shots impact. And that's it! Before the fear-chilled blood can heat into battle frenzy, that battle is over. An SP. It would have retreated even as we fired.

The effect of its one shot is evident on an infantry carrier which is now crawling round and round in circles like a cockroach with its back legs crushed. There is frenzied activity around the carrier, which slows to a halt facing back towards us. The SP's shot had probably smashed one track of the carrier. The driver had been hit or had baled out, leaving the carrier running in circles on its one good track. The distant figures of the infantrymen rise from where they had thrown themselves on the ground. Their steady advance starts up again, shadowed closely by 4 Troop. A Highlander doubles up and collapses. Another bends over him for a while and then moves on. A group of Minnies lands in the midst of 4 Troop, obscuring the Shermans. They sail through the dispersing smoke like navy destroyers through heavy seas.

Radio static dies and changes into the hum of an 'A' set switched to transmit. 'Hallo, Roger 3.' (David Bevan calling Bobby McColl.) 'Support Roger 4 at a distance. Roger 3 over.'

We trundle slowly forward. The Highlanders are now moving into the mists on the outskirts of the village. Well spaced out 4 Troop sit and watch 100 yards behind. We move halfway across the field and halt, also watching the infantry, watching 4 Troop, watching the menacing houses. The artillery has gone quiet for the moment. Another group of Minnies falls in the general area of 4 Troop. Two more infantrymen topple over. The ripple of a Spandau machine-gun filters through the tank noises. All the Highlanders throw themselves flat or duck behind carriers. Two of 4 Troop's tanks fire into the houses. There is a long pause. The Highlanders get up and move forward again, running into the shelter of the houses and out of our sight. Them 4 Troop moves forward a hundred yards. We follow suit.

A vicious clang and crash sets our tank rocking back on its springs. My forehead jars against the head-pad. Thick clouds of earth and smoke shoot up into the vision of my telescope. The entire moonlit world disappears. Snowie's knees grind into my spine as he ducks down. A succession of similar crashes and clangs all around the tank! A sound like rain or hail upon the turret top. The periscope gradually clears of the airborne refuse. Moonlight shows clearly again. Stan: 'Bloody Minnies! Where's our sodding artillery?'

Silence. Engines ticking over. Waiting. Watching. Shoals of shells skid through the air above us, groaning, howling, moaning, screeching, rumbling. Again we wait. Flashes in the dawn mists ahead. The thump, thump, thump of individual shells grows and merges into a continuous percussion beyond the nearest houses. As if in defiance, the Minnies hit back, once again creating their own black fog of smoke and dirt in the general direction of 4 Troop. We sit watching, motionless. There is nothing to shoot at. Somewhere among the houses and hedges the Jocks are moving forward. Machine-guns add to the general noise. The frantic blitz of Spandaus. The steadier stutter of infantry Brens. The hard, persistent thud of tank Brownings. Firing as they go, 4 Troop move to the side of the buildings.

Commander: 'Driver, advance. Gunner, hold your fire until you see a target. Loader, HE. Driver, right a bit. Steady. Left a bit. Steady ... slow down ... halt! Gunner, watch your front.'

My oblong of vision through the 'scope has apparently narrowed, although I know that this is an optical illusion. At first I had a wide panorama of the field with 4 Troop and the Black Watch ahead. As we advanced nearer the houses, I lost 4 Troop and the infantry, and then the field and the boundary woods. Now, as we draw even nearer, some of the houses slither out beyond the edges of my vision. We are down to two farm cottages with a lane running between them, just a rutted dirt track. Beyond is a strip of road crossing our front. Beyond that, an orchard wreathed in mist and mystery.

In the lane stands an empty hay wagon, the shafts pointing at the sky. Nothing moves. We hear the incessant din of artillery shells crashing into the cottages, orchards and gardens. But here close at hand the motionless, colourless scene exudes a kind of tangible silence, a visible silence all its own.

My entire universe now is a tiny cart track between two cottages in France. The world beyond, the world only just beyond, with its slamming explosions and rattling machine-guns, has been registered by my mind as a constant factor to be ignored. All that matters is any sudden change on my still picture, the subtle intrusion of a shape that was not there before. To me the silence, the emptiness of this lane is more terrifying than a field full of explosions. It is an emptiness pregnant with portent of some horrifying apparition. It is a lost place beyond the normal habitat of humankind. It is where Columbus stood when his men thought they were nearing the edge of the world. It is where the spy stands blindfold as the bolts click and the bullets slide into the breeches of a dozen rifles. It is where the tiny jungle creature stands as the coiling anaconda stares with icy eyes. It is the moment in mid-air of the mountaineer who has lost his grip on the precipice lip or the parachutist whose release has failed to work. It is all of us standing at the graveside clutching a handful of earth or a red rose.

As I sit and watch my narrow lane, my mind insists on thinking ahead of my eyes. Begins imagining ... it could be a sudden wave of SS infantry running into the lane ... and, before I can press the foot button and fire enough bullets, one of them falls on his knees, aims a bazooka, the rocket springs straight at the turret, blinding us in the explosion, sending sharp shards of steel slicing through the turret, cutting, smashing, paining, screaming ... or it could be the long muzzle of an 88mm appearing between the trees in the orchard, a huge, self-propelled gun and, although I get my shot in first, the massive gun gushes fire. I glimpse the black shot in flight. It smashes through the tank, sparks the engine into an incinerating blast of flame, burning, searing, seething ... or along that village street now could be crawling a 50-ton Tiger tank, and in a moment its great bulk will fill the end of the cart track, and I shoot but my shot bounces off, and its great gun turns. I shoot again but it bounces. My 75 shot ricochets hopelessly as the great gun turns, turns, turns. An immense flash with an instant concussion: flesh, bones, flames, blood, screaming apart into unconsciousness ...

For a moment I sit shivering, resenting the imminence of death (for somebody here, if not for me), the years of youth wasted, the years when I should be walking a pretty girl home, taking her out cycling in the idyllic green Herefordshire lanes, rowing her along the mirroring River Wye, rowing along the sky mirrored in the river, and strolling by the Eden-coloured flowerbeds of the Castle Green. All that is lost. Sixteenth, seventeenth, eighteenth birthdays surrendered to war, black-out, civil defence duties, troop concerts, volunteer work in canteens. Nineteenth, twentieth birthdays surrendered to parade grounds, tank-training areas, shooting ranges, slummy barrack rooms, night guards ... and now this! No pretty girl. No fairy lights. No flowers. No picnics. For the moment I feel bitter and resentful. And that gives me the defiance to continue sitting here watching. They say that perfect love casteth out fear. Not down a bedev-illed Normandy cart track. Perfect resentment casteth out fear much more efficiently. In this doom-packed lane between grimacing cottages.

'Hallo, Roger 4 Baker. Prisoners coming towards you. 4 Baker, over.'

'4 Baker. I see them, off.'

Rex chortles, 'That's against the Geneva Convention,' and Snowie responds, 'What is?' Rex explains 'Seeing prisoners off!' And before Snowie can reprimand Rex, Stan groans, 'Gawd! Put him out for the Tigers to eat.'

Silence. Each to his own thoughts. Lane still. Road clear. Orchards dead. I stare along my narrow province and begin to drift off into imaginings again. Movement! Movement imagined? Movement happening! Men. Khaki men. I consciously jerk my foot back from the fatal button. Khaki men. Jocks. Blessed Black Watch. More than one is *bloody* Black Watch. One man winding a field dressing around his own wrist. Coming along the strip of street across our front. Moving into the sullen orchard.

'Driver, advance. To the end of this lane. That's it. Halt! Gunner, that gives you a better field of fire.'

We have squeezed along the narrow dirt track between the cottages, crushing the hay wagon into shattered sticks. We are at the street corner. A straggling village street with a ruined church tower, a few houses, yards, barns, orchards, totally chaotic and unplanned. Small groups of Black Watch, rifles at the ready are moving along or across the street. In the street itself they advance slowly and deliberately. In the orchards they crouch and run in short sprints. Another Sherman pokes its snout around the far corner. Two Germans, bareheaded and with the usual baggy trousers over their high boots, walk across the road, their hands on their heads, looking shocked, grey, disconsolate. A Black Watch private guides them with gentle taps of his rifle (suggesting that he might have been a shepherd with his crook on some Highland hillside), grinning and urging them on with a steady stream of Gaelic which is incomprehensible both to us and to the prisoners.

The trees in the orchards are merging from blacks and greys into greens and browns. Daylight is superseding the moonlight. Daybreak seems icy cold to me. But again that must be some kind of psychological reaction, for here in the noisome tank we are all sweating.

04.45 hours: Numbers of Black Watch, perhaps up to a hundred, are standing along the street just waiting. There are no civilians. No Resistance fighters. This is a dead village, Saint-Aignan-de-Cramesnil, completely evacuated and militarized by the Germans. We roll along the street, grey cottages on our left hand, an orchard on our right. Once again we are moving out onto our exposed left flank. The church, very much like an English village church (Norman, of course), stands at the street end. Beyond the churchyard the road dips down to the plains which are still the hunting preserves of the Tigers. Over all that vast land the Nazi writ still runs. Those lanes are the freeways of the enemy's tanks and troop-carriers and self-propelled guns. Those woods are his assembly points and ammunition dumps. And we are exposed.

We move across the junction, swinging right, and are behind a wall again, protected by farm buildings. I breathe deeply. The benevolent odour of farm manure oozes in through the openings of 3 Baker. This smell is even more powerful than the slightly sweet stench of corrupting flesh with which we have lived for two months since landing. Through a gap in the buildings we glimpse a rather untidy, dirty farmyard.

Stan snorts, 'Gawd! Pull the chain! Home sweet stinking home, Tommy?'

Tommy snorts back, 'They wants to rake out and get that place mucked out. Poor mucking pigs and poultry, having to scratch in that lot.'

Stan persists. 'I thought pigs liked scratching in muck, Tommy.'

'Pigs are blinking sensitive animals with delicate stomachs, worse than

you or me. We always boils our pig food at home before we feeds 'em ...'
He swivels his periscope: 'Talking of pigs ...!'

I freeze as a German helmet appears within periscope vision. A helmet
on a Teutonic head. A *Wehrmacht* collar. A field-grey tunic. Before I can
stamp on the trigger my brain flicks 'All clear!' It is only a German
waxwork sprawled in a ditch beside an upturned motor bike. He cannot be
dead. There is no sign of violence, no tomato sauce splashes of blood such
as Hollywood would inevitably infuse into such a scene. Just an undamaged
waxwork dummy, left out in the sun and tumbled into a ditch. It cannot be
alive. There is no movement of limbs. No heaving of chest. No flicker of
face muscles. Hands outstretched, clutching at empty air in unnatural
tension. Eyes staring. Face blank. It drifts out of vision as we crunch past,
a tiny horror tableau in a ditch. I cannot imagine it as a hated Nazi, or a
mother's son, or a son's father. As a ploughman or a postman or a factory
hand. Or a member of a Lutheran congregation. Or a boozer in a
bierkeller ...

Just a sickening, yellowing waxwork illustrating the futility of human
life. Would it not have been kinder of a loving God to have created us all
as human waxworks with easily replaceable working parts instead of all the
travail of mother, toil of father, pains of growth, wild hopes and imaginings,
affinity with sunsets and sea breakers, the studying, wooing, loving, hating,
parading, fighting, starving, hiding, only to ride a motor bike round a
corner of some remote, stinking French farmyard, drive headlong into a
Black Watch bullet, fall grasping frantically at the new sun, and fade into a
clumsy waxwork in a ditch – a dummy of less value than the spare parts on
the motor bike which it rode? Now they will shovel him into a ditch as a
present for the worms, collect his badges as interesting souvenirs, appropriate his watch and field-glasses as useful tools, and utilize his motor bike
as a valuable asset.

Loud click as Ken switches to 'A' set, and a sudden blessed silence from
the unending radio static and far distant imbecile voices. 'Hallo, Roger 3
Baker. Track clear as far as we can see. Roger 3 Baker, over.' '3 Baker, OK.
Halt. Keep watching. Off.'

Once again we find ourselves in a little lane. Or, rather, this is simply the
beginning of a farm track running between an outbuilding and the main
basse-cour of a modest French farm. On our right the buildings open up
into a large and fairly tidy yard. A German lies at the precise centre of the
yard. Several Black Watch run into the yard, weapons at the alert. One of
them prods the German with a bayonet. No response. The Jock uses his
boot to turn the German over. Another broken waxwork.

Ahead of us the cart track winds across a level cornfield towards a hedge where the track dips out of sight. Farther on, the same track climbs back into sight up a slope between tall trees and disappears into a dense wood. There is no movement in the field or in the wood. The sun is now up. It is Tuesday.

05.30 hours: The story of Normandy, 1944. A cornfield. A hedgerow. A wood. Deserted. Nothing to see. No 7th Cavalry. No Light Brigade. No massed ranks of Brandenburgers. No Stukas.

Stan: 'What are we waiting for, corp – apart from Christmas?'

Snowie: 'Usual thing. Counter-attack positions.'

Stan: 'What for? Jerry's gone home long ago. I reckon you could have a game of football on that field without Jerry taking any notice.'

Snowie: 'Don't bank on it. He's probably down in that dip. Keep your sights trained that way. Watch out for unusual shapes. There's an SS panzer division out there somewhere. If Jerry's going to attack, he'll most likely do it sooner rather than later. No more idle chatter now.'

Rex: 'Commander! I can see a squared shape. Seven o'clock right, three trees close together. Right again, a single tree, then—'

Snowie: 'I've got it. A small building. Not a tank turret.'

Tommy: 'Chicken coop. Or a loo.'

Stan: 'What would a loo be doing out in the country there?'

Me: 'For passing pilgrims. Through the telescope it looks like a tool shed.'

Snowie: 'Operator, reload HE. Gunner, put one round HE through the door of the shed, coop, loo, strong point, whatever ... just in case.'

06.15 hours: Hurried scraping on the back of the tank. Commander Ken takes off his headset and climbs out. In a moment his head reappears and he picks up the mike. 'I'm off to a commanders' conference. Ken, come up top. Report if anything happens. Pull back under cover if you have to. Tommy, move over and gun. Stan, come up and load. Rex, get into the driver's seat. Give you all a change of position. But keep awake!'

I haul myself up into the cool, brisk morning air, a welcome change from the sweat-hole down below. Up here I can hear the constant noise of fierce battle from our right rear. But to our left and out front there is the undisturbed peace of nature. The Germans have failed to evacuate St-Aignan's birds, which chirp and whistle noisily. Somewhere an unmilked cow complains in anguished bellows. A small patter of human conversation filters through from the Black Watch just behind us who are digging deep into the rich Norman soil, dug over so often for more peaceful purposes these last two thousand years.

Tommy shouts up, 'August flaming Week. What a way to go holidaying in France. Churchill's ferking Tours Limited. A right Cook's Tour this has turned out to be.'

Stan calls back, 'What do you expect at the price, mate? And a flipping luxury Sherman mobile home instead of a rickety old "charabang", remember? With a door alongside each row of seats, and no springs.'

Loud clanging on the back of the tank. A Black Watch lieutenant is hitting the armour plate with an entrenching tool. Modern communications! 'Can I come up?' he shouts.

'Be our guest!' Trooper me bawls back. He climbs up gingerly.

'Can I take a look at the *Boche* country?'

'Would you like to borrow our glasses, sir? Not that there's much to see.'

'Thanks. It's a better view from up here ... Bloody good glasses they issue to you tank chaps.'

'They're not WD issue. They are best *Boche* supply. Zeiss. We borrowed them from a Jerry for the duration.'

'Good idea. Must get myself a pair.'

The sun is now climbing higher in the sky on our left. And the shadows shorten, drawing back into the bases of their objects. Where the woods opposite have been an impenetrable puzzle of trees and slanting shadows, now the stronger, higher sunlight penetrates and cleans up the lines of the woodland so that tiny glades and avenues become clearly defined. I turn my binoculars on each open space, green and glistening, and upon each clump of wood, sharp and black, searching for the odd squared shape or for the ominous hump or for the unaccountable movement.

Nothing!

06.50 hours: Stan, chewing a 'dog' biscuit, grunts, 'I think our Snowie has got a week-end pass. Or perhaps Hank has instituted morning prayers.'

Rex adds, 'Or perhaps they've all been captured by Jerry and there's nobody left except us. Is that wireless set still working? No messages for ages. Can you see anybody else, Ken?'

Stan yelps, 'There's a ladybird just walked right across my periscope. Red with white spots.'

Tommy groans, 'No good! I could go the lady or the bird but I'm a bit too old for ladybirds.' He passes more solid dry biscuits round the crew.

Silence returns. If you can call birdsong silence. Stillness. If you can call the gentle ballet of breeze, leaves and grasses stillness. Peace. If you can call the perpetual menace of fanatical storm-troopers snaking through undergrowth peace.

Stan feels compelled to speak, 'Hey, let's go home. There's nothing doing here. As boring as a jumble sale. Let's just sneak off. And then when dear old Corporal Ken comes back, chewing his moustache and looking for his tank …?'

07.05 hours: 'Here's Ken coming back,' I say. 'Get ready to play musical chairs again.'

Ken trudges along the farm lane behind us, a tired man with a tread closely resembling that of a farmer wearing boots heavy with sodden clay. He is carrying his map case under his arm and has both hands thrust down deep into his pockets. He is staring down at the ground and does not see the young Highland lieutenant who has come across to speak to him. Suddenly, he starts, retrieves his right hand from his pocket and salutes, his other hand still stuck incongruously in his pocket. The Highlander merely grins. They stand and chat (Corporal Ken will know more of the battle plan than the infantry officer). They chat in the empty lane. Empty lane, deserted farm buildings, silent land. But all around us the suspicious silence. Whispering, muttering, gossiping silence.

In Fleet Street this morning the war artists will be drawing arrows out from Caen and will not know that Ken and the Highlander and I stand at a tiny blob well ahead of their wildest-guessed arrow on the map. The two men exchange friendly salutes, not the slammed emphatic motions of the parade ground but the gestures of two passing desert travellers, sharing a moment of companionship in a lonely place. Our commander climbs casually up onto the tank. Pulls his left hand out of his pocket at last. The hand is clasping a pipe. He knocks the warm ash out against the turret, pockets the pipe and nods to me to drop back into my normal seat.

Click of the microphone. Snowie intones his briefing notes. According to Hank, either we have lighted upon a total vacuum in the German defensive system due to shortage of troops, or else any survivors from St-Aignan have simply gone to ground in Robertmesnil to wait for reinforcements. Nobody knows yet. But the entire Polish Armoured Division is coming through on our left, and a Canadian armoured division on the right, and they are going to smash right through to Falaise and join up with the Americans, encircling the Hun.

Stan, always argumentative, says, 'Why wait for them? We could get over to that ridge now. In a couple of hours there'll be batteries of 88s over there and all the armoured divisions in the world will only be walking straight into another high-class cock-up.'

Snowie patiently responds. 'The generals seem to think differently. Mind you, I don't know if they are right. I've got the feeling that Hank doesn't agree with them either. Anyway we have our orders.'

Tommy mutters, 'Bleeding generals. If we did away with them, the war would be over much quicker!'

We watch the continuing landscape. Rex recites, 'What is this life if full of care we have no time to *sit* and stare?'

08.30 hours: We reverse out of our cart track, between the farm buildings. We poke our tail back towards the church, then roar forward along the parallel minor track at the front edge of the village. Farm buildings protect us from the enemy's view. Just outside the village there is a small, dark wood with the density of a forest. At the rear of the wood there is a glade, almost totally secluded. The rest of 3 Troop tanks are already parked there.

Our commander orders, 'Driver, halt. Switch off. Unload all guns. Operator, get the earphones out and we'll keep wireless watch down at the side of the tank. Crew, dismount and prepare breakfast.'

We dismount slowly. After long periods in cramped positions inside the tank, we emerge like talipeds, shambling, sloth-like creatures whose limbs tend to bend in the most unexpected directions. Stan opens a tin of corned beef to fry, and we go gathering some of the abundant dry wood to make a fire, shielded by tall trees. One by one we take the spade from its brackets on the side of the tank and make our little pilgrimage into the trees, rendering unto Nature that which is Nature's. In this little wooded nook of Normandy the performance of natural functions is much more pleasant than in a crowded, stinking camp latrine or even on an open hillside. Supposedly in a perilous place, an enclave behind the enemy lines, the atmosphere is for a moment reminiscent of a boy scout camp.

Soon Stan has fried the corned beef in one tin, soaked hard biscuit in rancid butter in another tin, and in a third tin double-boiled some water to try to rid it of the appalling tang of chlorination. We sit down on the lank grass to eat. The battle noises are no louder than the anticipatory rumbles in our bellies. Youth erupts, and our jokes grow into imbecilities and insults. Tommy swings his mess-tin like a scythe. Stan ducks and the tin hits me. I overbalance from my crouching position, crash into the tank track and spill corned beef on the grass. Anxious for jollity, we all guffaw loudly. I scrape the corned beef out of the grass and spoon it back into the mess tin. I'm young, fit, hungry!

Stan comments, 'You've spilled some of your corned beef on the tank track, Ken.'

Tommy snaps, 'That's not corned BEEF!!!'

There is a moment of icy silence. Tommy crawls over to the tank track, picks something from it, holds it up. A tatter of field-grey cloth.

'Stan, you should look where you're driving. You've mashed up a Jerry.'

Stan stares at the track pale-faced. Snowie gets up and wanders away into the trees. Tommy drops the piece of cloth, wipes his fingers on his denim trousers and laughs weakly. Rex is leaning against a tree, bending over, retching, convulsed. I get up, go round the tank and … I'm young, animal, hungry, I finish eating my corned beef.

Troop Sergeant Wilkins strolls from his tank and advises us, 'Mr McColl says to brush up the camouflage. We may be moving in and out of trees and hedges later in the day.' We set to work lopping a few live branches out of the wood to transform our tank into that scene from *Macbeth* where Birnam Wood comes to Dunsinane. I mention the concept to studious Rex.

'Yeah, a mixture of *Macbeth* and the Wooden Horse of Troy,' he laughs. 'Once we get within the walls of Robertmesnil, Captain Agamemnon McColl and his trusty gladiators leap out and decimate Sepp Dietrich and his Trojan SS. Come to think of it, our night march might one day go down in history like the Trojan Horse.'

I scoff at that, 'Not a chance. Agamemnon wasn't in the rural yeomanry. He was a Guards officer, and his brother-in-law was editor of the *Athens Daily Times*.'

Snowie adds, 'And don't forget we're not even British now. We're Canadian Army today. All you'll get in the official history, Rex boy, is "Canadian troops, displaying the spirit that won the West, captured St-Aignan-de-Cramesnil."'

I suggest, 'What we need is a Xenophon.'

Tommy (trying to break into the conversation), 'Why? Can you play one?'

'Idiot!' Rex chortles, 'Xenophon was a Persian soldier who went on a famous forced march in ancient history. He wrote about it afterwards. And what he says goes, because he was the only one to write about it.'

'Hank draws pictures,' says Tommy trying to redeem himself.

'That should get us a mention in *Comic Cuts*,' Snowie grins. 'Let's get the Christmas decorations hung up on 3 Baker, lads.'

We stick branches into various projections and holes around the Sherman until it looks like an immense but rather moth-eaten bush. The idea is not to build an imitation tree but simply to destroy the clean, square metallic outline of the armoured vehicle. 'Have you ever seen a Bactrian camel?' asks Stan, 'Lots of humps! And all that wool hanging off, permanently moulting. That's Roger 3 Baker for you!'

'Come on, Roger 3 Bactrian camel,' yells Rex, slapping the Sherman on the rump. 'Gidee-yup the Camel Corps – with Corporal Ken Snowdon starring as Lawrence of Arabia!'

09.50 hours: We have mounted Roger 3 Baker and rumbled the hundred yards or so from our tiny woodland dell to the minor lane which runs parallel to the village street. This minor road is now the base line from which A and C Squadrons are slowly probing forward. We halt along the lane at a spot where, flat and devoid of hedges, it runs past the cornfields and orchards. Our troop waits in reserve. From where we are, the ground seems to dip away in all directions, here very gently, there more sharply, meaning that we are at the crest. Behind us now the little village of St-Aignan, in its orchards, and with the damaged church spire skewering up through one of the orchards, looks pretty in the bright sunlight. This is the same village which, six hours ago, looked bleak and perilous seen from the other side by moonlight.

Two other Shermans roll along the edge of the cornfield behind us and come to rest within hailing distance of our tanks. The squadron leader, Hank, climbs out of the first one, the second-in-command, Bill Fox, from the other. They walk forward to Bobby McColl's tank and engage him in conversation, pointing and waving riding crops about the deserted landscape.

Presently Snowie informs us, 'Hank is expecting a counter-attack. Our troop and HQ(F) [fighting headquarters] are going to sit in the centre, plug any gaps and resist to the last man. Or at least that's the idea.'

'Fine!' comments Stan, 'As long as I am not the last man.'

Again the silence, the immobility so rarely seen in war films or read in war histories. Tank engines ticking over quietly, almost emphasizing the otherwise silence. This emptiness is the major proportion of the war experience much as the empty black mass of the sky is vaster than the tiny sparkling stars. Death, doom, destruction may leap from any bush at any moment. But a disciplined informality pervades until that epic moment. Don Pateman, Hank's co-driver, walks the 20 yards to ask if he can exchange his tin of pork and veg for a tin of meat and veg. Hank does not like pork.

'Hey, lads,' Don shouts up through the co-driver's hatch, 'Have you heard about Bill Fox's secret weapon?'

'Sounds like a dirty joke,' Tommy shouts back from his higher post.

'No, Gospel truth! Cut me throat and let me die! Last night we passed right over a German slit trench. Old Bill says the whites of their eyes looking up was just like an Al Jolson number. So Bill puts his hand into the Mills bomb pouch beside him, takes out a bomb, pulls out the pin and throws it. "Need their bowels moving," he says. But no flash. No bang. Like a wet Guy Fawkes Night. Next day Bill gives poor Bruce Dickson hell. "No bloody flashes. Check the damn things." But Bruce checks the pouch and all the bombs are still there. Then Joe Watkinson snarls, "Who's pinched my pissing apple?" See, Joe had left his apple in the pouch, Bill picks it out, pulls out the pin, or rather the stalk, and throws. One frightened Fritz with an effing big lump on his head. Hank says that it's against the Geneva Convention to throw apples at the enemy.'

And in absolute precision the German guns weigh in with something much more substantial than apples. A row of black explosions runs, like spurts from the hoofs of immense invisible horses, across the cornfields beyond Bill Fox's tank. A direct hit on a cottage 100 yards away produces a murky white explosion, a cloud of ruptured stone and mortar. A whale of an explosion flares, gushes and batters the air between us and Bobby McColl's tank. I take the quick way into the turret, a standing leap, touch of a foot on the track, push of a hand on the deck of the tank, twist of the body and I roll across the turret 9 feet up in the billowing air. Only to find Snowie ducked inside the hatch, blocking my way in. Tommy tumbles on top of me. As I descend I get a field-wide vision of Bill Fox ascending his tank as though leaping Beecher's Brook without a horse, Hank disdainfully cocking one leg into his turret, Bobby McColl going down his turret like a Stuka dive-bomber. Several Black Watch privates roll over the lip of their machine-gun pit, mess tins in hand. One tall, solitary Black Watch officer stands at the edge of the orchard, watching the circus and sniffing the air as though aware of something burning.

'Gawd! I'll have scorch marks on my arse for weeks,' gulps Tommy.

'Have you been hit?' asks Snowie anxiously.

'No, just friction sliding over the turret. I could smell my effing trousers singeing as I went.'

'At least I had some potatoes to show for it when I got shot in the arse digging them up at Noyers,' chortles Stan, safely ensconced down below.

10.20 hours: We have moved only a few yards forward from the minor road into the field but the move has opened up for us a complete panorama of our front. A cart track runs down into a wooded gully across our front, twisting on and up through the cornfields to the hedgerows and tall roof of Robertmesnil farm. To our right a small orchard with a gap allows us to see the vague line of the Falaise road. Behind us are the scattered cottages and farms of St-Aignan-de-Cramesnil. (If we can view the whole of that panorama, anyone out there can view us!)

In the centre 2 Troop tanks (Wellbelove, Stanley and co.) are making their way down the track into the dip. The gully is deep enough to hide the lead tank as it crosses and climbs up into a maze of hedgerows from which it can monitor Robertmesnil. To our left 4 Troop are extended in the trees, and 1 Troop appears to have moved to cover the extreme and empty left flank where we kept watch earlier this morning. Behind them is the local chateau.

On our immediate left, in a finger of orchards, the Black Watch are well dug in. Between us and them is one of the HQ(F) tanks, commanded by the squadron captain (third in command), Ken Todd. That is the tank on which I did most of my training in England. The tanks of A Squadron are judiciously spaced in orchards on our right, with B Squadron completing a circle to our rear. We are a considerable little army, but we are out on our own (while other troops move up on our right) in unknown territory with untold numbers of enemy reinforcements, tanks, guns, SS, somewhere up the road.

Stan contemplates, 'Sitting here like this, we might just as well be watching a cricket match. Nothing happening, nobody moving, bloody monotonous, soul-destroying waste of time. Might as well go home. Hey, corp, what about it? Let's turn the tank round and go home. Maybe everybody else would do the same. Jerry as well. We march on London and they march on Berlin?'

I chip in, 'Sounds like a more sensible way of ending the war.'

Snowie snorts 'Sounds like kids' talk to me.'

We are now closed down for action, Stan turning the engine over from time to time, so that the normal noise of warfare does not intrude into our consciousness. There has been an increase in the steady drumming of artillery shells from both sides. We only sit up and take notice when we hear the brief, abrupt, SLAM-CRASH double impact of anti-tank weapons.

'Hallo William to William Able …' Someone starting to talk before they were ready. That was the colonel's call-sign, calling his second-in-command, Wykeham. But it was not the colonel's voice.

Rex: 'Probably wanting to borrow a spoonful of sugar from the 2-in-C.'

Stan: 'More likely the Coleman's mustard to put on the ham, I say, don't you know, old chap, what?'

'Hullo William to William Able. Medical half-track immediately for Big Sunray. Over.'

'William Able, coming immediately. Off.'

In spite of the artillery outside and the rising heat of the sun, a chill silence seems to have crept over the field. It is the silence, the telepathic intensity of sixty tank crews sitting listening. It is a silence which is in the mind rather than the ear. Sunray is the tank term for commander. And Big Sunray on William tank is the colonel himself. And the call for the medical half-track has only one possible meaning.

Tommy: 'Christ, corp, that's the colonel bought it, surely?'

Me: 'That's rotten luck. Coming right through the night march, then getting wounded before the battle even starts in daylight.'

Rex: 'It must be the bloody shelling. I hope the old man is OK.'

Far to the left in my periscope I see the front of the squadron leader's tank. A jeep pulls up. A tall figure vaults off the tank into the jeep. The little vehicle spins in a tight circle and speeds away.

Tommy (shouting, not on I/C): 'Bloody SS. Shit on you, rotten buggers. Shooting our colonel. Why don't you ferk off back home and shoot bleeding Hitler.'

Rex: 'How will they get him back across open country with Jerries still around there?'

Snowie: 'It should be easy enough to follow our track marks, a real Oregon Trail we'll have left behind us. And the jeep will just have to rely on speed.'

I pull a tiny notebook from my pocket and note the time when the colonel was wounded. We are specifically ordered NOT to keep personal diaries. There seems to be a theory that the personal musings of one 147 Tout K.J. might materially affect the outcome of the war should they fall into enemy hands. Squadron joker Harry Graham tells an interminable story about a German spy finding a personal camera on a burnt-out British tank, after which the developed film passes through numerous adventures before reaching Hitler's bunker. Hitler then studies the print avidly and, after some time of private meditation, emerges waving the photos and shouting '*Ach so*! It is ze Britisher *schwein* we are fighting against. Why haf never anybody told me zis before?' Our high authorities certainly have an undue obsession about secrecy when any German intelligence officer beyond our gully can have heard on the radio and guessed that our colonel has been wounded.

'Hullo Victor. Hullo Victor. Sunray hit by HE. Urgent medical orderly please. Urgent! Urgent! Victor, over.'

'Hullo Victor. OK. Off.'

Rex: 'Victor? That's B Squadron. B squadron leader, Major Brassey.'

Stan: 'Jesus! Jerry's working down the Army List. What the hell's going on? The colonel and the Honourable Peter both bought it and the battle not started yet?'

Tommy: 'They're hitting the ones at the back before they hit the ones at the front.'

Snowie: 'Today, we're all at the front. There isn't any back at St-Aignan.'

Nobody behind us. I stare out over my patch of virtually undamaged French agriculture and, to divert my thoughts, compare it with the scenes of 1914–18, blasted, destroyed terrain, when the static trenches ran eternally across the same piece of land. My patch of Normandy looks almost cosy in the ascendant sun, except for one menacing roof at Robertmesnil. For some reason, buildings behind the enemy's front line always look hostile and malevolent. In fact, in 1944, hedges, bushes and small woods are much more treacherous than buildings, for they give much less obvious cover for tanks, SPs and mobile infantry with bazookas.

Down the track in front of us and into the wooded gully hops a large brown bobtail rabbit, looking much bigger than its English cousins. Unperplexed by shells and mortar bombs it hops along until its white tail disappears in the tall grass towards 2 Troop.

Rex: 'Hey, Ken, did you see that? A rabbit. Why didn't you shoot it for dinner?'

Me: 'I thought maybe it has rabies and will bite a Hun.'

Tommy: 'If I'd had my old double-bore with me, that rabbit wouldn't have needed nothing but a bit of salt and pepper and a few onions.'

Stan: 'Live and let live, that's me. I don't believe in all this shooting business. I'm just a glorified bus-driver, a non-combatant. They wouldn't let me be a conchie so I drive a tank as the next best thing. Live and let live. That's the tank drivers' union rule, and even the *Boche* sticks to it.'

Me: 'As long as you don't call on the gunners' union for support when the Jerry gunners come back from strike.'

11.15 hours: Some of our early training was useful, even if the long weeks spent on Morse was a total waste. As taught in the training regiment I make mental inventories of everything on my landscape, especially trees and bushes. Above the point where the track finally disappears (left to right): three bushy-top trees in a solid hedgerow with light between the tree stumps; then a patch of solid wood with no light showing; an open horizon with no hedgerows; four tall trees; two large bushes; part of a gate or shed showing through a gap between two more bushy-top trees. If that light or gap or bush moves or disappears it means danger, action, deeds before words, and words before thought. Fire! Report! Adjust! Fire!

'Hallo, Roger 2 Baker.' (Hitler-mimic, Corporal Stanley.) 'Alert! I seem to see movement half-left, a hundred yards left of roofs, but cannot yet identify. 2 Baker, over.'

'2 Baker,' (Lieutenant Heaven) 'keep looking. Report as soon as you are sure of movement. Even if you cannot see what moves. Fire on suspicion. Over.'

I screw my eye up close to the gun sight and slowly traverse along the 2 Troop area, taking advantage of the considerable magnification to explore the intimacies of that little wilderness of trees and shadows in front of an even darker hedge. Nothing moves there ... except green fear. The fitful jazz beat of explosions behind us have merged into our consciousness until we disregard them. They become like the shading of woodwind, strings and percussion, inconsequential continuing music waiting for the soloist to enter with his first clarion note.

The SLAM-CRASH of an aimed shot – direct, violent, massive, close – smashes across the humdrum background of barrage. Close! Where? What? '2 Baker, I'm bloody hit! Bale out! Hornet at … Gawd!' (God, that's Stanley gone!)

Hornet – enemy tank or SP. Where? Where? Where, where, where … I squeeze the grip right … left … traversing quickly, staring into the camel-shaped trees. Hornet at … where, where, where, the hedge, solid-topped, fairly level … has a gap, a gap. A gap? Why? What? 'Charlie, left of roof, hornet in hedge over …' I adjust left, down, crosswires on! Stamp! Flame at muzzle. Frustrating smoke. Smoke. Smoke. Clearing to show spark of tracer leaping high into gap but another tracer from near gully flies into gap ahead of my tracer as Tommy slaps my leg, loaded, down a bit, fire! Tommy slaps. Stamp. Fire. Traverse. Sight. Slap. Stamp. Fire. Other flashes than mine festoon the far hedge with artificial flowers, blooming, dying, red as Flanders poppies. And as quick to wither. Normandy has poppies too.

Snowie orders, 'Gunner, cease fire. Operator, load AP again.'

I gasp, 'I feel better for that little bit of anger', but Rex responds, 'I hope Corporal Stanley feels better too.' Stan comments, '2 Baker didn't brew up altogether. No column of flame or smoke over there. Maybe they all got out.' Tommy is not optimistic. 'Jimmy Stanley broke off in mid-message. I reckon he's had it, poor bugger.'

Rex's voice sounds pensive, 'I hope nothing's happened to Stanley. He's such a bloody funny bloke. Who's going to make us laugh if he's bought it? Who's going to impersonate Adolf? Who's going to shout, "Ve haf goot torture for you. Ve vill your nails pull out and your balls shoot off"? You can't win wars without the Corporal Stanleys.'

Snowie breaks in, 'We're going to have to win it without the colonel and B squadron leader and Corporal Stanley and any other poor sod that gets in the way of a Jerry shell. Wait on, though. I don't see a Sherman blaze but I think we hit the Jerry gun. Thicker smoke and no flames.'

Stan tries to joke, 'Big Chief Sioux, him read smoke signals.'

Snowie's commander voice snaps, 'Yes, well, we're fighting a war, not running a children's party. You may be the next who has to bale out in a hurry, so keep your eyes and minds on those woods.'

Again I secretly rehearse my exit for that fatal moment. Once hit we shall need no other incentive to leap for the free air. The explosions of our ammunition, which is sufficient to knock out fifty tanks, will serve us as a humane killer before the Sherman furnace has had time to grill us as we sit. Something in my being revolts more against the slow grilling of my flesh after death than against the sudden swift shattering of mind and body in a massive explosion.

'People moving. Ours!' I cry. My periscope picks up movement down the track in the gully. A black beret appears. Another. A third … four! The figures trudge up the track into sight. I swing my gun to cover the four figures. Squint through the magnifying sight. Grey, waxen faces come into focus. One with blood on his forehead. Blood on his chest. Four well-known faces. Sad but relieved. Hurt but unbowed. I count them again. Recognize them. Try to make four into five. Press the mike switch. 'Corporal Stanley is not with them.'

Tommy snarls, 'Who's going to take the piss out of bloody Hitler now then?'

So Corporal Stanley, an orphan with no family to mourn him, will never again twiddle his moustache, shout 'Hoch, Hoch, mein Gott' and give his impersonation of Hitler. Hitler has gained his revenge. Something evil has again entered this high summer's day. Only a thin curl of smoke now rises as a memorial to Jimmy Stanley where his knocked out tank snuggles into the forest beyond our sight.

5 Tiger Terror!

8 August 1944:

12.35 hours: Full noon. August heat. Smoke and dust. A static skyline. Crowded with green shadows. Empty of people. One distant, menacing roof. Hidden fires. Ourselves watching. Intense. Silent. Sweat-soaked. Odorous. Poised between tiredness and fear. Crackle of static. Voices of distant battles. Crash and shatter of shells. Ours. Theirs. Brilliant blue skies. Torrid sun. I wipe my eyes with sweat-soiled cotton waste. Wipe the periscope rubber. Wipe telescope. Eye to telescope again. Empty oblong world. Smoke bursts. Crash and shatter of shells. Mainly theirs. Birds sing in sudden silence.

'Hullo, Oboe 3 Charlie.' (A Squadron) 'Hullo, Oboe 3 Charlie. View Hallo! Three Tigers, moving north, line ahead near road. Twelve hundred yards at one o'clock. Oboe 3 Charlie, over.'

'Hullo, Oboe Able to 3 Charlie. Hold your fire if you can till I join you.' (That's Tom Boardman.) 'Able to 3 Charlie, over.'

'3 Charlie, holding fire. Off.'

Tommy: 'God, man! Tigers!'

Now the moment of true fear has struck. Tigers! They say each Tiger will take out five Shermans before it succumbs, if then. They say one Tiger took out twenty of our tanks way back. Now the huge steel hand of fear clutches and squeezes my lungs, heart, throat. Like molten metal pouring down the throat and behind the eyes.

Snowie: 'Driver, start up. Loader, check loaded with AP. Gunner, traverse right. See what you can see. Co-driver, keep watch ahead.'

I see Oboe Able making his way to the right flank to take direct control of the shoot-out with the Tigers. The German 54-ton tanks (almost twice as big as a Sherman) are heading down beside the Falaise road towards Caen, oblivious of our presence. I swing my gun onto the short stretch of road which I can see across a distant cornfield. No Tigers there. Not yet.

In any case at this range my 75mm would be like a pea-shooter against a concrete wall.

'Hullo, Oboe Able to 3 Charlie. I see them now. Keep under cover and hold fire until about eight hundred yards. Then fire at the last one while I pepper the others. Over.' (Charlie is the big gun seventeen-pounder Firefly whilst Oboe Able has the smaller but quicker firing 75mm.)

'3 Charlie. Will do. Off.'

(Stan: 'If Oboe Able is going to take on the first two Tigers with his 75, he needs to be ready to duck.' Rex: 'Or jump. Or say his prayers.' Snowie: 'The 75 shots will make the Tiger commanders close down inside their hatches.')

'Oboe Able to 3 Charlie. Near enough. Fire! Over.'

'Charlie, OK. Gunner, fire!' (In his excitement Charlie commander has forgotten to switch back to I/C but his gunner can hear 'A' set clearly.) 'Gunner, on! Fire!... Got him, you golden boy. Got him. Charlie, got him. Over.'

'Able to Charlie. Reverse and go into new cover. Get the middle one. I'm hitting the first in line to keep his head down. And use your I/C. Off.' I see a thick sprouting of smoke over the trees beyond my range. 'Oboe Able to 3 Sunray. Charlie's Sunray has been hit. Get over there and keep Charlie shooting. 3 Over.'

'3. On my way. Off.'

I traverse gently back and forward but can see no more of the road. The growing cloud of smoke shows where one of the Tigers is blazing.

SLAM-CRASH of an 88mm! Almost simultaneous crashes. Flat trajectory. Tremendous muzzle velocity. An anti-aircraft gun used point-blank against tanks. Firing and impact explosions coming almost together. No smoke in A Squadron positions. SLAM-CRASH! Another Tiger fires unseen. A Squadron's 3 Troop leader will be dodging through the orchard trees. Lifting the sergeant commander from the turret. Giving orders. Bearing on the middle Tiger. One Tiger blazing and the other two swinging round to look for shelter and still not sure where the pesky Shermans are. We see it clearly in our mind's eye. The reverse of normal Normandy procedure – the hunters hunted. The Tigers affrighted.

BLAM-CRASH! Slightly different sound, equally imperious, of the seventeen-pounder.

'Oboe Able to Oboe. Second Tiger brewing. Am keeping third busy while Charlie brings to bear. Over.'

'Oboe, bloody good show. Over.'

Black gush of smoke over trees hiding road. Another Tiger burning. SLAM-CRASH of 88 almost together with BLAM-CRASH of seventeen-pounder. One … two … three crashes nearby. An answering roar of sound. New spouts of flame beyond the distant trees. I shout 'They've got him. They've hit Tiger three!'

'Hullo 3 Sunray in 3 Charlie. Got the second Tiger first shot. Hit the third with three shots. Charlie Sunray hit by falling flap, result of near miss. Send van for Charlie Sunray. Oboe 3 otherwise OK. Over.'

'Oboe Able to 3. Good shooting. Off to you. Able to Oboe. Can see first two Tigers smoking and abandoned. Third Tiger blew up. Beautiful fireworks. Over.'

'Oboe to Able and 3. You earn a Tiger's tail each. Off.'

(Stan: 'Hear that? Three bloody Tigers gone up in smoke for none of ours!' Rex: 'I reckon it's Joe Ekins gunning in 3 Charlie. A cool cuss.')

I chew a boiled sweet and fold the paper. The chewing of the sweet is incidental. The folding of the paper is critical. The brief, unseen but uncomfortably close clash with the Tigers has been exciting, stimulating but also terrifying. A split second's delay or a yard's error by Oboe 3 Charlie and the Tigers could have been in among us by now, at 100 yards range, smelting some of us into writhing ash. But where Tigers lead, others must follow – Panthers, SPs, Mark IVs. The hedgerows ahead may be thick with enemy tanks, pressing their guns through hedges, ranging on us, firing; smashing us in the turret, driving compartment, gun-shield, engine; tearing us limb from limb; sealing us within our own crematorium tomb; sparking the conflagration that nothing can douse. So, to stop my soldier's hands from trembling, I fold a sweet paper. Therapeutic. First fold. Double fold. Further folds harder to square off. Fingers engaged and steady. The mind gathering in that 50 per cent of its capacity which always wanders away, concentrating on the task, compressing my own fears and anxieties into the stubborn paper while my eyes continue to scan the empty world outside. Empty except for three Tiger pyres, near enough for us to smell.

12.55 hours: 'Hullo, Roger 1.' Our 1 Troop leader, Tony Faulkner. 'I can see our little strange telegraph friends on the left. Dozens of them. In a cavalry charge across country. Roger 1, over.'

'Roger 1,' (Hank responding) 'Good to know they've arrived. Keeping our left secure. Leave them to get on with it. Over.'

'Roger 1. OK. Off.'

Tommy: 'What the hell is Roger 1 talking about? Telegraph friends?'

Snowie: 'Poles, of course. Telegraph poles!'

Tommy: 'Then why can't he say Poles? Surely Jerry can see them by now.'

Snowie: 'Always use code names. Jerry isn't supposed to know that there is a Polish Armoured—'

'Hullo, Oboe 3. Number of nasty hornets straight ahead. Crossing from left to right. Some turning towards us. Ten … twelve … fifteen or twenty I can see. Over.'

'Oboe 3, OK. All stations Oboe, did you hear? Fifteen to twenty hornets ahead. Oboe 1, 2, and 4 over.'

Snowie: 'All crew watch half right. Nasties should be moving behind hedgerows either side of gully. Check loaded AP.'

Tommy: 'Christ! Twenty of the buggers!'

And now SLAM-CRASH, rather lighter guns than before, again and again, unseen but all too near. Ours and theirs intermingling whilst we watch and wait and shudder.

'Roger 2 Charlie. Have brewed one Mark IV. Two more in sight, right of me, three o'clock. 2 Charlie, Over.'

'2 Charlie, good shooting. Off.'

(Stan: 'Hey, that's little Ernie Wellbelove. Bloody good shooting, Ernie. That's paying them one back for Corporal Stanley.')

'Roger 2 Charlie. Tally Ho! Number two brewing. Watch for it. Here goes number three. Third Mark IV flaming. That's all we can see, 2 Charlie, over.'

(Tommy: 'Good old Ernie boy. Bash 'em for the colonel. Bash 'em for Jimmy Stanley. Bash 'em for the bleeding V bombs.' Snowie: 'Cool it then. Watch out. That's only three gone.')

'2 Charlie! Behind you! Behind you, I say! 2 Able, traverse right! Charlie! Charlie! O my God, 2 Charlie is brewing. 2 Able, can't you traverse right? Right! Traverse … Oh my God … bale out … bale!'

Fire shoots skywards across the gully, not where the Germans should be. Where 2 Troop should be. The slam-crash double explosions overlay each other, and the day degenerates into chaos, noise, flame, smoke, grilling sunshine, stinking sweat, searing fear, billowing blast; and our tank shuddering and juddering even as it stands still on the exposed, oh so exposed ridge crest.

Rex: 'That was a Sherman.'

A second fire blasts even higher a few yards to the right of the first. Not where the Germans should be. Where 2 Troop should be. Two towers of flame gushing into the sky, spilling out foul black smoke.

'Roger 2 Able. Both Sunray and Charlie gone … Hullo! Roger 2 Able. May I do … Christ, I'm hit … baling.'

(Me: 'Ernie's had it, then?' Rex: 'You never know. There's always a chance …')

'Hallo, Roger 3.' (Hank calling Bobby McColl.) 'Move up to cover Roger 2's front. 3, over.' 'Roger 3, OK. Off to you. All Stations Roger 3 move up in line with me. Off.'

Snowie: 'Driver, advance slowly, ready to reverse. Gunner, I think all 2 Troop tanks have brewed. Any vehicle you see moving will be enemy. Shoot first. Ask after. Co-driver, do not, repeat, do not fire on walking men. They may be 2 Troop survivors. Have you got that?'

I work my gun along the known hedgerows and woods. From this new angle I can see more of the woods across the gully. Trees. Undergrowth. Branches. Intricate, twisting tracery of branches, twigs and leaves. Those twisted variegated shapes are safe. I count them. Assess them. Trees and branches. Twigs and leaves. A box shape. A box ... BOX! Jab gun elevator, twist grip, crosswires ON! STAMP! (Snowie: 'Hornet! Hornet! Front!')

Suddenly everything seems to slow to a thousandth of normal speed, like a film running down. A single second is packed with so many thoughts, so many sensations, so many occurrences, each one fully comprehended and savoured to the full. The bulbous gush of fire from our own gun muzzle, dazzling the telescopic sight. The huge recoil of the 75 gun by my left cheek. The clang of the breech block springing open and belching out heat and sulphurous fumes into the turret. The hellish thunder hammering at my left ear drum. The entire tank lurching back in the agony of the firing act as the great gun gives birth to the heavy shot jammed tight within it. The agonizing drive of the shot up the rifled gun barrel, the curving grooves grasping the shot as it gathers speed, acceleration fighting against deceleration, the shot twisting into a spin which hurls it from the gun at tremendous velocity. The spark of tracer racing across space.

Whilst my tracer is still in mid-air, a brilliant flash lashes from the box shape in the hedgerow, identifying it as a gun turret. A shot fired at us or ours. Then our tracer dipping in slightly towards the enemy tank and, in the last moment of its flight, another twin tracer speeding in from another angle, merging with it so that both tracers hit almost in the same instant and within inches of each other.

There is a tiny puff of smoke from the box shape. It jerks back into the wood out of my sight. Even as it does, thick black smoke spouts around it, black smoke tinged with crimson. Tommy slaps my leg and I stamp again, holding the gun on the base of the ascending smoke pillar. Slap. Stamp. Fire again.

'Hullo, 3 Able. Have brewed a Mark IV in the area of Roger 2. Roger 3 Able, over.'

'Roger 3 Able, good start, more to come. Keep your eyes open. Off.'

Stan: 'What the hell! Ken got that one. The two shots landed together. But ours hit first. What is 3 Able talking about, just because he is a sergeant and we are only a corporal?'

Snowie: 'What does it matter, as long as it burns?'

Tommy: 'Go on, burn, you buggers, burn!'

'Hullo, Roger 3,' (Hank to Bobby again) 'can you get one of your people forward to cover exit of Roger 2's people? Also to check on possible move across gully to 2's position. 3 over.' (Tommy: 'Uh-huh. Bloody glory calls. And who do we think little Bobby will be sending up to do that ferking job?' Snowie: 'Shut up! They're transmitting.') '... 3, off to you. Hallo, Roger 3 Baker. Did you hear? Go do it. Take no risks. Get back here if in doubt. 3 Baker, over.'

Snowie: '3 Baker. Understood. On my way. Off.'

We roll gently down the green slope towards the thick belt of trees which seems to rise up to the sky as we near it, obliterating the view across towards Robertmesnil. A jungle of trees and uncut hedges. An orchard appears to have collided with a copse, and a mortal battle has been taking place between opposing species of trees. The space beneath is rank with the casualties of broken branches, rambling undergrowth, groping thorns and last year's leaves. Stan picks his way carefully through the trees. The 30-ton tank could easily smash down these lanky trees but in the process we could damage one of our guns or the gun-sight. We might also pick up loose wire and other litter in our tracks, and that might temporarily halt us. In a place where quick retreat might be all-important.

Snowie: 'Rex, come up and gun. Ken, come up top. I'm getting out for a look-see. It's impossible from up here. My head is stuck up among the branches. And bring me up a Sten gun.'

I wriggle up beside Snowie. The turret is pressing back a large branch of one of the trees so that the top of the turret is swathed in twigs and leaves. Snowie drops over the side and treads softly towards the gully, 15 yards in front of us. I get out of the turret and crouch low to get a view through the branches. I ask Stan to switch off for a moment so that I can listen for trespassers and poachers, on foot or in vehicles.

Furtive movement on our right. Not the way that Snowie went. Nobody but Jerry on our right now. Only a patch of uniform holding a bassoon, a patch of field-grey uniform holding a large bassoon, a contra-bassoon ... cannot be a bassoon ... who comes playing bassoons in this uninhabited ghost world ... not a bassoon but a bazooka to blast tanks with ... my bewildered mind clicks for action ... into the turret! 'Tommy, reload with HE! Rex traverse and fire! Even if you cannot see anything. Traverse right and fire. Fire!' The compact HE shell hitting a solid branch almost under our noses and blooming into tree-high flame and fury, releasing screaming torrents of red-hot shrapnel and charred rubbish, splashing and scratching at our turret ... opening a glowing hole in the trees ... but no bassoons ... no bazooka ... no bazooka man now.

Snowie has come aboard over the back of our tank. 'What goes?' I report and Snowie snaps, 'Get in and get ready to skip. I saw at least three tank shapes across the gully. No go there. As soon as 2—'

I point out, 'There they are. 2 Troop.'

Out of the gully, well to our left: berets, heads, shoulders, four five six Yeomen of Northamptonshire, forlorn, running, stumbling tiredly. Six of them when there should be eight or ten. Their officer is with them, arms linked with two bloodied troopers. He seems unwilling to walk, his body and legs spastic, not co-ordinating. They wave to us. No Ernie! They head up the slope for home.

Snowie: 'OK, driver. Let's go. Back where we came from. In reverse, but *fast*!'

13.00 hours: Amid the reverberations of guns and mortars a new sound distinguishes itself, a high screeching whine. Then an immense earthquake explosion that sends the tank swaying from side to side.

Tommy: 'That's a bomb. It's an air raid.'

Snowie: 'Pass me the yellow smoke. They're American.'

Tommy: 'Flaming Yanks!'

Another almighty concussion. Tommy passes a yellow smoke-bomb to Snowie. On the flat decks of our tanks are painted large white stars which are supposed to be visible to bomber pilots. If, as sometimes happens, we are attacked by short-sighted pilots who have not been provided by the RAF with spectacles, or by illiterate Yankee pilots who cannot distinguish between Allied stars and Nazi crosses, then we let off yellow smoke as a further identification sign. As another minor earthquake denotes the fall of another block-buster bomb from a Flying Fortress high above us, I see a row of yellow smoke-bombs burst into autumnal glory among the orchards as annoyed commanders take simultaneous action.

Stan laughs, 'That won't stop them. I'm sure air force pilots believe that Jerry has clicked onto the idea of yellow smoke. And so when we eject yellow smoke, they imagine we are Jerries trying to deceive them. So they bomb us all the more violently.'

'Or maybe if they're Yanks above,' continues Rex in the same vein, 'they're descendants of Custer and they think we are Sioux down here making smoke signals. White man, him heap big god flying on metal cloud up sky and dropping thousand-pounder turds on Big Chief Sitting Bullshit.'

A funnel of dense smoke and flame rushes up out of the ground 50 yards ahead of us, mushrooms high above the trees and then cascades dirt, smoke, jagged iron in all directions. The invisible express train of blast howls and drums and smashes into 3 Baker. It is like being in a crash with a ghost vehicle. My head jerks back from the rubber pad, recoils forward and whiplashes against the iron turret wall. I feel as though I have run into Joe Louis's fist. Too late I grab the levers to steady myself. A sound like hail patters on the outside of the tank as the lethal cloud of rubble begins to fall. I feel Snowie duck into the turret behind me. As usual his knees jab into my back. A lump of smouldering shrapnel as big as a golf ball, but not so smooth, bounces on my left shoulder, ricochets against the breech of the gun with a pinging sound and tumbles to the turret floor. Descending dust, ever-present smoke and charred dirt drift into and around the confined turret, causing us all to cough and retch.

Tommy shouts vainly, 'Go home, you sods. Go back to the States. You've pinched our girls and drunk all the effing beer. What more do you want?'

'Hullo, Oboe 1 Able. Two Mark IVs on main road. Eighteen hundred yards. Am engaging. Oboe 1 Able, over.'

Snowie asks me, 'Gunner, can you still see the Falaise road?'

I traverse: 'No, it's out of sight since we last advanced.'

'Hullo, Oboe 1 Able. One nasty down. The other hit ... and whackho! – there she blows!'

'Oboe 1 Able. Give your gunner a pat on the back. Eighteen hundred yards is good shooting any day. Off.'

Stan muses, 'But that still leaves anywhere from twelve to seventeen Jerry tanks ... hiding out there ... somewhere ... according to what somebody reported a while ago.'

For a few moments there comes one of those strange lulls which descend on battlefields from time to time. Maybe a dozen German tanks are sitting in those woods watching us. What are they thinking? Why are they not acting? When will they act? They do not refrain from nastiness unless there is a much bigger piece of nastiness being planned. Fritz is not a lazy soldier.

This silence makes me feel naked. I have a couple of inches of armoured steel in front of my face, thicker steel in front of my legs. Yet I sit out in the open, high above the ground, imagining that a 75mm gun from a Mark IV is lining up on my gunner's seat. And a Mark IV from 200 yards is as lethal as a Tiger from half a mile. Some enemy gunners go for your tank track in order to disable the Sherman. Some go for the engine, if visible, to produce an instant inferno. A few sophisticated shots go for the commander's head protruding from the turret. But the majority go for the gun and gunner. My own aim, if I get an enemy tank in my sights with open options, is to put his gun out of action first. No sensible German will give me a chance to shoot back by aiming at anybody else, anywhere else in the tank, but me!

Discipline, learned through foot drill on parade or through endless shining of brasses and peeling of spuds does produce an instinctive reaction to commands in the heat of battle. It does *not* affect the dreams that come in the night, or the drift of thought in the idle moments of days behind the line, or in the long hours of inactivity in the line. All the horrors of war resurrect from time to time and pass across the mind's colourful stage like a procession of ghosts from *Macbeth*. Some tank crews gain relief by discussing their fears and, in the process, exacerbate the agitation of wildly imaginative people like me. Would I prefer a smashed leg, or a tearing stomach wound, or an arm ripped off, or a shaming gelding in sensitive places, or a chest wound that could vary from trivial to critical within a fraction of an inch, a fractured skull, an eye plucked out, a scarring of the face for life? (It's happening NOW! All around me!) Is it really true, as they say, that the shock of wounding prevents one feeling the pain at first? The worse the wound, the less the feeling?

Rarely is screaming heard in battle in the way it is related in fiction. But I may be the odd one who screams! And what shall I be feeling then? And if a shot hits us at a certain angle, it can knock the turret flaps shut, weld them tight and leave us trapped, immured. If the shot hits the engine, there are two chances. In the case of the tank brewing totally in a 20-foot torch of flame, we shall grill alive, medium to well done, in three seconds flat – that is, just as we are being blown apart by dozens of our own 75mm shells spontaneously exploding. Alternatively, if the shot misses the petrol system we may emerge into oxygen-rich air as human torches soaked in oil.

These messages lie coiled, compressed within the brain, like snakes dozing in the sun. Then, like the unseen, striking snake, they unwhip and flash across the mind in their entirety within a fraction of a second, biting their poison into the mind – bleak, glaring ideas against a lurid background of remembered incidents and unremembered dreams and present events. At that point fear emerges in all its symptoms. The clutching feeling at the heart, piercing sensation in the throat, ice-cold prickles up the nape of the neck and under the ears, burning fire behind the eyes, within the cheeks and across the eyebrows.

But fear is not to be equated with panic. Fear is a companion which one sits with, converses with, tolerates and resents. Panic may be devoid of fear and is a sudden, unpremeditated and often totally illogical reaction to a sudden, unexpected occurrence – the puma springing from the tree. Fear is all too often only too logical, and related to the well-expected. This silence is the worst time. No sound or movement to distract the mind from the hurrying, busybody whispers of doubt and apprehension. Silence is a time for loving, for two people in the moonlight, for the shepherd on the hill, for the poet in the pine wood, for the student in the library. Not for the front line with its thoughts that lurk in legions under every bush. Especially here straight out front where thin smoke marks the spot at which Ernie Wellbelove and Jimmy Stanley must lie dead.

Pray for noise! It comes! Our own artillery stonk. Correct to the yard. Right on top of US! Snowie's knees hammer my vertebrae as though playing a descending scale on a xylophone. More grit and blazing filings shower on us – from behind. We lurch forward – battered from behind. I see another Sherman disappear in an explosion which looks like a great ball of coal dust blown from under the earth. When the dust subsides, the tank is still there.

Tommy objects: 'Flipping hell. That's our own artillery. Let 'em all come. Let 'em all have a go. If Jerry can't hit us, perhaps the Yanks can. If not the Yanks, then the Royal Artillery. Who's next? Roll up, roll up! Penny a shy!'

Stan grunts 'Jerry must be pissing himself with laughter. There'll be more Huns carried off to hospital with cracked ribs from laughing than are wounded by this lot. If I were a Jerry, I would pack up and go home and leave us to it. We don't need them to be in a war.'

I venture, 'There's always the navy!'

Stan retorts, 'If Nelson could see this, he'd do his nut. "England expectorates ..." Heads down! Here they come again. Housey Housey!'

Black shell-bursts play among the bushes and trees precisely along the edge of the gully in front of us. If the first artillery stonk was extraordinarily bad, the second one is extraordinarily good. Shells in rapid, drum-roll succession flicker and puff along the entire length of the nearest woods. A tree catches fire, the flames running up it like re-shirted sailors swarming up a ship's mast. Another tree totters and falls. A third tree lifts off, like a rocket zooming upwards, then loses momentum and topples over upside down. In a brief pause in the artillery barrage I hear a new outbreak of the distinctive double-impact noise which indicates tank or anti-tank guns. And this noise comes from behind me. As I am now traversed right, that means the noise is from the left. Where there is nobody. Except maybe the Poles.

'Hullo, Roger 1. It looks as though our telegraph friends are coming back from their picnic and will not be travelling farther today. Roger 1, over.'

'Hullo, Roger 1. Can you give more detail. Over.'

'Roger 1. I would say fifty or more doing a Ronson. Over.'

Tommy groans, 'That's it then, ain't it? That's bloody IT! "At 13.00 hours the Poles will pass through us" but what they forgot to say was that at 13.01 hours the Poles would be going back where they came from – some of them.'

'Oh, skip it, Tommy,' Snowie intervenes. 'They did more than you should expect from any human beings, charging 88s head on. Anybody else but the

Poles would have beaten a retreat half a mile sooner. There's nobody tougher than the Poles. Not even the SS.'

Rex observes 'It's the generals to blame, handing out "missions impossible". It's Balaclava all over again. Waxed moustaches, blood, glory and sheer catastrophe.'

'The Charge of the Light Brigade was a Boy Scout Jamboree compared to this,' is Stan's summing-up.

'Some of those bloody generals couldn't milk a cow,' adds Tommy with that kind of logic which stalls any conversation.

13.25 hours: The barrage comes and goes like violent gusts of rain on an equinoctial day. At the extreme left of my traverse arc I can see the squadron captain's tank spewing up clouds of corn dust as it rushes past and stops level with us, twenty yards away. Captain Ken Todd waves at us as though telling us to pull back a bit. His crew are all my bunk-room pals from HQ(F) training days, older soldiers, kindly mentors, Lance-Corporals Eric Marchant, Harold Hoult and 'Robin' Hood.

Their tank 'Brixworth' stands stark and immune, motionless a moment like a painting on an art gallery wall.

Then one horrific pulsation of the mind records a ball of flame and smoke shooting off the side of that tank, the fearsome crash of an 88mm gun after the flash, the even more terrible crash of the explosion on the Sherman. People eject from the tank, one with clothing on fire, another smouldering. They fling themselves to the ground as a gusher of fire soars skywards from the turret. Another mind-numbing explosion from the inside of that turret. A fire so intense that it sears the retina of my eye to the exclusion of all else momentarily. Eric, Robin, Harold!

That tank is 20 or 30 yards away. If the 88 can see them, it can probably see us, its invisible gunner choosing Ken Todd's tank rather than ours. Its gunner now refocusing on us. I rip the turret right! Think! Lines of fire. Eric, Robin, Harold! Lines of fire. Not from the left because the impact was slightly right. Not from the extreme right because we would have been in the way. Robertmesnil! I glimpse a straight line in the intricate hedgerow. Brake turret. Up gun. Stamp. Consciously look at the crosswires *after* I have fired. But a part of the mind was registering the crosswires accurately and unasked – as one drives a car without thinking. Smoke and flame die from my muzzle and I see our tracer stab into the area under that straight-lined shape. The tracer bounces off solid mass at the centre of a bright explosion. Another 88 fires from the same hedgerow. Fires at us and somehow misses. The second 88 is so well hidden that I can see no trace of it. I shoot at the approximate spot where I glimpsed a muzzle flash. Fire again! (A Sherman fires much faster than the SP can.) Adjust, slap, stamp. No response ... but another ... and another 88 fire towards us. Brief vision of muzzle flashes in far hedgerows, blur of something flying angrily towards me, furious howl of displaced air alongside us. No explosion. Yet. (I think: 'They're not very good gunners. Four, five shots at all our tanks. All missed. Unless they're fighting someone else out of my sight.') Eric, Harold, Robin?

I fire again and again at remembered flash points. Other guns alongside and behind me are sending tracer arrows into that same area of confused hedgerows. The 88s are not replying. Only two rising spirals of dense smoke respond. (Snowie: 'Gunner, cease fire.')

Traversing automatically I see the medical half-track skid up to Ken Todd's tank. One figure is half collapsed, holding a shoulder, against the tank track. Others bend over a bundle which they have rolled on the grass but which is still smouldering. Above them Brixworth sends up its supreme firework display of exploding ammunition 20, 30, 40 feet into the air. The cremation inferno rages out of the engine plates. A bundle lies on the turret roof.

I press my mike, 'Commander, is that somebody lying on the turret top? I can see a bundle ...' Eric, Harold, Robin?

'Don't think so. If it is ... he will be dead by now.'

'Shouldn't we go over and help. Just in case?' But as I speak I move my eye from wide-angle periscope to close-up telescope. The bundle emerges as a bedding roll rapidly being consumed by the widening flames, now covering the entire tank and its camouflage. 'There but for the grace of God ...' And the medics gently cradle one body into the half-track, which immediately slithers round and slides away fast. 'Eric,' says the telescope. Watching still. Harold and Robin lift their fifth man, new recruit Johnny, link arms with Ken Todd, and begin the rough trek back to first-aid treatment, and the even longer trek back to the Forward Delivery Squadron to collect a replacement for Brixworth. Clean new Shermans are queuing up by the dozen to replace us as we are incinerated one by one.

'Hullo, Roger 1 Sunray. Roger 1 Sunray reporting that Roger 1 was brewed by SPs from the farm. Roger 1 Able is now Roger 1. Over.'

'Roger 1. Understood. Off.'

'Hullo, Roger 4. Hullo, Roger 4. Sunray wounded. Urgent half-track, please. Roger 4 still functioning. 4 over.'

'4, OK, will arrange, off to you. Hullo, Roger 4 Able. Did you hear? Take command of Roger 4. 4 Able, over.'

'4 Able, I heard. Will do. Off.' (Tommy: 'What the hell's—')

'Roger 4. Hit again. Gunner wounded. Can you send half-track back. 4 over.' (The temporary commander calling.)

'Roger 4. Will do. Off to you. 4 Able, your 4 needs another pair of hands. Over.'

'4 Able, will see to. Off.'

Tommy: 'I say again, what the hell's happening? That's one troop leader unhorsed and another pissed off looking for a more comfortable neck of the woods. And the third has already gone home.'

Stan: 'And that leaves just us and Bobbie and Hank between fifty-five SS panzer divisions and the thousands of English virgins who escaped the Yanks.'

Rex: 'What I can't understand is how those 88s on the ridge missed us half a dozen times before they retreated – some of them?'

Snowie: 'Probably our artillery bombardment or the American bombs knocked their sights off true. They say some of the Jerry tanks have a weakness that way.'

My eye is attracted by a tracer from one of our tanks shooting at the skyline. ('Gunner, Mark IV hull down on strip of bare skyline one-clock.') I traverse. Target so small the fine crosswires almost blot it out. Only a squared-off dirty fingernail paring showing over the crest. I stamp on the button. Two more of our tracers fizz in, almost combating my shot. A modest puff of smoke on the skyline. The tiny edge of turret disappears. But immediately a large puff, plume, geyser of crimson smoke broadens, climbs, and then clouds the skyline. 'What idiot Jerry commander came poking his head over a bare skyline?' I ask myself. Pity the poor German gunner, my *alter ego*.

Stan agrees vocally, 'Poor sods, with a bird-brained commander like that. Didn't stand a chance.'

13.50 hours: 'Hullo, Oboe 3. Masses of enemy infantry advancing through cornfield, nine o'clock. Oboe 3, over.'

'Oboe 3, act accordingly.' A Squadron's Major Gray Skelton. 'Off to you. All stations watch for infantry observed by Oboe 3, nine o'clock from him. All stations Oboe, over.'

And then, 'All stations Roger.' (Hank.) 'That will be one to two o'clock from us. Off.'

With the abrupt impact of a true August storm (blue skies above), thunder rolls out of the sky and transforms into steel rain. Cumulus clouds of smoke roll across the fields and through the orchards. Lightning flashes out of the ground at a hundred different places. After the feeble response of last night and this morning, the overwhelming enemy barrage comes as a double shock. I am mesmerized by the frantic succession of explosions, the separate puffs appearing faster than a steam engine could produce them with the throttle wide open. Sudden dirt squalls, miniature tornadoes, erupt out of the ground all along our front (we are still partially isolated behind the main enemy battle line). Again and again we are showered with filth. The air is purple-black with smoke from outside, brown with the dirt haze and blue with the smoke of our own firing as well as our petrol fumes. And the sun strikes on steel armour in full summer intensity.

'Hullo, Roger 3 Able, Roger 3 Baker.' (Bobbie sounds an immense distance away beyond the cannonades.) 'Move forward to that nearest hedge to brass up advancing infantry. 3 Able, Baker, over.'

Snowie guides Stan into a tangle of trees with a view beyond more trees towards open areas this side of Robertmesnil. The first movement across the pleasant golden cornfield is of tiny dark spots appearing and disappearing in the more distant corn. The spots grow into helmets. And under the helmets are faces. Two, five, ten. A dozen, a score, a platoon, a company, surely. Still more and more. Flame and smoke obscure my view. I realize that I have fired the 75mm, and my foot is now jammed on the Browning button. The multiple tiny blips of tracer from the machine-gun chase the larger, sizzling tracer of the 75HE into the cornfield. A raw, red cabbage of flame blooms amid the corn, and the dotted line of Browning tracer whips to each side of the main explosion as I go into the hosing routine. I see a German soldier standing perplexed in the corn. The telescope magnifies the detail and reveals him in his sloppy tunic, baggy trousers and large tin hat, a tragicomic little man hardly typical of the elite SS whom we have come to fear.

My Browning jolts, stopped, its ammunition exhausted. Tracer from Rex's gun sprays short bursts farther right. But my sole German still stands for a second, wondering what to do, where to go. Then he drops as a 75mm HE shell from another Sherman explodes in front of him. I am not sure if he threw himself down before the burst or if he was blown down. He does not reappear. I feel a brief, strange sense of bereavement.

Tommy slaps my leg. I fire both guns. Lines of tracer are sweeping the vast field from other tanks and from various directions. HE flashes spurt from points right across the field. The German infantry move forward in rushes, still mainly discerned as movements in the high corn rather an as recognizable human bodies. When no explosions or tracer are to be seen in one part of the field, it comes alive with stealthily moving enemy. When we switch to that point, they go to ground. The movement there ceases. But other groups rise and rush forward. I quickly decide to fire short bursts at moving groups, then switch to other places to catch other groups as they rise. As quickly as Tommy slaps my leg, I stamp out more HE hell for the men in the field.

Enemy in the cornfield. Our own Browning thudding away. Tommy reloading HE and slapping my leg. Stamping on firing buttons. Adjusting crosswire sights. Our own flame and smoke. Alien flame and smoke. Enemy barrage rocking our tank. Rex firing away downstairs. Snowie reporting. Frantic wireless traffic. Thunder such as no Norman summer has known, their thunder, our thunder. Lightning of shell bursts, briefer, brighter, more angry and more frequently fatal than God's lightning. Our tracer sweeping cornfields and miraculously colliding with someone else's tracer. A dozen lines of tracer. 75mm bursts flaring amid the corn. Men stumbling, crawling, hesitating, falling, flaming, running, hiding.

But where are their tanks?

'Oboe 3. My Baker has brewed. Oboe 3 ov— I'm hit ... I'm bloody hit ...' (that's where their tanks are!).

'Hullo Oboe. Can anyone tell me what is hitting Oboe 3?' (Skelton again.) 'Oboe, over.'

'Oboe 4 Able. Now 4 Charlie has brewed. I think there is a nasty down in gully about ten o'clock. I can't see here high up in the apple trees. He's down ankle high. Can't see ... s'all gone dark ... all gone cold ... Somebody please, 4 Able, somebody please, ple—'

'Hullo 4 Able. Are you there? Are you there? 4 Able, over.'

'Come in somebody, we're on fire ...' (a different voice.)

'All stations Oboe. Follow procedure. Identify yourself first even if you're brewing. Otherwise we can't help. All Oboe, off.'

'Oboe 1 Baker. Our Sunray killed by exploding shell. Otherwise OK. 1 Baker, over.'

'1 Baker, carry on if you can, off to you. Hullo, Oboe 4 Able, are you there? 4 Able over.'

Our tank rocks and shudders at another near miss. I fire both guns again. Hit an area of furtive movement in the corn. Movement stops. Two other HE shells explode within feet of mine. A triple flailing death. Winnowing the grain. Harvesting the hate of years. And the corn begins to burn. And my Browning stops. Remains silent.

Tommy: 'Misfire, co-ax!'

Snowie: 'Get it going again then. Use your drill!'

Tommy: 'I am using bloody drill, aren't I? It won't move – cocking handle. It's the heat. Gun is red hot. Jammed. Useless.'

Snowie: 'You must get it going. Must! Must!'

Me: 'Let me have a look.'

I pull off my headset, squeeze out of my seat, double myself up into my own leg space, crawl under the breech of the 75, scalding myself on the blazing empty 75mm cases spilling out of the bag under the gun, coming up close to Tommy. I tug at the cocking handle. Solid. I shout in Tommy's ear. 'Get the oil. Water. And a hammer.'

Tommy: 'You'll burst the bloody thing. Court martial offence.'

I drop down on the floor and scream at Stan down below, 'Hammer! Hammer! Get me the hammer! Misfire up here!'

Tommy passes me the jerrycan of water out of the storage sponson. I pour tepid water over the Browning breech. Not done! I pour a thick stream of oil over the same area. Not done! I grab the hammer. Bash at the cocking handle. Not done! The handle bends slightly but remains frozen. Panic now. I slash away with the hammer like a frantic murderer at work. The handle moves. I hit it again. It jerks back. Two of us grab it and tug it back and forward sluggishly. More oil. More tugs. I put my finger under the ordinary manual trigger of the gun. Pull the trigger. It fires. Rapid burst. Does not blow our faces to smithereens. 'Crazy bugger!' laughs Tommy.

Back to periscope. Smell of corn burning. The entire cornfield is burning. Small individual picnic fires and widening holocaust fires around scurrying infantrymen. Still enemy advancing, some firing wildly, some running towards the rear, some bursting into flaming torches, some waving and shouting, visibly cursing, frying where they stand.

'Hullo, Oboe 1 Able.' (Major Skelton). 'We're not going to let this bastard in the gully brew up the entire squadron. You go right. I'll go left. Look down at ground level for him. One of us will get him. Oboe 1 Able, over.'

'Oboe 1 Able, going right. Cheerio and off.'

While the infantry attack disintegrates in the burning cornfield and a new smell of charred flesh permeates the tank, the German barrage still tears viciously at the woods around, scattering plumes of blazing earth across the fields and into the orchards. Now our own artillery comes down in a series of red-eyed, smoke-aureoled explosions at the far edge of the cornfield, cutting off the retreat of the infantry. Those little grey men run in all directions now, their fear of our guns superseded by the nearer, more urgent and atavistic terror of total incineration. The Black Watch machine-guns and rifles, from their tiny pits behind us, add to the chaos. A few Germans stop to shoot back, the very intensity of the inferno about them at least providing some smoke or haze cover for those who have not become blazing human faggots or been butchered by our bullets or fallen suffocated by the fumes of grilling grain.

'Hullo, Oboe 1 Able.' (One of Skelton's tanks attempting a pincer move.) 'Mark IV at two o'clock from you, ground level, aiming my direction. Get him fast. I will ... we're hit! Bale, lads, bale! Oboe 1 Able, closing down. Off.'

'Hullo, Oboe 1 Able, if you're still there. Dismount at leisure. He won't hit anyone else. I got him up the backside. A severe case of metal haemorrhoids for one Fritz. Off.'

'Hullo … squawk … squawk … see 1 Able's full crew coming back safely … squawk …'

Stan: 'Tommy, have you got an empty Browning tin? Urgent!'

Tommy: 'One coming down. Don't forget to pull the chain when you've finished.'

Me: 'In the next war they'll build tanks with chemical loos.'

Stan: 'Tommy, and pass me the hammer back at the same time.'

Tommy: 'If you've got constipation bad enough to need a pissing hammer …?'

The August sun beats down. The tank engine is running. Our own guns are blistering hot to the touch. Each of us is sweating from fear and exertion. We can fairly feel the heat from the burning fields and brewing tanks. Combined with the mounting torrid torture there is the smell of roasting fresh from outside as well as the animal smells and cordite fumes within 3 Baker's own grimy bowels. The total effect is stupefying. Almost anaesthetic. In spite of the frantic, mortal battle activity, I am finding it difficult again, in this oxygen-deprived oven, to keep my eyes open.

Traversing right, I see motion. One man. Khaki. One of ours. An officer walking. Towards us. Out of a small orchard. Something intrigues me about him. I look through the telescope for a closer view. Recognize him. From A Squadron. His face is set in a fixed, shocked grin. I realize what is wrong. His arm is swinging loose. His hand is hanging the wrong way round. A patch of red shows beneath his shoulder. A pang of pain, sympathetic, compulsive, shoots through my own shoulder. I shudder. The cloth of his upper sleeve is ripped away. He moves like a sleep-walker in a hurry. And grins. At nobody in particular. Someone leaps off a nearby tank and walks beside him, catches him even as he stumbles. Out of my vision.

Stan: 'Poor bugger!'

Tommy: 'Even though he's an officer. Anyway, who's to say? Would he be better off dead like Ernie? Or waiting like us for a worse one in the guts or cobbles? He's got a Blighty one, mate, and that's not the worst thing happening around here.'

Me: 'He might have been *Oberleutnant* Fritz van Boche frizzling out in the cornfield.'

Tommy: 'Yeah! Corn on the cob!'

Rex: 'Oh, can it, Tommy! Isn't it enough to brass up the poor bleeding Jerries and leave 'em to roast without insulting them afterwards?'

14.10 hours: 'Hullo, Roger 3. Move your people left and forward to cover gaps, and watch for little men infiltrating. 3, over.'

Snowie: 'Driver, that means we go through this hedge, slightly right and come to another hedge which angles into trees. Can you see? Advance now.'

Stan: 'My whole world is HEDGE down here. Guide me, O thou great Jehovah!'

We suffer a nerve-jarring bump as 3 Baker climbs the steep bank under the hedge. And then we are through into another miniature jungle of lush greenery where hedges and woods are impossibly jumbled. But this position allows us a glimpse into the deep gully through which enemy tanks have been slinking, a gully deeper than the height of a tank. A gully the width of a race-track, with a steep tree-crowned bank, like a grandstand of spectators, blocking off the far side of the green ravine.

But my immediate telescope view seems to be filled by a monster apparition of utter dreadfulness. A horrendous death machine. A bomb or an aerial torpedo or a great rocket, a gigantic unexploded egg; so big that I rub my eyes, look again! It seems as long as our Sherman tank.

I yelp, 'Commander, can you see that bomb right ahead?'

Rex intervenes, 'Can see. That can't be a bomb. That's a bloody battleship.'

Commander orders, 'Wait for me a mo' to close down. And shoot it!'

It happens too fast. I fire. Here, looking from above and only a few feet away, the muzzle flash from my depressed gun is a sky-splitting, eye-gouging flame. Before the muzzle flash has fully burgeoned, the answering flash from the shell's impact flares against the bomb, more angry and more diffused. A heartbeat's pause and then a full-size version of Hell races from the ground up into the sky, flame wrapped around flame like the petals of a crimson artichoke, enfolding one another. A tree in the hedge explodes in sympathetic reaction. And comes the almighty triple concussion: muzzle roar, shell burst, bomb blast! A noise so intense it darkens our vision as it cudgels our brains. An umbrella of sods, filth, shrapnel, tree branches, fire missiles, opens over our tank. A hail of lethal rubbish rattles down over our heads. Four distinct versions of ultimate blasphemy surge from within the tank after a sudden, stunned silence.

'Hullo, Roger 3 Baker.' (Snowie's voice at his most school-masterly.) 'Just blowing an unexploded bomb, a gift from friends on high. No damage. Roger 3 Baker, over.'

'3 Baker, you had us worried. Off.'

'Roger 3.' (Hank's voice at its most sardonic.) 'Tell your Baker there's enough noise going on without him advancing Guy Fawkes' Day by several months. Off.'

(Stan: 'OK, Hank, take the micky. You're not deafened, blinded and shitting yourself.')

After a moment Stan reflects, 'Good job you closed down for that one, Snowie. They're not paying you trade union rates for sticking your head out, twelve feet up in the air in the middle of a bloody big battle. Think of all the ruddy staff captains at HQ who would be scared to show an eyebrow within a mile of the front line. You ought to be at least a sergeant, if not a little lieutenant to command any kind of tank.'

Rex agrees, 'That goes for the whole crew, too. I can't see why in the RAF you can have a flight lieutenant who is not even the commander or pilot of his plane. You can have two or three officers to one bomber. And just to fly the ass-end of the plane you have to be a sergeant, minimum. But we, Fred Karno's Army, have to sit right out in a field within yards of Jerry's 88s (the same anti-aircraft guns that they can fly thousands of feet above) – and what are we? Highly qualified, oh yes, but unwanted, unsung, unrewarded troopers.'

Snowie cuts off the dialogue, 'Simple solution, lads. Join the RAF next war. Keep watching that gully.'

I look at my watch again. Shakespeare wrote that famous passage about time moving at different speeds for different people in different situations. I know for whom time crawls along at its slowest. For the tank crew posed high above an alien battlefield for all to see; all of us desiring, but not endowed with X-ray eyes, to penetrate the scowling woods, anxious to discern the invisible enemy who can no doubt see us only too well. Waiting for the sudden flash of agony, and seeing all the time the thinning smoke palls rising over other tanks which have brewed up and cooked their crews alive.

Tommy begins to sing his favourite song on the I/C. 'I love coffee. I love tea. I love the Java Jive and it loves me …' Senseless! Like war!

14.30 hours: Still only 14.30? 2.30 p.m. That's twelve, fourteen, fifteen hours on from start time last night. Twenty-four, twenty-six, twenty-eight, Lord! Thirty-two hours on from reveille yesterday. And watching.

Gunfire nearby. Sudden, spaced, buffeting. 'Hullo, Victor 4 Able. Have brewed one hornet. Another in sight, over.' '4 Able. Good show. Charlie coming to help. Off.'

'Victor? That means,' muses Snowie, 'Some of B Squadron have come up alongside us to fill gaps. Ken, look left.'

'Traversing past farm. Nothing yet … I can see smoke on skyline but not—'

'Bloody hell!' from Tommy who has screwed his periscope almost to left rear, 'see that? Talk about Ronsons. That was a Jerry turret blown right up in the air.' And I am in time to see that a gusher of fire has catapulted the unmistakable outline of a tank turret, twisting and spinning 50 feet above the ridge, before plunging down again into the vortex of flame. And, as though the falling turret had been a lid slammed down on a furnace, the fire goes out. In its place a spreading chestnut-tree pattern of oily black smoke oozes up into the sky. I do not permit myself to wonder if the enemy crew members were still inside that spiralling turret. How not? Nobody else comments.

Another tank comes up astern, its turret topped by an officer's cap jammed square on a stolid, pushed-forward head, our squadron second-in-command, Bill Fox. He leaps across to our tank, takes Snowie's mike and speaks on I/C so that we all can hear his rasping voice, deliberately aggressive (a baronet's son, upper-class) but we know kindly old Bill too well to resent it.

'Job for you, lads. Take your tank quickly across the gully. Find our KO'd tanks. Check probably three people missing. Corporal Stanley, young Wellbelove and Trooper Judge. Officer wounded, in shock, not sure. Go check. Absolutely sure. I don't want any of our lads left to the bloody mercy of some damn SS butcher on holiday from the concentration camps. Be quick. Take bloody good care. They *are* SS out there. If it moves, shoot it. Off you go.'

As Bill jumps back to his own tank, Snowie orders, 'Driver, take it as fast as you can across the gully, but ready to slam into reverse. All guns front. Go!'

Stan whoops, 'OK, boss. Berlin, here we come. *Hoch, hoch, mein Gott ...*' and as he crashes through the gears, Tommy finishes off the much varied hymn, 'What a bloody fine lot, are the Northants Yeo-man-ree.' 'Shut up!' snaps Snowie, head exposed to the entire German army.

The track dips violently down to the race-track space and climbs even more precipitously through trees. To an open space half the size of a football field. Surrounded by hedgerows thick enough to be called woods or woods straggling enough to be termed hedgerows. A waste, a wilderness with spaces between the boundary trees. Ahead brief views of cornfields blackened by fire. Nosed into the trees at nine o'clock, eleven o'clock and three o'clock are Shermans, two of them still sending up fruitless smoke signals. Behind at five o'clock is a narrow gap from which a Mark IV must have shot up the troop. Nothing moves. Here or beyond.

'Rex, come up and watch,' says Snowie. 'Ken, have a look at those two Shermans out front, and I'll go check the farthest one. Fast's you can!'

I can already see Corporal Stanley sprawled in the turret of this nearest Sherman. I stop myself from shouting to him. It is a long, long weary way to his tank, however near. He watches me all the way. His eyes are like one of those Rembrandt paintings in the National Gallery – the eyes follow you wherever you go. He watches me climb onto his tank but says nothing. His right arm, caught in the turret flap, is extended in one last parody of the Hitler salute that he himself would have enjoyed. Hesitantly I touch the hand. Cold already. Unfamiliar. No sign of blood. Just shock. Shock to the body. Shock in the eyes. I no longer know him.

Hurry, hurry, hurry on, then, to the next tank watching forward, the nearest tank to Paris and Berlin, the tip of the arrow point on the war maps. This one still sends up thin trails of smoke from the blackened engine. I look into the turret. Nobody. But through the turret I can vaguely distinguish someone … sitting in the driver's seat. This tank did not explode. A shot hit the gun and twisted it in the mounting.

I open the driver's hatch. And wish I hadn't. Trooper 173 Judge is sitting there. All of him. Except his head. What happened to his head is explained by the stipples of mincemeat on the walls of his compartment. From the shoulders down he sits upright. Holding the sticks firmly. Feet in place. Ready to drive to Berlin. Men of one of the smart Hussars regiments, the 'Cherry Pickers', wear cherry-coloured cap and trousers. Trooper 173 Judge's blouse is smart with the same colour. The mess on the floor is black. Flies have already found it. I hold my handkerchief to my nose and close the hatch quickly.

That leaves Ernie Wellbelove. Missing. His tank lifeless and reeking of smoke and burnt explosive. A desecrated temple. Something stirring in front of the tank catches my eyes. I freeze. Then relax. A movement only of shadows on the grass. Shadows cast by trees in the bright sun and persuaded into gentle motion by a hesitant unmartial breeze. On the grass someone is lying, stretched out in the sun as though sunbathing on this high summer afternoon. In the lush Normandy grass.

Ernie Wellbelove is lying asleep, engulfed in peace, his hands folded over his chest, a pleasant look of satisfaction on his face. I bend over him. His denim blouse is warm in the sun. The delicate shadows give movement to his breast. Only his cheek is chill in the ultimate hypothermia. I look for his pay-book but his pockets are already empty.

The last time I saw him, a few hours ago, generations ago, he was pretending that all the noise of battle was his fault, playing drum rolls on an imaginary set of drums. He is twenty, a few weeks younger or older than me. (He *is* twenty? He *was* twenty. He *will always be* twenty.) A little old to be playing at drums. A little young to be playing with guns. Far too young to be lying here, where he will ever more lie in a 'corner of a foreign field', damn the poets!

I cannot resist a quick peep through the front-most bushes. A German officer grins at me from the turret of a Mark IV tank, its great gun pointing at me five yards away. Sheer fright sends me charging up the front of the tank, waving my puny pistol idiotically. But the mind has already registered the familiar blackening of the tank, the gun askew, tracks broken, staring eyes of the commander with his set grin. But panic operated more swiftly than sense. Suddenly everything is totally unreal and fear loses its sting.

I can see that what happened to Trooper Judge happened to the bottom of this German tank commander. His elbow, vice tight on the turret, holds his trunk in place. Blackened, shrivelled creatures squat and stink inside the tank. The flies exercise their loathsome neutrality. There are untidy lumps scattered over the burned cornfield, like sacks of manure dumped by the farmer. Only the sacks are of field-grey cloth, their contents panzer grenadiers. Nothing moves, nothing hisses. Nothing pings.

Snowie waves and I run back, vault onto the tank, slide into the turret, bumping my feet on Rex's back as he wriggles down through the fretwork-style turret cage into his seat. The tank roars in the agony of acceleration as Stan takes us home, down the dip, across the race-track, up into our nook. Again I keep watch and Rex wriggles up, while Snowie goes to report in detail to anxious Bill Fox.

We have inserted ourselves again into the static tableau of battle: infantry dug into holes in the ground, tank commanders peeping through tree branches high up, Fritz over yonder bandaging wounds, our artillerymen way back, piling more shells ready to hand. All waiting for the silence to rip apart. All wondering whose name is on the next bullet or shard of shrapnel, Britisher and German alike. All in the infinite lottery of war.

15.00 hours: 'Hullo, Mother. Where's my sugar? Over.'

'Mother, we're trying to get some sugar for you ...'

'My batteries are as flat as a snake's belly and still no goddamn sugar.'

The voices are faint, increasing and fading away across the ether. Completely blocked out when one of our regimental stations speaks. These voices have been in the background all day but, over the last hour, have become clearer, perhaps as a unit draws nearer to us.

Stan: 'What silly ass is asking for bloody sugar in the middle of a battle?'

Tommy: 'Sounds like a Yank. It's a wonder he's not asking for ice-cream as well.'

Snowie explains: 'Your Yank is probably a Canadian. One of their columns working up on our right.'

The mass enemy attack has gone to ground. But whilst a mass attack is frightening we can see it clearly and deal with it. We worry more about the single, unobserved attacker moving stealthily through the undergrowth to loose off a bazooka bomb point blank. Even, in all this rank grass, to climb up the back of the tank without being seen. So Snowie stands up top worrying most about the unseen clumps of bushes and long grass right there behind us. And we sit imprisoned within, worrying about Snowie keeping awake. We have been in action more than fifteen hours, with seven hours still to go before dark. But those seven hours will be a long, long time as the summer day swelters on in all its thirstiness. Down here inside the tank it will be like the stoke-hole of an old coal-burning ship.

'Hullo, Mother. Any news of my sugar? Mother, over.'

'Ferk your mother!' snarls an anonymous voice.

15.15 hours: In the long dreary silence I am losing touch again, drifting back to the little glade across the gully, so like that painting by Constable: a small field mainly in shadow but patched with golden sun; tall, thick spreading trees; cornfields beyond, wide and brilliant for harvest; and a boy lying there drinking at a pond; a boy with the face of Ernie Wellbelove drinking at a deep, cool fountain of peace …

Whoosh! Crump! Whoosh! Crump! Whoosh-oosh-oosh! Crrrump-p-p!!! And FIRE, immense, infernal, thundering! … light searing the eyeballs … noise of the universe splitting apart … heat of a belching volcano … flame and pelting steel raging out of the turret wall 3 feet from my face … crackle of fire taking hold … stench of cordite and burning material … thick, choking smoke spattered with blood-red flame on the turret, in the turret … God, we're going up … three seconds to get out … if … 'Bale out! Bale out!'

I jack-knife up onto the turret top, Snowie grabbing my elbow, Tommy catapulting past me. We jump clear, sprawl on the ground. 'Where are Stan and Rex?' I ask. 'Saw them going for the escape hatch underneath,' gasps Tommy. Snowie shouts, 'Stan, Rex, where are you?' Stan's ever cheerful voice responds, 'I'm here, trying to be a bloody rabbit down a warren,' and Rex adds 'here behind this bush, doing my bit for king and country but I'll never need Epsom salts again.'

We look up at the tank. The turret is hidden in smoke, but … three seconds gone … none of the gushing, horrible flame that so often marks the death of a Sherman. Bloody but not brewed. This fire seems more smoke than flame. Strange!

Stan: 'What the hell goes on?'

Rex: 'No fire in the engine.'

Snowie: 'Must have been HE not AP. It's our camouflage on fire. Get the fire extinguishers, lads. Save the old girl!' And oblivious to enemy snipers we jump back in, grab fire extinguishers, exit again and crawl around on top of the tank, spraying camouflage, blanket rolls and each other's denims. ('No need for hot-water bottles tonight. Blankets all warmed up,' laughs Stan in obvious relief.) Fifty yards away Bobby McColl is running towards us, sees that we are safe, waves, trots back to his own tank. Two Black Watch men in a slit 30 yards back give us the thumbs up sign. Our fresh green camouflage has been reduced to a few twisted branches charred black and sprinkled with white ash.

Inside the tank the wireless waves continue chattering away. Messages from our own regiment loud and clear. Distant messages identifiable only as human, but lost in the ether, their language, nationality or service arm indistinguishable. Farther beyond, indecipherable crackle which could be insurgent aliens or disembodied spirits released from the battle, an incessant traffic of the dead trying feverishly to maintain contact as they drift farther and farther away into the empty wastes of eternity?

'Hello, Mother. Where is my damn sugar?' (Terse, rude, exasperating.)

'Ah-hullo, Roger Able.' (Bill Fox) 'Can't somebody tell that bloody Mother idiot to keep off the air. We're fighting a battle not being invited to tea at Buckingham Palace. Over.'

'Hullo, Roger Able.' (Hank.) 'I've had a word. "Sugar" is not sugar but code: what cockles live in. Over.'

(Tommy: 'Still don't get it. Cockles live in the sea, don't they?')

(Snowie: 'Shells, boy. Cockles live in shells. The Canadian is only asking for more ammo.')

15.45 hours: Silence. Stillness. Heat. Stench. Fear. Weariness. Then the woods seem to burst apart with a thundercrack 50 yards to our right. A tree rises into the air, poised on a bright expanding finger of flame. Noise hits 3 Baker with a series of sledgehammer smashes as explosions erupt with the velocity of a Bach fugue. Even here inside the armoured vehicle the constant repetition of concussions drives the breath from my lungs and claws at my chest. The enemy is still resilient. We are still exposed at the farthest point of advance. Still no protection on the left. Still the thin screen of Black Watch filling in the perimeter of which we are the watch towers. Still our position feels precarious. In the gruesome intestines of the tank it is a heroic effort just to maintain consciousness. Fumes from two direct hits, from a wood fire, from fire extinguisher foam, from pints of human sweat, frequent urination, festering faeces, battle weariness, lack of sleep.

But wakefulness brings back the ghouls to haunt us, ghouls now wearing the grim, grinning death masks of Jimmy and Ernie and 173 Judge and that legless German commander across the gully. They were sitting as we were sitting a little while ago. Now their bodies are desecrated, their death pangs unimaginable, their spirits out there in the ether trying to keep in touch. And the shot that has *my* name on it will arrive before its sound. From any direction. From any angle to the vertical. However much I watch. And its flash will be my darkness. And its pain …?

Then I see Major Bevan taking an afternoon stroll – in the continuing thunderstorm of battle, whose rain is jagged iron splinters, whose lightning strikes again and again at the same places, whose thunder continues, peal overlaid on peal. Am I seeing mirages? Has he been killed and is this his ghost coming to haunt?

Aristocratic Hank, tall, lean, languid, swishing his riding crop at tall weeds. He pauses and waves his riding crop at a thicket about 50 yards from us. Presumably another of our Shermans is nestled there, invisible to us. As another regulation group of six Moaning Minnies descends and fulminates between us, and the smoke evaporates, he is still standing there. For miles around everyone has gone to ground, German grenadiers and Black Watch in their fox-holes, Yeomanry inside their tanks, artillery in their gun-pits. But Major Bevan chooses to walk above the earth. Rather than an anonymous beret, he is wearing the normal officer's cap, visible to any enemy sniper 800 yards away; a khaki shirt, a cloth crown on each epaulet; and an old loose pair of corduroys. At the gap in the hedge to our rear, which is our escape route, he pauses again.

I touch the traverse lightly to follow him in the periscope's eye. Snowie has probably saluted him for Hank touches his cap with his riding crop in a familiar gesture. Gives 3 Baker a friendly wallop across the rump as though the tank were a horse. He looks critically at the burnt camouflage branches still adorning our front and flicks away a dead branch. Knowing that the invisible crew is watching he screws his face into a combination of a grimace and a grin. Then continues his idle ramble back through the hedge. I see his cap beyond thinner patches in the hedge as he strolls across the cart track which is the focus of our world war at this moment. Sporadic explosions continue as he turns and heads up the slope, still at the same Sunday afternoon pace, towards where HQ(F) tanks must be. 'Good old Hank, even if he did put me on jankers once,' breaths Tommy.

Stan asks Snowie, 'We don't have any infantry out front of us, do we? There's a man's face staring at me from ten o'clock, twenty yards, clump of thick nettles, just a face at ground level. Spooky.'

Rex answers, 'I've been watching it too. It's ghostly. It's just a head. Staring at me. I've been staring back. But it hasn't moved, hasn't blinked, hasn't breathed in ten minutes.'

Tommy agrees, 'I see it. So what? We've seen lots of things flying around today. Tank turrets, trees, unexploded bombs. Why not a few spare heads? There's probably a body somewhere belongs to it.'

Stan repeats, 'Spooky. Gives me the bloody creeps.'

Normally the apparition and the conversation would have had me meditating on ghouls again. On death and wounding and pain and fear. But if David Bevan can take a stroll, sauntering coolly across these fields under blood-curdling fire, then I can square my shoulders, ignore the evil spirits and keep a clear watch a while longer.

6 Evening Requiem

16.30 hours: Teatime at home. Or Evensong in Hereford Cathedral where, in another life, I might have been singing. Here, on I/C, Tommy hums 'I love coffee, I love tea, I love ...'

Rex: 'Hullo ... wait ... definitely a Jerry helmet, infantry crawling, five hundred yards, one o'clock of woods ...'

Snowie: 'Hullo, Roger 3 Baker. One o'clock of woods beside track. Furtive movement, five hundred, probably men crawling. Roger 3 Baker, over.'

Bobby McColl: '3. Hold fire. Let them come on a bit. Get a good view. Off.'

From our various vantage points the views of Rex (5 feet high), myself (8 feet high) and Snowie (11 feet high) are dictated by the thickness and intricacy of branches and leaves. Stan and Rex, low down, can see best. Stan: 'Jerry in cornfield. Gone again. Crouching or crawling.' Rex: 'Nobody above the gully yet.' Stan: 'There, and there, and gone.'

Snowie: 'Gunner, fire when and where ...'

Me: 'Wait ... I see. Little men coming out of bushes above, beyond the gully. Six. Ten. Regiments. Firing!' Although needing to press the mike switch to talk, I can fire both guns by foot pressure on the buttons.

More little men in staggered line, high in the 'racetrack spectators' trees above the gully. My first instinctive high-explosive shell bursts high in the trees. Strictly inaccurate but deadly for anyone beneath. Rex's gun is strumming away, tracing to the right, so I shift left a bit and, as Tommy slaps my thigh, bang off another big one, still holding my Browning's series of 250 bullets without pause. Other tracers, large and small, sweep in from left and from behind us. In a moment's pause I vaguely hear a Black Watch Bren zipping much faster than the Brownings. Our private little argument with Naziism grows into a general confrontation. Little grey figures in the woods, formerly moving towards a common goal, are now split into smaller groups or individuals. These make short, quick rushes in conflicting directions. Some rush right, some sprint left, some crawl to the rear, some slide down the bank forwards. Not easy to shoot at.

Into the intense din there bursts a higher, louder, compressed screaming and slamming as a Typhoon rocket plane (I see it peripherally through the trees) hurls itself perpendicularly at the woods, the rockets fizzing out from it like smaller planes given birth, diving into a sea of fire and smoke that must mark the residence of German tanks invisible to us, but naked to the all-seeing eye of the RAF. Then another 'Typhie', diving vertically until an almost impossible last-minute U-turn back up into the sky. And another. We throw out yellow smoke bombs a perilous 50 yards from the Typhies' targets.

The grey men on the gully slopes have lost any sense of co-ordination. Some keep on moving down to where the 'racetrack' in the gully must seem welcome shelter. Some fall in unco-ordinated spasms. Many lie still. Snowie: 'Driver, move a yard or two forward so gunner can put HE straight into the gully. I'll fling a few grenades to help.' So many explosions I cannot mark our own shell bursts. A fleeting shadow across the sun. More rocket planes. Less movement of grey figures.

Rex has already shifted his aim into the farther burned cornfield. Blackened patches amid the yellow standing grain serve as markers and cause retreating figures to race across the gaps. I now focus on the tiny figures leaping across those ghastly open spaces. Gaps requiring perhaps a 50-yard sprint. An eternity for the fugitive running. A split second for the focusing gunner. And always the sense that those brave, terrified, leaping, falling, writhing figures are somehow comrades of our own horrific experiences.

17.00 hours: Mother will be passing the biscuit barrel and the choir will be chanting the psalm.

We have been watching in case one or several panzer grenadiers slither through the bushes and long grass to attack us in a do-or-die reaction. I feel the commander's knees smack into my back as he ducks instinctively for a moment. Three German soldiers have stood up on *this* side of the gully. Before I can fire I note a white handkerchief which one is desperately waving. The others have hands raised high. Mouthing the universal surrender plea, '*Kamerad*!'

Snowie resumes his perch. 'Ken and Rex, you're the linguists. Get out a moment and see if they can tell you how many of them are left in the gully. Intentions?'

I squirm out of the turret and find that Rex, from his private hatch, has already motioned two of the enemy towards the troop leader's tank where Bobby is waving 'Come on!' I pull out my revolver and Rex has brought his Sten gun. I feel more confident with only one real live enemy, he unarmed, and we both armed. And backed by a 30-ton Sherman tank. 'Do you speak English?'

'*Nein.*'

'Your name? *Name? Zuname?*'

'Grüber. Heinrich Grüber. *Kamerad! Non parler anglais. Peu français. Ich ... non SS.*'

'OK, Heinrich. Give! *Vos amis? Deiner Kameraden?* Where? How many? *Ou? Wo? Et combien?*'

'*Kameraden? Tot! Zwanzig* [He counts twenty on his fingers] *morts. Deaded. Poof-poof-poof. Alles kaput!*'

'And what about panzers? *Panzerkampfwagen?* Tigers?'

'*Nein. Keiner. Marché.* Falaise. Paris.' He flaps his hand vaguely at unknown destinations beyond Robertmesnil. '*Deutschland.*'

'OK, Heinrich. On your way. Not Paris. London, Chipping Sodbury, Salisbury Plain. *Heraus.*' I wave dramatically towards the beaches and accidentally pull the revolver trigger. Bang! Heinrich throws himself to the ground and gabbles German prayers for mercy. Rex seizes his epaulet, pulls him up and utters the ultimate imperative, 'Oh, come on, mate, skip it!' He takes a cigarette out of his pocket, stuffs it into Heinrich's blouse pocket and gives him a friendly push. 'Your war's over. Thank God for that. Our ruddy picnic goes on.' Heinrich smiles weakly, turns forlornly and heads towards his comrades, who are no doubt rendering similarly negative reports to Bobby.

17.20 hours: Snowie suggests we move around a bit to counter boredom and ease sore buttocks. I swop over to Tommy's larger province. Tommy squeezes into the gunner's seat. Rex takes the driving sticks while Stan goes into a doze.

Rex: 'Look out ... movement – cornfield, behind trees right and forward of Robertmesnil. Big disturbance. Too big for a man. Not a tank. Looks like a blimming elephant.'

'Cow,' corrects Tommy at the gunner's telescope. 'Sort of brown colour. Hurt. Limping. Dragging a leg. Missing a leg. Stumbling on three. Tits brushing the ground. Ferking bloody crime, treating animals like that.'

Snowie decides, 'We'll have to shoot it. A burst of co-ax should do. Tommy!'

Tommy swings round in his seat. 'You're not asking me to shoot a cow? I can't shoot a dumb beast. God's creatures? I've never hurt a bloody animal in my life.' The cow is now moving into view of all of us, standing crookedly and, though inaudible from here, obviously bellowing in pain.

Snowie abruptly, 'Gunner, don't argue. Shoot it. Put it out of its agony.'

Tommy revolts. 'I can't, I tell you. Men, yes! Bloody *Bosche*, yes! Ferking Frenchies too, if necessary. But, animals? No! Never!'

I see Snowie's lips purse and begin to curl, but Stan, now co-driver, wakes fully, pulls his trigger and, with a wide, circling, erratic burst of machine-gun bullets, eventually locates and splits, butchers, hurls the cow into flying, bloody fragments. Stan keeps on shooting madly at nothing. Another furious animal lover. Shooting God up the skirts for a hell of a mess-up with the creation frolic. An entire belt of bullets rackets through the gun, blasts from the spout and hurls into the blue. Click. Silence.

We all relax a little. But then six Valkyrian shrieks wake the air above us. Snowie ducks and pulls the flaps shut. Six Moaning Minnie bombs crash down in a neat box around us. Sods and iron shards spin up and rain down upon us. Six mortar bombs. Then nothing. Nothing. Clearly the mortar corporal over there can see us. Equally clearly he himself is hiding from our Typhies, Spitfires and artillery spotters. A lethal game of chess. And we are pawns.

Tommy growls, 'Why didn't that effing Moaning Minnie bugger shoot that cow himself. It was in his flooding field, wasn't it?'

17.55 hours: 'Hullo, Roger 3 Baker.' (Hank's voice.) 'Can you see movement in woods beyond gully? Roger 3 Baker, over.' We are now back in our normal seats. Snowie reports to Hank that we cannot see any movement. HQ(F) must have a more lateral view than we do of the deeper part of the gully. Hank persists, 'If it moves, shoot it!'

Then I see one, two, possibly three field-grey figures, no weapons visible, working their way from tree to tree and from bush to bush above the gully, extremely slowly and apparently unconcerned about being seen. Why only three men? And what have they lost?

Snowie reports even as I reach enlightenment. 'Roger 3 Baker. Three only men. Wearing Red Cross armbands. Checking for wounded. Over.'

'3 Baker. Maybe. But watch carefully. Those are SS out there, Red Cross or not. Don't trust 'em. Shoot first. No questions asked. Off.'

The three men are halfway down the slope. At this moment I spot another man about 50 yards to the left. He is the tallest soldier I have ever seen. Huge. 6 feet 8 at least. And as wide as he is tall. SS uniform, tin hat, rifle slung carelessly from his shoulder. Strutting slowing along the bank as though on sentry-go. The prototype Nazi.

Rex sees him too. 'Hey, look! Mr Atlas. *Gefreiter* King Kong. Ten foot tall at least.' Snowie responds, 'Gunner, left. Chase that big fellow away. Fire!' I object, 'Too near to the Red Cross people.' But Rex has already opened fire. The trees are so thick that Rex's shots from low down ricochet off in all directions. The tall SS trooper is unperturbed. At the same steady pace he turns and begins to head back towards the top of the gully, away from the ambulance party. 'Lost him' groans Rex.

'Gunner, then, no danger to Red Cross. Give him one HE to encourage him on his way.' I fire. Damn! The 75 was loaded with AP, solid shot, instead of HE. But, at tremendous velocity and short range, the shot hits the ground just below the big sentry, goes spinning into the trees, flinging up an inordinate mess of dirt, branches, leaves and smoke. And leaving an incredible swathe of broken trees in its wake. Slowly the whirling mess descends. The big man is no longer there. Has he retreated at the double? Has he taken cover? Has he disintegrated?

Tommy sums up. 'Gawd Almighty. If he survived that lot, he'll be picking wood splinters out of his ass for the next fifty years.'

'Hullo, Roger 3 Baker. Spotted a non-Red Cross prowler. Seven feet tall. Opened fire. All movement ceased. 3 Baker, over.'

'Hullo, 3 Baker.' (Hank again cutting in.) 'Seven feet tall or ten feet tall, chase 'em! I don't want the enemy to establish a claim to those gully slopes. Off.'

18.10 hours: Rex: 'The three stretcher-bearers are back.'

Me: 'What about *Standardtenfuehrer* Hercules?'

Stan: 'I reckon we'll find him hanging up in the top of one of those elms, like the fairy on the Christmas tree.'

The day is now definitely in a state of decline. A cooler breeze filtering into the turret takes the worst of the heat out of what has been a very hot afternoon. The sun is still high but westering. Shells and mortars burst with no more frequency than a fit of hiccups. Most of our remaining tanks seem to have switched off their engines, enabling commanders to listen for infantry approach. Birds chirp anxiously, exchanging views about what has been happening down on earth and making feathered assumptions about whether it is now safe to go hunting food. In the tank only the constant atmospherics and the hum of the wireless set itself continue. When I remove the earphones I can hear Stan softly singing, 'There's a small hotel, with a wishing well; I wish ...'

Rex: 'The Red Cross Fritzes have found themselves another customer.'

The three Germans in the wood have been crouching in the same spot for some minutes. They load something heavy onto a stretcher. The two bearers lift their burden and head slowly up into the woods, stepping over huddled bundles beyond their care. The third man, presumably an MO or trained orderly, stands up holding a bag. He turns very deliberately in our direction, shades his eyes with one hand. Then waves to us. Turns. Plods off towards Berlin.

18.25 hours: Snowie suggests that Rex take a breather behind the tank, at the same time making some tea on our Primus stove, which is petrol fuelled by means of a tiny hand pump. Rex groans 'On my way. Pass me my crutch.' Rather than risk his own forward hatch he crawls through the turret cage and up through the turret. I catch a glimpse of his face. The face of a man of seventy, grey, dry, creased, gaunt and wasted. I suppose all of us look the same. And our premature ageing is exaggerated by the filth of 5 miles of battle and the weariness of two days and a night of extreme foreboding. Shall we ever be young again? Rex drops to the ground, stumbles with cramp, massages his legs. Hops up and down. Runs back and forth like a footballer warming up before a match, whilst some Black Watch men in a trench not far behind us make signs to him that he would be more comfortable in their little hide than in a tank.

Rex slaps me on the back, and I jerk wide awake! He has made tea and climbed back in, offering mugs all round. Rex sits in Tommy's seat while Tommy risks his skin making another brew of tea to offer to the infantrymen, who are not as well equipped as us. I ask Snowie if he wants to sit in the gunner's seat and drink his tea while I do look-out duty. Still half asleep I ascend into purer air. Or rather, less sullied air. In our present state it is fatal to stare at a tree which is swaying gently in the breeze because it can hypnotize, seduce, beckon the mind into glorious, fatal sleep. And whilst I am breathing this fresher air, I am still perched in the main ventilation outlet of the tank where the steaming, reeking air from within is soporific. The SSM, our witty Sid Turton, always says that commanding a tank on a hot day is like standing at the door of an over-heated brothel.

'Hullo, William 3 Able. Crew member with suspected appendicitis. Griping pains. Hard, swollen belly. High temperature. Do I jig? 3 Able over.'

'3 Able. You jig. Will get a robber to your little house immediately. Off.' (That fine service, the Royal Army Medical Corps, has, from its initials RAMC, derived the unfortunate nickname 'Rob All My Comrades'. Hence a 'robber'.)

Stan: 'I don't believe it. It must be against King's Regulations to catch appendicitis in the face of the enemy.'

I can hear Snowie sipping his tea in the pure, mysterious silence.

Unknown insects buzzing. Here at the extreme point (still!) of Allied advance the silence is too good to be true. It could be evidence of sinister intentions on the part of the persistent *Boche*. So I resume the routine of searching the skyline, the cornfields, the woods, the gully, the skyline, the cornfields, the woods the gully the skyfields the cornlinethewoodlythe …

19.22 hours: One moment an empty cornfield, scarred by blackened patches. The next moment – one, two enemy half-tracks, crowded with troops wearing the big coal-scuttle helmets … Snowie, back up top, snaps 'Gunner, cornfield … right … right … on! Both guns. Fire!' And my first hurried snatched shot lands well up in the woods beyond the targets.

Ten, maybe fifteen infantrymen are sitting huddled and crouched in each vehicle. They are retreating fast, probably at 30 mph at 500 yards range and increasing, the rear tracks of the carriers slithering around as the front wheels jerk this way and that in efforts to swerve and confuse our gunners. My first 75 shell wasted, my continuing Browning tracer loops down to the level of the half-tracks as I depress the guns. One of the Germans in the rear vehicle jerks visibly (one out of two million still to go!). Tommy slaps, our 75mm flashes, roars, smokes and its single tracer, apparently sliding along the dotted line of the co-axial tracer, hits low on the rearmost half-track. It leaps into the air, with men falling, diving, leaping, rolling. (Tommy: 'Whoops! Crickey! Shit on the buggers!') The vehicle lands right way up. Bounces. Spins in a circle. Goes on spinning. One German miraculously sitting in it! Possibly the driver. He looks over the side, jumps out, runs and crawls towards a patch of standing corn, which then catches fire.

The leading carrier is now bucking and bouncing towards a gap in the more distant hedges. It scuttles into the gap. I fire again and the tracer seems to take a tremendous time to plane across the cornfield but other tracers fly ahead of mine into the gap. The half-track has disappeared but several tracers pursue it cleanly through the hole in the hedge. A billow of flame! A rush of smoke! We shall not know any more about that explosion until we catch up with those shells tomorrow, or in a week's time. Meanwhile, as yet more tracers home in, the other carrier, encircled in an orange balloon of fire and reduced to a lump of tortured metal, bounces amid the corn, rolls over and, mimicking a human death, somehow shudders and lies still.

19.50 hours: Silent wireless. No, not silent. Indistinct rumblings and cracklings of a far-away war. Or perhaps it is still the echo in our ears of earlier wars. Whispers out of an unknown planet. Even the conversation within the tank has languished and we have come to the end of our script of imbecilities. I find my mug still half full of tea. Horrid chlorinated mash gone cold. My thirst overcomes my nausea. I take a swig of the liquid. Pure rat slime. Another swig. It is liquid. It is wet. It is obnoxious. But, like many bitter things, it has a thirst-quenching quality.

Tommy is asking, 'Stan, is there any food left?' to which our driver chirps, 'One lousy tin of sardines and six yellow-brick biscuits. Just doing the chef bit. Coming round with the refreshments.' And through the turret cage he hands us our poor man's caviar.

'Hullo, Roger 3 Able and 3 Charlie.' (Bobby McColl to our other two tanks now behind us out of sight.) 'Nasty hornet thirty to forty yards right of farm. Fire to my command. One AP, one HE and bursts of co-ax. Report when on. 3 Able and Charlie, over.'

'What did the bugger say?'

'He said, "Thirty to forty yards right of farm."'

'Does the Heeland Laddie expect me to pace it out?'

'HULLO, 3 Charlie. SWITCH to I/C, OFF!'

'Charlie, OK, Sorry! Off.'

Tommy: 'He, he, he! Charlie will be for the ferking high jump! – leaving his set switched to 'A' like that!'

Rex: 'Oh, I expect the Heeland Laddie will put it down to battle panic. Our Bobby's very sweet like that.' And we listen as, still unseen, our Able and Charlie fire off several rounds with the responding welcome sight, beyond the gully, of the familiar upsurge of thickening smoke, commencing black and slowly blending with a crimson glow.

Stan (now sitting in the co-driver's seat): 'I think all the Fritzes have gone to the gold-lined slit trench in the skies. I'm going to have a snooze.'

Rex: 'Hey, Stan, you know that spare head we saw ages ago? It has gone all sort of pink. And still watching us. Unblinking. I reckon it will follow us around when we move. Sort of ghostly.'

Stan: 'That's done it. I never could sleep after my Mum had told me a ghost story in bed. Who else wants a snooze down here?'

20.15 hours: Cautious movement behind us. A Black Watch corporal, Sten gun at the alert, comes suspiciously through the hedge, sniffing like an over-grown golden retriever. Behind him is a Black Watch officer with drawn revolver. They relax, wave to us, tread carefully over the rough vegetable field to our left. Today's infantrymen do not trudge like clodhoppers but tend to do ballet steps over ground likely to be infested with deadly anti-personnel mines. They prowl along the hedgerows looking for suitable machine-gun posts and fields of fire. Another man follows them and begins sweeping the ground with a mine detector, quite laconically as though hoovering his parlour carpet.

21.00 hours: The sun is now dipping towards its sunset point. It touches the extreme tip of the tallest tree beyond the gully. Huge shadows point towards us like gigantic anti-tank guns. The tracery of leaves on trees resembles a stained glass window already beginning to blush with the most resplendent hues of sunset.

A click of the microphone, and it is Lieutenant McColl's voice on I/C, his face framed in the turret opening. 'Right, lads! The good news: we're pulling out. The bad news: not until 23.00 hours. Our troop last. Your tank bringing up the rear. Laager at Hubert Folie. Night march form: wireless silence. Green marker lights. White tapes already around minefields. Tail lights only, except your tank – nobody behind you, except the Highland boys who stay. Corporal Snowdon to go in jeep with Sergeant King to mark out rendezvous sites in village. Tout, come up and command. Keep awake still. We may still stir the odd *Boche*. That's it. Come with me, corporal.'

As I climb up top a file of Black Watch (blacker than ever in the shadows) keeps good step down the track behind us. Their captain issues instructions. The files split up, spread out and begin to dig. In the quietness, bruised only by delving spades, I hear desultory conversation from within the tank. 'That Omar Bradley's a good bloke – the best of the Yanks' ... 'Alexander the Great? Wasn't he with Monty at Alamein?' ... (Tommy's voice:) 'Who's this Annie Ball and her elephants? Is it a circus act?' (and Stan) 'If we pulled out after twenty missions like RAF crews, we'd be due out now.'

The infantry captain exchanges salutes with his sergeant, acknowledges my own gesture and walks away west with his lieutenant. The sun is now lodged like a burning bird's nest in the branches of a tree along the gully. The two Highlanders' backs are purple-black in the eye of the setting sun, their heads shimmering in a haze of light. The individual shadows of the two moving figures trail behind them like the extended trains of wedding dresses, long, crow-black, sinister trains. And the golden halo around the head of each ebony figure completes a parody of a wedding in Hell. The silence erupts and a horde of screaming lost souls flies over our heads. The earth spits blood. A splurging overflow from Hell blazes up along the hedgerows. Late evening enemy spite. The Black Watch sergeant and his party look up, duck a little, listen, bend again to the task of secreting their own little pieces of infernal machinery deep within the innocent Normandy undergrowth.

21.45 hours: Epic tardy moment. Emblem of our possible survival. The unseen sun touches the earth's rim and sets off its own conflagration in the sky, shaming the day's human efforts. In peace, sunset is a time for poets to dream, shepherds to close the gate of the fold, and lovers to go walking. In war, sunset is the moment which changes the battle from the grand panorama of massed manoeuvre into a stealthy, creeping feud of individual hunters carrying on their bloody craft in the dark. The 1944 tank is of little use as a defensive weapon after dark, so we withdraw most nights to clean guns and load up with ammo, petrol, water, food. So sunset is a moment of truth for the tank man. He has up to an hour more to survive. Guns fire, soldiers die in the gloaming. At long last nightfall, for the tank man, means a daily armistice, a safe refuge, a retreat into thankful obscurity. Hope wakens again after the torrid terrors of the day.

Again, the shrieking birds of prey swoop from the skies. Minnies! Duck quickly. Listen to the neat crump-crump-crump-four-five-six. Six carefully placed gouts of flaming anger behind us. One waspish shred of shrapnel buzzes over the tank and expires in the hedge in front of us. Then our own artillery rumbles away, fishing along the skyline for the German Minnie master who won't go home.

22.15 hours: Like the eastern RAF fires of last night, the sunset has lit chains of incandescent colour behind the western trees. We watch the sky fires burn down to night-grey ash. With my field-glasses I can still see the German bodies on the gully slopes, formless blobs of duller grey on the darkening slopes.

This little nook in the hedgerows has become a personal possession for us. Stan, Rex, Tommy and I have known more terror in an hour here than a human being should experience in a lifetime. But there was nowhere safer for Snowie to take us so we clung to our primeval refuge in the hedges, fearing the latter-day armoured dinosaurs coming against our fragile bows and arrows, realizing the vulnerability of our nest, but appreciating its warm gift of furtive concealment. Home. Owners.

The last light takes moth flight from the highest leaves and branches. Black creepers of night have wound upwards around all but the tallest trees. I get down briefly to tell the Black Watch that we are moving.

The lieutenant nods, 'Aye, well, fade into the night. But we'll be glad to see ye again in the morning.'

The sergeant calls to his men 'Right, lads. Tanks are moving. Ye'll need to depend on your ain eyes the noo.'

We donate them a tin of bully and a packet of biscuits because we are going back to replenish.

22.40 hours: 'Stations Roger 3,' clicks in Bobby's voice. 'Move as ordered. Off.'

Our 3 Baker is only a dark shape, detaching itself quietly from the darker mass of a hedge and gliding back on gentle murmurs of its engine.

'Driver, about turn and follow Charlie's rear light. Gunner, traverse to rear and keep watch for tracer. Loader, keep an HE up the spout. Let's go.'

23.00 hours: Our artillery is putting down a general stonk, presumably to cover our withdrawal, although Fritz will notice the noise of many engines in between the individual shell bursts. In any case, Fritz himself is addicted to clockwork systems and will be expecting our tanks to move back about now. Sure enough, a screeching shower of mortar bombs falls in the orchards which A Squadron have just vacated. Then a heavier sound, like an aeroplane coming into land too fast, rushes close overhead and dives into a deep, concentrated thunderclap in the village. Its twin grinds overhead. A third monster shell mills the air close down over our heads, lashes tornadoes of explosion out of the village lane. Our cart track shudders up through the very springs of the 30-ton tank.

I can now discern Bobby McColl's tank lit by rolling waves of light, the tank appearing to be rocking on the tide. Bobby's head protrudes from his turret. Red wrath war-paints his face, Red Indian style, and he too is staring fascinated at the flames streaming like blood down the burned-black sky. Beyond him another ghostly galleon sails the crimson-tinted night. Then the guns stop. Blackness slams down on us like the closing of a vast oven door in the night.

Stan chuckles to Tommy, 'There you can see it now. Your favourite sign, a red light,' and suddenly he is accelerating past village cottages, across a smooth field. Hedge 'Fly by Night' looms solitary, forsaken, superfluous, rather like Beecher's Brook after the National Hunt season has ended. And now, across last night's empty landscape, there stretches a highway, pricked out in merry green lights and bounded by clean white tapes. Tanks avoid circuitous medieval lanes and blaze new trails of Roman directness, straight across country. Julius Caesar (once here) would have been at home in a tank.

23.30 hours: We are now way out in the emptiest deserts of darkness, monotonous, mesmerizing, enervating. The land dark. The tank dark. Ourselves dark. Hardly enough light to blanch the Nubian darkness of our skins. And this dark, rumbling, gently rocking vehicle sways us, levitates us, leaves us weightless, feelingless, purposeless, absorbed into its warm, stinking fetid obscurity ... like a drifting boat ... like a floating bed ... like a rocking cradle ... like a pulsing womb ... like a snug shroud on a slow hearse ... a warm, descending tomb, a long barrow in which to rest to sleep for the mind to disengage and go drifting along darkened tunnels, warming, pulsing, sinking … looming … glooming … drooming … swooming …

CRASH! Tank hits a crater, then noses down, wrenches up. The ground is torn and battered to the extent that it is impossible to say where ground level is. There are no visible horizontal lines. A squandered heap of bricks, once a cottage, is strewn across mounds and into craters so that the floor level of the cottage could be anywhere within a couple of feet, higher or lower. And here the stench is as bad as anything I have encountered in Normandy's hot summer. Purposeless shells drone and rumble overhead, perhaps travelling round and round the earth's surface without ever landing. And everywhere the incalculable proliferation of mess, of imbecilic inventories, of millions of particles, every pile of earth as full of detail as a mine dump alive with gleaming pyrites. Flickering impressions as far-off artillery flashes stipple the immensity of darkness. A place of massacred warriors and wasted materials.

Day's end. Battle's rest. Deserted land. Tired eyelids. Rancid mouth. Aching ankles. Vacant stomach. Ceaseless crunching of tracks on rough ground, ceaseless screeching of tracks over sprockets, ceaseless booming of engines, ceaseless calling of lost voices trying to reach us through the ceaseless atmospherics of the wireless, ceaseless … swaying … swinging … swooning …

9 AUGUST 1944:

00.05 hours: It is like turning out of the Sahara Desert into the railway terminus of a great city. One moment we are travelling across a barren formless land, the desert theme accentuated by the clouds of dust as we navigate the trackless wastes where camels might have seemed more indigenous.

A huddle of buildings appears on the left. We hit a solid road and run between two houses. And are in the midst of frenzied activity. 'Infernal' is a word which has sprung to mind frequently over the last day or two, but this scene is like a stage representation of Hell indeed. Lurid light struggles against omnipotent darkness. Small hand-torches wave their yellow rays by the dozen. Cooking stoves flicker furtively, orange and red, on all sides. Two or three large trucks manoeuvre with the aid of black-out lights, the normal headlights covered with black patches in which tiny crosses are cut. Somewhere in the background a larger bonfire diffuses a crimson- and maroon-coloured glare: probably a dump of inflammable materials set ablaze by tracer or incendiaries. An almost unbearable stink of burning rubber sterilizes the normal stench of putrefying flesh. Against and within this kaleidoscope of hesitant light, hordes of human figures, black silhouettes, hurry to and fro between the massed vehicles.

The buildings of Hubert Folie are, almost without exception, ruined. There are roofless cottages and floorless cottages which have sunk into deep pits. There are buildings with three walls, two walls, one wall. Doors hang loose, doorways have been enlarged into ragged gaps, windows jut askew, oddly positioned new apertures give the walls the appearance of having been designed by crazy architects for dwarfs and giants. Here and there stands a shattered vehicle. And everywhere the day's passengers, cramped from long journeyings, leap about in a grotesque ballet, exaggerating their activities in order to exercise neglected limbs.

The first recognizable figure is a lanky English gentleman, waving a riding crop to direct traffic: Hank, the squadron leader, counting us in. He waves us to stop. Shouts. 'Are you definitely the last in line?' I shout back, confirming. In the intolerant, distressing light his shoulders seem to sag a little and he looks behind us, body language denying hope. In front our own Corporal Snowden beckons us on.

At Snowie's signal we halt. Jumping to the ground without due thought, I stumble with cramp and tiredness and hang onto a welded storage box for support. Out of the darkness an excited, sweating man runs towards me. Throws his arms around me. Embraces me in a most un-English manner. I push him away. Recognize him as Corporal Aris, the squadron cook. He is weeping and laughing at the same time. 'Young Ken! You got back. You're safe. You made it. A lot of other lads bought it. And the colonel too. Bugger Hitler! But you got back!' A rugby scrum of echelon lads – cooks, fitters, signallers, armourers, clerks, spare crews – engulfs us, enfolds us, enthuses, roisters, riots.

Amid the hubbub a great voice booms and a large smiling face thrusts its way through the common herd. The RSM himself! Burly, bustling George Jelley, boy soldier of the former war, terror of minor criminals, uncle to front-line crews.

'Come on, my merry men. Father Christmas is here. See what you've got in your Christmas stocking. Petrol, ammo, water, rations.' And grabbing a large 75mm shell in hands which could juggle a beer barrel, he hurls the live shell at a lad on the next tank with such force that it nearly knocks the catcher over.

A different voice cuts in, more shrill, more abrupt. 'C'mon, c'mon, c'mon, you admin wallahs. Another thirsty tank here. Don't bother the driver. He's been fighting the Hun. Get the petrol cap off. Get passing the jerry cans. Get pouring that petrol. There's a bloody war on. Didn't you know?' The ferocious staccato of words pours from the ferret of a man who contrives to look immaculate even at this hour, the SSM, Sid Turton.

As RSM George passes up the last few ammo boxes to Tommy on the turret, I hazard a gentle vote of gratitude. 'Thank you, sir. It's been a great help at this time of the night to have so many echelon blokes willing to help.'

'Willing, lad? Willing? *I've* been willing them, with a boot up their pants. Did you hear? The Yanks bombed us back there. The most accurate bomb-aimers I've ever met. Right down our throats. Right up our backsides. Blew up a three-tonner and HQ squadron leader's jeep. Only we weren't the enemy! Huge great Flying Fortresses and Liberators. I looked up to see once. I didn't look up the second time. I was halfway to Australia down a slit trench, digging with these ten great shovels called fingers.'

'Sorry about the Forts, sir.'

'Nothing to it. Except we lost three good lads, that ginger-haired fitter, and the signaller with glasses, and a new lad-never-knew-his-name. A thousand-pound bomb right on top of them. No trace of 'em afterwards. Not even a hand to shake goodbye, like you found in the old 1914–18 trenches. Gone in tiny globules all over the field.' He slaps the tank. Pulls out a big khaki handkerchief. Blows his nose. Wipes his eyes. Grins sheepishly at me. Then turns and growls at the echelon lads, 'Right! You lot on strike? Haven't you got homes to go to? Knock off now. This is the last tank in. Get some kip. Early day tomorrow … today.'

00.25 hours: An anonymous voice shouts from another laager of four tanks. 'Put that light out! The air raid warden's coming.' Another disgruntled voice from another direction: 'Oh, go visit a taxidermist and get stuffed.' Replies: 'There's supposed to be a black-out.' Not so angrily: 'Well, then, go get the fire brigade to put that flaming great blaze out in the village.'

Just beyond HQ(F) laager someone has draped a large waterproof tank cover over the walls of a ruined, roofless barn. Dim lights glow. The floor is uneven with glinting, tumbled straw. Hank is seated on a camp stool, cap straight, knees together, jaw set, doodling in pencil on a map cover. Bill Fox, cap pushed perilously back, knees splayed wide as though on horseback, jaw chewing industriously, sits flicking a riding crop at evasive flies. The SSM stands behind them. Bobby McColl squats on the straw. Only one other lieutenant, Tony Faulkner, has survived, out of our original team of eight subalterns. Suddenly I am back with Stan's Pop in the 1914–18 lot, and tales of forever marching back from the front line with pitifully few survivors.

Normally this 'O' (Orders) group would be closed, sacrosanct. Tonight those of us who are not yet asleep hover around unchecked. We have shared the day. Hank says, 'You can all count. We have ten tanks left out of nineteen. Tomorrow we of C and the remnant of A merge as one squadron. Counter-attack positions as the Poles go in again. Sad about so many ... But we have destroyed at least twenty enemy AFVs (armoured fighting vehicles), including probably five Tigers. We have carried out novel tactics with total target achievement, more success than was seriously anticipated by higher authority.' He glances at a paper in his hands: 'A message has been received from the Supreme Commander congratulating us all on achieving ... a significant victory.'

He breaks off and listens as an unseen singer changes from 'Red Sails in the Sunset' to 'Tell Me the Old, Old Story'. Hank joins in the general laughter. 'Sergeant-Major, do you think our singer could hear what I was saying?'

'No, sir, I regret to say that the choice of hymn was purely coincidental.'

'Perhaps it is fair comment anyway. The old, old story is true. We reached "Fly-by-Night". We repulsed the counter-attack. But the remainder of the battle seems to have come unstuck. Some of you saw what happened when the unfortunate Poles were sent on a cavalry charge in Shermans across open ground in broad daylight towards 88s firing point blank. A damnable massacre.'

'Bloody shambles again! Balaclava and all that,' growls Bill Fox.

David Bevan continues: 'Tonight no tank crews will stand guard. Rear echelon will find all guards. Tomorrow, by which I mean today, reveille at 03.30 hours. That's nearly three hours away still ... start up 04.30. 3 Troop lead. By 05.15 back in same positions along the gully. Right! I'm off to bed. What about you, Bill?'

'Ruddy good idea, David. Shame I never thought of it myself.'

The night is purple black, the twinkling stars above and the flickering stoves beneath only serving to accentuate and confuse the sepulchral darkness, vaguely bulked out by ponderous tanks, shaped like oriental mausoleums. Three or four troopers crouch around a hissing Primus stove plaintively singing, 'the blue-hoos ... in the night'. I turn my bleary eyes up to the sky, find the Plough, the North Star. Beckoning home.

00.50 hours: I take the spade and head for outer darkness. Count the paces. Ten, sixteen, eighteen, twenty ... We go around France doing our best to strew the countryside with dead bodies, spent shrapnel, murdered cattle, ruined houses, but at the same time we have rigid sanitary regulations. The regiment insists that those responding to the baser call of nature dig, and fill in, a hole at least 25 yards away from the nearest tank.

01.05 hours: At last. We sit down to supper. Not strictly correct. If we sat down we would fall asleep, keel over and sprawl there, like so many dead cockroaches. Stan does sit down and goes through the motions of a sinking ship. So we stand and gobble. Double rations because so many did not return to share. I wolf the food, thankful for the decency of darkness. Another salvo of shells slides overhead, does a rub-a-dub-thud well beyond us. A voice calls, 'Dear God, turn 'em round and ram 'em up Hitler's ass.'

Tommy finds the energy to scramble, monkey-like, up the track, onto the engine covers, loosens the rope and kicks our bedding rolls off the back of the tank. I lean against the tank, mug of horrid tea in hand, and stare at the stars. In this moment I feel a wild exhilaration. Relief! I am still alive. Drinking in the chill night. Seeing the vast jet canopy of skies, with stars big and mobile and flickering like a plague of silver, luminous moths. I am alive. Safe. Young. Running wild in a strange country, hazarding life, wolfing food, escaping fate, enjoying the undemanding but loyal companionship of other youths who, like me, are quick to fun and slow to anger.

'Our camels sniff the evening and are glad,' quotes bookish Rex.

I know that one: 'We take the Golden Road to Samarkand.'

'I'm ferking off to bed,' unquotes Tommy.

01.15 hours: 'No digging a trench tonight, lads,' Snowie orders, 'Sleep where you collapse. Worth the risk for once.'

'Lost something, Tommy? Has your ball rolled under there?' asks Rex as Tommy crawls clumsily under the tank.

'I'm flooding well not sleeping in the open. Last time I slept in the open somebody pissed on me in the middle of the night.'

Stan has woken and climbed on to the warm engine covers, his favourite place. He calls, 'Warm up here! Room for two, Ken.'

'No thanks. My mother told me to beware of strange men.'

'It was your sister she told that to.'

'I never had a sister.'

'Lucky sister!'

01.20 hours: Bumpy ground. Two hours to sleep. Comes another day. Sleep, I must sleep. How sleep? Count sheep? Count German tanks crossing a gully? Count brewed-up tanks? Pillars of smoke? Broken waxworks? German war widows queuing up for pensions?

01.26 hours: A soft footfall in the grass. 'What's up, mate? Can't you sleep?' It's Jack Aris, corporal cook. Normally cooks would never dream of standing guard. They are privileged persons. But tonight is different. He squats beside me. 'What was it really like up there? Was it bad?'

'Well, really, in the line you don't see much at all. Just trees and occasional puffs of smoke. No blood or anything. You hear more. But there is little to see. If it sticks its head up to be seen, it gets its head promptly shot off. Of course, in another sense, it is all rather horrific because you can hear the wireless reports and you can visualize what is going on. Like floating over the battlefield, watching with your ears. Our tanks brewing up. German tanks milling around. Half the regiment blazing. Masses of German infantry crawling through the corn. Then burning.'

Jack straightens up, 'Glad you got back, anyway. Sorry about little Ernie, Jimmy, others. Must go patrol a bit. Give Jerry the shits, see me with this gun. Gives myself the shits, this gun. But got the book of instructions in my pocket. Go sleep, old son. Don't worry about this 'ere war. I'm winning that.' He moves off across the grass, crouching slightly, rather like a superannuated Red Indian.

01.31 hours: Dimly, luminous watch hands mean ... one hour fifty-nine minutes left for sleep. Can't sleep. Stan can. Little Ernie certainly can there beyond the gully. Ground hard, uneven, penance couch for back, hips, shoulders. A corner of my haversack pillow sticks in my ear. An excess of corned beef sets my gullet on fire. And now ghosts marshal themselves down the subterranean corridors of my subconscious: a battered waxwork in a motor cyclist's uniform, a panzer tank commander curtailed at the waist, a British commander frozen in a mock Hitler salute, a headless thing wearing 173 Trooper Judge's uniform, a bevy of Moaning Minnies transformed into real witches, riding the skies and able to home in on the target human who runs hither and thither but cannot escape ...

Today, yesterday I have seen people killed. In a tank one does not so often see people die. The tank is a nice, clean, hygienic and civilized method of slaughter. Press a button and the enemy drops out of sight, but undoubtedly safely dead. You don't even have to wipe your bayonet or wash your hands. A kind of 'humane killer' device which causes no pain at all – to the killer. (The night breeze swings to another compass point and catches the stench of some human cess-heap.)

01.34 hours: At this hour, if awake, my mother will be putting her faith in a Supreme Power who can divert bullets. (Ernie Wellbelove and the Fritz motor-cyclist probably have mothers praying too, with less success!) Pray for sleep, at least.

01.37 hours: Someone screams in the night.

The voice burbles into incomprehensible muttering. A second voice grumbles, 'Bloody hell! Stuff a blanket over that man's head!' A third voice rejoins sleepily, 'Oh, leave him. It's Lankie. He's probably dreaming about that Jerry he shot.' The argument babbles on in three voices: 'I shot some effing Jerries meself, din' I? All right, so you're a bleeding adult. Lankie's only a kid still. No, I didn't. No, I didn't. Don't shoot. Don't shoot. Do'shootshooshoo. Aw, pull the bloody trigger pull your own it's big enough I tell you I din' I Gawd fetch the vet aw leave the kid can't musn't shoot a white flag 'tsa white flag, ruddy mother's boy, did 'ave a mother anyway ...' and the three voices overlap, gradually subside into sleep, leaving three unfinished sentences hanging in the gently pulsing night.

The far-distant thunder, of guns or of August storm, now produces little more reverberation than a highly strung bass drum responding to the caress of a child's finger-tip. Little more disturbance than the failing pulse of a dying man. Empty your mind, they say. Empty ... then the bumps go bumpbump-bubump ... 2 miles away? Five miles away? Flashes that are lightning. Or not lightning? Or both lightning and not lightning? Empty your mind. Ernie Wellbelove, of course, his face not covered ... another, a waxwork in a ditch ... gullies and gaps in hedges ... Hank out strolling ... bloody shambles again!

'Hullo, 4 Able. Hullo, 4 Able ...' But 4 Able never did answer. And somewhere out on the ether, escaped pulses of radio carry the message on for ever – on, on through a void, racing to where 4 Able is and will ever be ... 'Hullo, 4 Able ...'

Remember then! Fill the mind! I hold on to the day that is now yesterday because that day is safe. In that day I live and do not die. Do not become mashed into a ball of writhing pain. So that day is mine. To hold on to. I turn my guns on the advancing field-grey masses of sleep and fight to hold on to this island of time, this melting iceberg of moments. Tomorrow is alien territory ... no man's land ... enemy country ... a new St-Aignan. So I hold on by remembering while chill battalions of sleep rustle through the undergrowth of my mind, waiting to take me unawares, waiting to leap, waiting to explode vast mines of nightmare ...

'Hullo, 4 Able' ... I wonder where his spirit has gone, playing imaginary drums ... little grey sacks in the woods ... a pale German boy in a trench, nameless and forever unmoving ... you've mashed up a Jerry ... *mon Kamerad Heinrix, smoken Sie that* ... a rugby scrum of cooks, fitters, signallers, armourers, clerks ... laughing and crying at the same time ... give Jerry the shits, sees me ... 'Hullo, 4 Able. Can you not ...' trying to keep in touch ... trying ... 'Oboe 2, nasties, right front' ... walked all the way from

Alamein ... keep away from them kipper-smoking furnaces ... forty-one hours, forty-one minutes, forty-one seconds ... sleep ... sounds like rat's claws scratching on the side of the tank ...

'Bale out! Bale out! 4 Charlie has brewed. O God! O GodGodGod! Hullo 4 Able 4 Able 4 Able are you there? ... will you ever be there? ... any more?' ... Radio pulses from over the world's edge, the universe's edge, oblivion's edge ... trying to keep in touch ...

You're not asking me to shoot a *cow*? ... a man, yes ... Oh 4 Able, can you not hear me ... 4 Able ... 1 Charlie ... Roger 3 Baker ... THAT'S *US*! ... Roger 3 Baker ... answer, can't you? ... my hands frozen ... cannot press ... cannot speak ... cannot halt the pulse of radio, speeding away, away from me, speeding for ever through the empty unknown wastes ... oh, my God, answer! Shout! Scream! ... calling for those who are trying to keep in touch ... through the gloom. Past innumerable worlds ... forever night ... beyond ... Oh, 3 Baker, 4 Able ...

No trace of 'em. Not even a hand to shake goodbye to, like you found in the old trenches ... Hark!listen!silence! ... 4 Able? Is that *US*? ... a pulse ... forever more ... trying ...

Oh, hullo, 4 Able, report my ...

Hullo, 4 Able ... hands frozen ...

4 Able ... cannot ...

4 ...

4give them, Father ...

4 they know not ...

4 Able ...

trying to keep in ...

trying ...

7 Tank Command

9 AUGUST 1944:

04.00 hours: In a sleeping daze we rose, scalded our fingers trying to make a hurried cup of tea, piled clumsily onto our tanks. Now we are on the road back to St-Aignan before the light has conquered the darkness.

By some dispensation of fortune our troop appears to be the only troop in A and C Squadrons which is numerically intact. Hank has moved up to second-in-command of the regiment. Bill Fox is our new squadron leader, a major now, with his new 2 i/c Ken Todd, only slightly burned yesterday (Eric Marchant was terribly burned). There is no spare officer, so the SSM, that perky, humorous, sardonic man, will be coming up to take the third HQ(F) tank when it is replaced. (The major usually has two captains in HQ(F), the second one going by different names in different units, sometimes 'rear link', but for us squadron captain.)

The modest cottages, the tall (if battered) Norman church, the rambling farm buildings, the fruitful orchards of St-Aignan, all present a holiday brochure picture in the summer sun. Only a closer examination reveals smashed walls and bullet-pitted trees, yellowing bodies of man (enemy) and beast and blackened burnt-out tanks of yesterday's strife. Today the Black Watch stand boldly about the village street where yesterday they ducked and sprinted. Their cooks tend roaring fires where yesterday the shells of both sides spewed flame.

We take our place among the trees on the very slopes of the gully, yesterday a race-track for German tanks and forbidden territory for us. Our tank still smells of smoke. We renew our green camouflage. My head aches from a wasp sting gone unnoticed in the battle. We watch forward and loiter one by one behind the tank. Bobby McColl approaches and beckons me. He switches on his rather shy, reticent sixth-form smile.

'Do ye still have that stripe ye wore coming over? Put it up again. Ye're promoted in Orders this evening.' I get stripes, needle and cotton out of my aptly named 'housewife' pouch in my small pack; and have a vision of John Pearson, corporal clerk, sitting somewhere in the orchards, typewriter precariously perched, faithfully typing away, *'to be Lance-Corporal, 147 Tout, K.J.'*, and maybe ducking out of the way of a mortar bomb or stray aeroplane bullet, between typing the 'K' and the 'J'. As we heard from the RSM last night, the lottery of danger is only slightly weighted in favour of the troop corporal's tank as compared with the quartermaster's truck. And when death strikes it is as final for the clerk as for the gunner.

10 AUGUST 1944:

Sergeant Len Wright, wounded at La Taille, breezed back into the squadron today. Together with other reinforcements, tanks and humans. Somebody has discovered a huge Nazi banner. We display it on the back of a tank. Somebody else produces a clandestine camera. We all give the Nazi salute, the camera clicks and we laugh with the pent-up fury of psychiatric casualties from St-Aignan. Some German gunner, telepathically aware of our idiocies and resenting the slur on the swastika, sends over a few random shells, precisely aimed at our gully. We disperse and grovel before the gods of cordite and TNT.

As the noise of the Polish advance distances and merges into evening quietude there is a promenade concert on BBC radio to which we can tune, now that we are off watch. About ten of us, who like classical music, squeeze into our turret to share the headphones as there is no loudspeaker. Operator Tommy is bribed with a spare tin of corned beef to go and sit elsewhere. Now and again the orchestra's percussion is reinforced by unmusical drumming from German guns. One comedian chooses to add his own windy notes, from a nether region of the anatomy, although the composer scored only horns – 'a bit flat' comments a critic. But we have been near enough to profound tragedy to appreciate Tchaikovsky's sentiments. As the sublime descending tones of that most moving finale of his Sixth Symphony drift away into the ether, we squeeze back out of the turret, giving an imitation of one of those comic films where an inordinate number of people emerge from a tiny automobile. The SSM, Sid, happens to be passing. He goggles at us, yelps 'What's this then? Keystone Cops on parade? A bloody secret caucus of the revolutionary IRA?'

13 AUGUST 1944:

Some of our people have been touring the battlefield and peering into knocked-out tanks. I risked a glimpse into one German Mark IV, thinking to examine its mechanical equipment. But death had posted a grisly guard inside in the form of a decapitated and already mouldering driver. The Lord of the Flies, entire nations of them, held sway there. I lost my enthusiasm for German mechanical ingenuity.

They say the offensive ran into problems. The incredible 'great leap' achievements of the first day of Operation Totalize, the epic night march and the devastating St-Aignan battle, were followed by less gainful daylight attacks on either flank. For us, not so much a defeat as a delay. For the enemy, not so much a stay of execution as a further dripping away of scarce warrior blood.

I am telling myself that I should write home and say that I am safe. But there is an empty void between my battle self and my filial duties. I get my notepad and pen but my wrist is petrified. My fingers clasp the pen but my brain is dead. Ken Lyke, who was at school with me, comes past in his petrol lorry. He says he will write to his parents and tell them to tell mine that I am well but 'out of reach of a post box' for a day or two.

16 AUGUST 1944:

SSM Turton is the Olympian messenger who ends my service with 3 Baker, with Ken Snowdon, Stan, Rex and Tommy. 'Right, get your gear, lad. You're moving,' chirps the irrepressible Sidney. 'I'll whistle up a pantechnicon while you get your grand piano and euphonium out of the old homestead. Sar'nt Ginns has caught the in-flew-bleeding-ensa. So Corporal McKenzie steps up to be shot at and you, being the only trained Firefly gunner left standing, must go and give Jerry hell with that bloody big gun.'

I report to McKenzie. He is the comedian who, with the late lamented Jimmy Stanley, dressed up as an SS panzer grenadier at Demouville. 'Hello, Mac,' I shout up as he stands on the turret, 'which country's uniform are you wearing today?' He grins, 'Any one you like, kid, as long as you fire this 'orrible gun on target. Get in and try it out. We advance in an hour's time.'

The Firefly tank is an ordinary Sherman but, in order to accommodate the immense breech of the seventeen-pounder, the co-driver has been eliminated and his little den turned into storage space for the huge one-piece shells. The electrical traversing gear makes it easy to swing the 8-foot-long gun with a twist of the wrist but heaven help me if ever I have to traverse by hand! The flash is so brilliant that both gunner and commander need to blink at the moment of firing. Otherwise they are blinded for so long that they will not see the shot hit the target. The flash spurts out so much flame that, after a shot or two, the hedge or undergrowth in front of the tank is likely to start burning. When moving, the gun's overlap in front is so long that driver, gunner and commander have to be constantly alert to avoid wrapping the barrel around some apparently distant tree, defenceless lamp-post or inoffensive house.

St-Pierre-sur-Dives is our first objective. Before leaving 3 Baker I heard lustful Tommy chortle, 'Dives! Real French Dives at last. And "Peer-sur-Dives", does that mean the dives have little peep-holes where you can watch the action?' We pass round the town and the road rises steeply through orchards and woods. We advance so slowly that the Black Watch infantry alongside us have to halt and wait, before plodding on again at something much less hearty than a Highland fling.

The first intimation of trouble is the sight of Sergeant Wilkins' crew from 3 Able walking back down the road. All of them grin and wave but with that pallid, zombie attitude which tells that their tank is somewhere up ahead, 'brewed up'. Sure enough, Bill Fox's rasping voice breaks through the atmospherics in our earphones. 'Howe 2. Break off to the right and find a way around the bottom of the hill. Howe 3 Charlie, follow and support 2. Over.' (That's us now, Howe 3 Charlie.)

On the right of our road the hillside falls away through an open field and an orchard, beyond which are more trees thickening into a wood. We crash through a fence and down through the field. Left a thick hedge, tall trees above the hedge, a great gap in the hedge. A mighty armoured steel machine in the gap. Huge gun pointing away from us but beginning to traverse. A Tiger? No, a Panther. As bad!

Mac sees it, yells, 'You can't traverse. Trees in way. Just fire! Anywhere. Scare the bugger away. Fire! Driver, advance.' I fire the seventeen-pounder and the world goes dark with its flame, raging, blinding, terrifying flame. Wait for sight to return. The Panther has disappeared. 'Put another round into the hole in the hedge where the bugger was,' says Mac, as Howard Reid drives us free of restricting trees.

I fire again. Close eyes. Open. Tracer speeding through gap and into oblivion. One round of seventeen-pounder flying on and on. Up the road to Paris. Five, 6 miles farther. Must land somewhere. Some poor headquarters German will get a surprise if it lands on his foot. But no Panther.

I have been vaguely conscious of wireless voices reporting snipers in trees. Trees in my telescope. Ropes dangling. 'Snipers must be up those trees, using ropes to shin down,' observes Mac. 'Can't see 'em. Too high to elevate gun. Load HE and knock those trees down by the roots.' (Pause because Firefly has only limited HE ammo and loader Lou must wrestle a round from the hull.)

I aim at foot of one of the trees. Fire! Blink. Watch. An immediate furnace of red-hot steel seems to flare at the tree's base. The tree, killed instantly, takes a tired leap, like a shot deer, topples and crashes flat. 'And the next one!' – Mac. As I aim I see at the margin of my vision a field-grey figure swarming down his rope. The muzzle flame breeds another grossly distending furnace fire. The second tree splits apart. The smoke clouds clear. There is no tree. No rope. No field-grey figure.

We seem to have wandered into a seething hotbed of enemy activity. As darkness comes, the human beings hiding from us out there become bogeys invested with supernatural powers of speed and destruction. Sitting behind a gun whose sights are now useless I feel vulnerable, scared, haunted. And now begins an experience compared with which the night march of 7–8 August was child's play. We are lost in meandering orchards, bounded by intricate and vast hedgerows, lapped by troublesome brooks and invisible swamps. Now we are strung out in single file through the trees, our flanks unguarded and the fragile link of sight with the tank in front and behind us likely to be broken by the slightest interruption, such as a ditch or a stalled engine or a German mine or a sleepy tank commander.

So I sit at my periscope and watch an oblong patch of blank void. And my mind supplies the vacant dark with gliding armies of spectres and ghouls. All my childhood horrors come back to mix with the known hazards of the battle – and the clanking of tank tracks mingles with the clanking of chains of ghosts coming down the dark attic stairs of childhood, and First War Germans grunting under my bed at midnight and a German waxwork sprawled in a St-Aignan ditch.

The tank roars and trundles on, stopping and starting. And somewhere ahead Bill Fox walks in bow-legged imperturbility through the perilous orchards, guiding the way. Silence buzzes in my ear-drums. Engine stopped. Wireless off. 'Home!' cries Mac.

Later McKenzie, returning from a conference, finds me fast asleep, leaning up against the tank. 'Wakey, wakey,' he crows, once again the comedian. 'Breakfast up.' SSM Sid's voice breaks in, his face only a paler blotch of night like a faint moon behind clouds. 'Leave the poor lad alone, Mac. Get some proper kip, lad. Jerry's on the run. Piece of cake tomorrow.' Mac climbs on the tank, throws my bedding roll down ...

Blizzards of sleep drown me and snowdrifts of unconsciousness wrap me around.

17 AUGUST 1944:

After a very late breakfast we have moved up beyond the hill of last night's adventure. B squadron is advancing on St-Julien-le-Faucon, and we sit in reserve in a large field behind a farm. Mac says that Bill Fox says that Hank says that we have got ahead of the rest of the army and that these few fields are another arrowhead of advance. Over in those woods to the right and over in that other farm to the left there may be enemy troops. I try again to write home.

I sit staring at the green fields and orchards. The silent tanks and the recumbent troopers. The smoke puffs. *The smoke puffs*! Six puffs of smoke as innocent as though from a pipe-smoker's mouth. Men roll over into slit trenches or leap up and run to hide under armour-plated tanks. I vault up and into the shelter of the turret. As I drop I see another six puffs. The scream of the falling bombs this time penetrates my vacant ears. Six screams, six puffs, six playful bangs like blown-up bags bursting, six cyclones of sods, iron, flame, smoke. Then six and six and six. And one flashing under the very nose of the squadron captain's tank.

Screams now, not in neat stitches of six, not linked to smoke puffs and blasts. Detached, arhythmic, agonized screams. Human screams. We are not nearest. Others run before us. Duck, kneel and grovel by the squadron captain's tank. Bruce Dickson staggers up from where he was sheltering underneath – battered, bruised, horrified but alive. Men dragging a person from farther under the tank. Poor Len Wright. Back a few days from a head injury in our first battle. Now wounded again in almost the same part of the head. Bleeding, cussing but alive. Now they wrestle underneath and drag out a mashed, minced, murdered tangle of clothing with an SSM's crown on its sleeve.

Bill Fox running, pointing. 'You! – run for the ambulance. You two! – stretchers. And you two! – field dressings, and you and you. Lay him down there. Get back and give him air.' Hank appears through the hedge from RHQ, pulls a medical orderly away from a pile of clothing saying, 'He's damn well dead. Get a stretcher to Bolton here.' With the tenderness of worshipping nuns, the rough-clad troopers move George Bolton, signals corporal, onto a stretcher. 'Damn well get him better,' snaps Hank to the medical corporal. 'He's too good an operator to lose.'

The savers of lives rev their mechanical charges and race away down the one liberated road towards the hospitals and beaches and Blighty. And the troopers bring spades and a blanket and a wooden cross and an indelible pencil to render the only service now left for the fast-joking, darkly sardonic, immaculate squadron sergeant-major, Sid, who will call no more parades on this earth.

As I am back on the tank top Don Pateman, Bill Fox's co-driver, pulls my foot. 'Bill Fox wants to see you. Immediate. Come just as you are.' I have been sitting bare-chested, bare-footed in the hot sun, but Bill Fox requires no spit-and-polish response. I jump down and follow Don across the grass which again sleeps peacefully and unremembering of the storm, except for one oblong of turf which is up-mounded above the rest.

Bill Fox and Hank have been chatting beside the tank. Bill turns to me with weariness shading his face and growls, not unkindly, 'You commanded a Stuart coming over. Think you can command a Sherman?'

'I'd have a good try, sir.'

'Ah, yes. You know the sergeant-major was killed there? Damn bomb bounced. Wouldn't believe it. Can't happen. Damn bomb bounced right over young Dickson. Turton was third one in. Exploded right over him. Damn bomb. Damn good sergeant-major.'

'I saw it, sir.'

'Ah, well. Choose to fight bloody wars, people get hurt. Take over the spare tank, lad.'

'You mean ... the squadron captain's tank, sir?'

'Of course I mean the squadron captain's tank. Ah, I see! Only a lance-corporal and all that? No officers left, lad. Squadron captain's only a messenger boy half the time. You command that tank. You go my messages. Get your kit. They know you on that tank. Straight away, lad!'

I collect my kit. Mac goes to find another gunner. In England I crewed with the men on the squadron captain's tank. The gunner (Eric Marchant) was burned and evacuated from St-Aignan. Otherwise they are the same people on a replacement tank. Now Lance-Corporal Harold Hoult, the driver, who is much older and senior, greets me with a cheerful groan. 'What have we here? This is a tank, boy, not a pram. We'll have to strap you into the turret so you don't fall out. Welcome home to the old troop.'

'Old troop!' I growl in faint imitation of Bill Fox's voice. 'Bill Fox said that everyone on this tank is so old that they need a commander who's not blind, deaf and bed-wetting, to care for all the old fogies.'

The co-driver, Robin Hood, also an older lance-corporal, intervenes, 'They shouldn't appoint a person as commander until he's had his first shave. Come on. Let's settle you into your new luxury cruise ship and I'll make a cup of tea. Drink to Sidney's memory, poor bugger.'

18 AUGUST 1944:

St-Aignan was a dead, evacuated village. But in this area the French people are still living in their houses, taking refuge in cellars or ditches when the battle approaches. Today the extended family from the farm and nearby cottages forms into a simple procession and, arms loaded with summer flowers, comes to decorate the first grave of SSM Sidney Turton.

The SSM's grave is still under close mortar fire. German big guns shell us. Infantry Moaning Minnies bombard us. Anxious to get in on the act, both British and American fighter-bombers strafe us, in spite of the white stars on our tanks which proclaim our Allied loyalties and the yellow smoke bombs which send up messages of Allied desperation.

A group of us sit in the corner of the field, keeping close to the hedge as though that fragile barricade of leaves could protect us from various kinds of fiery extinction. We study each other's faces, and the messages of distress and weariness and apprehension on each face add to our individual distresses. The conversation advances in fits and starts, like a night march by tanks, and meanders endlessly, like a river full of ox-bow lakes.

'Ferking fool's game, war. Not so bad shooting Jerries. It's when the buggers shoot back …'

'Fool's game sitting 'ere, mate. Waiting to get your goolies shot off.'

'Why don't we just get up and go, instead of sitting here like swallows in the sunset?'

'Swallows don't sit in the sunset. They fly.'

'Course they bleeding sit sometimes. Can't fly all the time.'

'Swallows can't land on the ground. They have to keep flying. Like sea-gulls.'

'Don't be a dumb twit. I've seen seagulls sitting on the flooding sea. And anyway where'd swallows lay their eggs if they can't sit?'

'Still say we should all get up and go home. They could only shoot us. And we'll get flaming shot, sitting here.'

'I'd rather be a bleeding idiot taking the chance of being shot for deserting than a bleeding hero being shot for certain by Jerry over that hedge.'

'You're safe if you go bonkers. If you go pissie-cologically sick. They can't shoot you then.'

'Well, why don't we all go bonkers. All start braying like pissing jack-asses? All start tickling our armpits and legpits, like gorillas? All sit 'ere and stare and drool with our mouths open and refuse to eat.'

'That's mutiny. That IS a shootable offence. If you ALL go pissie-colog-ically sick, it's mutiny. You can only go one by one. Every man to pissie-college by himself.'

The imbecilic conversation meanders on, but so near the borders of stark truth that I wonder if the slightest push, or just one more bomb, will send us all hurtling down the mental precipice on whose lip we teeter.

20 AUGUST 1944:

We pass through the picture-postcard town of St-Julien-le-Faucon. Black-and-white houses like the Welsh Marches of my childhood. The villagers are out on the pavements, cheering us by. Many of them carry pails of wine, buckets of apples. A boy runs out of the grocer's shop of Monsieur Gazareth, his arms laden with Camembert cheese. He throws a cheese to each tank as it goes by. By the church the column halts. Laughing Frenchmen hoist a girl up to a turret and she kisses the blushing commander.

The column rolls. I miss a kiss. I stand tall because it is an imposing thing to be located here in the turret of a moving Sherman, watched by admiring crowds. Perched tight in the turret, head and shoulders out in the air, it is as though the body has grown a monstrous, bulging, armour-plated belly, like a grossly exaggerated Buddha, but omnipotently warlike where Buddha is pacific. The great, challenging gun protrudes with connotations of virile masculinity and earth-destroying wrath. The legs, the grinding tracks, crunch the very ground into submission. The two machine-guns, at a word from me, spray scarlet flames of death across the fields. Through the wireless microphone my voice penetrates into unseen distances, and through the earphones I eavesdrop on mystic mutterings and weird whisperings out of eternity. And in this landship, this mobile community, this death machine, my writ runs, my word rules, my command utters fire and steel and smoke.

Yet fearful: because the internal husk, myself, is a frail human being, able, in a fraction of a second, to transmute into a screaming maniac or a heap of blood-stained khaki tatters with a stripe on its sleeve. Or an evil-smelling cinder.

21 AUGUST 1944:

We cross our start-line in the pre-dawn dark, heading up the main road from St-Julien to Lisieux. There is no mayoral farewell committee to see us on our way at this hour. There may be a reception committee. The Germans know it is the day and the hour for us to advance. Around some leafy corner an iron monster of destruction waits. A dinosaur, its wicked telescope eye gleaming in anticipation of its prey, its fiery breath ready to spit, its whole body coiled for the strike. The Germans know the date and the hour and the place. We only know the date.

We turn left into a lane. No. 3 Troop methodically leapfrogs ahead. We wait in the lane as Black Watch infantry prostrate themselves and peer through the roots of the hedges, some of the highest hedges I have seen, even in Normandy. The Black Watch colonel walks up to Bill Fox's tank behind me and Bill gets down to meet him.

Leaves fall around my ears as though in an accelerated autumn. Lounging infantrymen dive into ditches. The Black Watch colonel and Bill

Fox hurry around the other side of that tank. Our engine is still running, its booming reverberations filling my ears. So the momentary panic has no meaning for me.

'Ah ... hullo Queen Baker.' (Bill's voice and our code-sign.) 'Do your best to see off that pesky Hun machine-gun. Ah ... Baker, over.'

In this nether Norman jungle the fields on either side are alien country. I am not sure which way the bullets are flying, north or south. Bill Fox gets into his tank and retreats as does the colonel in his jeep. The Black Watch infantry seem to have a majority inclination towards a danger from our left. I climb on to the tank top. Fully extended on tiptoe, my eyes probably some 14 feet above ground level, I can just peer over the top of this Beecher's Brook *in excelsis*. An innocent black-and-white farm in an orchard. Or is it the last citadel of a weary SS detachment, determined to halt here and bear the ignominy of retreat no longer?

I tell the gunner to traverse and fire our Browning through the hedge. I am aware of somebody tapping my arm. Harold, the driver, has climbed out of his little hatch. 'What the hell are you doing standing up here?' he shouts over the rattle of the Browning gun. I grin, 'I'm looking over the hedge. What do you think I'm doing? Watching a football match?'

'You'll get yourself bloody killed, you idiot. You can be seen for miles around.'

'Wrong! Hedges too high. Get back in your cab, reverse and we'll try a shot through that gateway.'

I see the flash from our muzzle as the tank itself hurtles back on its haunches, keeling over on the springs and then reasserting itself. A ball of tracer emerges from the muzzle flame, darts across the orchard and crashes, an unwelcome visitor, right through the front door of the farm. It explodes somewhere inside, belching flame, smoke and dust back out through the doorway. Two more shells follow and boil over into cascades of torrid flame. No reply from house or orchard. Black Watch men in the ditch cautiously lift their heads, shoulders, bodies. One of them, a sergeant, gives me a V sign.

Bill Fox's tank reappears, halts at my tail. He beckons me over. 'Good show. Now I want you to take that left turn. Explore for about four to five hundred yards. If it is clear, pull back and the infantry will dig in. If anything stirs get to hell out and we'll call down an artillery stonk. Take care but don't hang about.'

At the corner we leave behind our escort of Black Watch. Harold steers the tank carefully into the narrow bend. Now is not the time to slide into a deep Normandy ditch. The new stretch of lane opens slowly before us. Dark and dappled with heavy shadows, the hedges encroaching from both sides. The far hedgerow, 50 yards ahead, where the road bends again, is almost indistinguishable. A lovely place to site an anti-tank gun.

There is a moment in which I can still reverse. Retreat and leave the infantry to explore the darkened jungle track. Tell Bill Fox it is too risky for a single tank. Fifty yards – total destruction distance for an anti-tank gun, if the dinosaur is such. Fifty yards – irresistible target for the hand-held bazooka, if the dinosaur is such. Trees overhanging, for the panzer grenadier bandits to swing down onto our turret and lob their bombs. I can feel the bullets tearing, the shards of armour-piercing shot smashing bone, the bombs burning and gouging my flesh, the Vesuvius of white fire opened behind me as the engine erupts. The sweat of fear obscures my eyes as I try to decipher the shapes in that dim, sneering lane. What dinosaur ...? I am primitive man again, my uniform, weapons, armour-plated fortress stripped away and my body exposed to the roaring beast. To go or to come? This is the worst place. I am killing myself by degrees.

'Driver, inch forward. Slowly ... now, go! Go! GO!' We charge along the brief lane and Harold tickles his way round the next corner. A longer stretch of road. 'Operator, reload with HE. Gunner, put two rounds of HE into the neck of that far bend. Just in case. In your own time. Driver, halt.'

Surprises still in store! The first shot blasts a large hole in the distant hedge. Three Germans leap from the ditch beneath the explosion and sprint like Jesse Owens for Berlin. Our second shell follows them and sets up a vision of Sodom and Gomorrah and the wrath of God in the centre of the bend.

'Gordon Bennett!' ejaculates Harold, 'We hit something there.'

We sit in our mobile castle and make the entire surroundings uninhabitable for foes. A Black Watch lieutenant climbs up the back of the tank. Shouts in my ear. 'Some explosion! That should scare away any poachers.' They dig in.

Back on the main lane of advance in the wake of 3 Troop, I glance at my watch and am astonished to see that it is afternoon. Then the afternoon is ripped apart by a vicious high-powered double crash which says 88mm. Anti-tank. High-velocity. Tiger?

'Hullo, Queen 3.' (Bobby McColl.) 'Queen 3 Able brewed. Anti-tank gun was firing down side lane. Nasty appears to have retreated. No further firing. Queen 3 over.'

Walking along the lane towards me are four, yes only four men in black berets. One missing. I scan the faces as they pass me. Waving despondently, their eyes still full of instant terror unwinding its ghoulish film across dilated pupils. Spearhead crew again. Brewed again. Wilkie's there. And Michael Pryde, his driver. Co-driver is missing.

'Hullo, ah, Queen Baker. 3 Able's co-driver not accounted for. Be a good lad. Go check co-driver's alive or dead. Baker, over.' So that is what messenger boys do? Ahead, 3 Troop's Firefly has swung into a lane leading diagonally back in the direction from which we have come. There is room for us to squeeze past his rump. Another 75mm Sherman stands a few yards beyond the corner, on our lane, in our way, its gun cocked at an unnatural angle. The Sherman points to the right, facing down a long, narrow, dark bridlepath between high hedges.

On my right the bridlepath looks and smells sinister. Wisps of smoke hover above the ruined tank. Explosion stench soils the air. Just minutes ago an 88mm shot, or maybe two or three, howled and hurtled along this narrow leafy channel, homing in on the target of the exposed Sherman called 3 Able. 'Driver, we will not halt just here. Squeeze past the brewed Sherman and then halt. Gunner, keep your 75 pointed up that path. Loader, check loaded with AP.'

But we are sliding. Harold bangs on the revs, brakes the right-hand track. But we are sliding and tipping, the left front dipping, the right flank jolting upwards, the tracks scrabbling at the bank, the ditch collapsing, taking us down, skewed, tilted.

'Hold it. Get out and look before you try again. Robin drive as Harold signals.' Randy Ginns, in the Firefly behind, makes signs that he will reverse and tow us out, while I approach the still smoking 3 Able from the driver's side. If a German tank or SP appears now along that fatal bridlepath we will be helpless. Hurry!

The wrecked driver's hatch is open. So is the co-driver's eye as I look in from his left. Open eye. Staring. He might be alive. Petrified with fear or paralysed with pain. I move over and lift the co-driver's own hatch. And age many years. Become world-weary. Too tired to be terrorized any more. There is no face at all this side. Familiar corned beef mash splashed on the inside wall. I touch the shoulder of my so young mate and the already cold body falls forward.

I jump off the tank. Wipe my hands on my denim trousers. Stamp across the road, crunching underfoot the silver trumpets and silken banners of my boyhood dreams.

Tomorrow our recovery vehicle will tow away the burned-out tank. A burial detail will dispose of the body of the co-driver. And the cows will once again exercise gentle rights of occupation of the lush fields and the quiet orchards. What was it all about? My first day of command in battle. A co-driver's last day of living.

Back in evening laager, Ken Squires, who has taken over from wounded George Bolton as wireless corporal, comes with the call-signs for tomorrow.

'Tomorrow we are Baker,' he says. 'That makes you Baker Baker. Sounds like a baker with a stutter. Or the beginning of a nursery rhyme. Daft, ain't it?'

'Yeah,' says Robin, 'but how much dafter can you get than fighting a war anyway?'

24 AUGUST 1944:

We drive through Lisieux, the streets thronged with jubilant people. We see how difficult it must have been for B Squadron to ascend the narrow streets by the cathedral, especially when they had been ordered not to shoot at the splendid basilica dedicated to local Saint Therese. Beyond the big city we camp. Somebody mentions echelon talk about Jerry high-tailing it to Berlin.

'Ah, bloody gossip,' growls an aristocratic voice behind us – old Bill Fox himself. 'Don't you, ah – damn well believe it. Better face facts. Some bloody fighting to come yet.'

'Jerry doesn't give up that easily,' adds Dick Bates, portly, elderly, once a gentleman's servant and now troop sergeant.

25 AUGUST 1944:

Lined up on an anonymous French road. No evidence of warlike activity. But war there is for, in a ditch alongside us, lies a young German, his face waxing white and fragile as a magnolia blossom, the blood drained away by an invisible wound, and the sunburn diluted in the catharsis of death.

I get out to look at him. Harold emerges from his driver's hatch clutching a water-bottle. No last rites and only chlorinated water from an enemy instead of communion wine from a priest. 'Hitler Youth!' grunts Harold, uncorking his bottle of precious liquid.

The young Nazi snarls. His lips and nostrils are impeded by the weakness of ebbing life but impelled by the rictus of death. His weak right arm lifts upwards and in the hand is a revolver. Yellowing fingers squeeze about the butt and trigger, aiming at Harold. I grab the revolver from a baby's grip and hurl it towards enemy bomb-bursts in the field. Harold remains a moment. His eyes seek the blearing eyes of the boy but find no human empathy with the mind raped from birth by the Nazis.

'Damn that bloody Hitler!' gentle Harold shouts at me, as though the Nazi boy, young enough, were his own son.

Soon we are bypassing an enemy roadblock through a thickly planted orchard of heavily pregnant trees. The boughs of the trees, totally armoured in layer upon layer of thick green leaves, commence about 6 feet above ground level. My vision is restricted to millions of chubby red and green apples like pixies hanging in the branches. Mischievous, hindering, dangerous pixies playing amid the leaves as our bruising turrets set the trees dancing. The steel turret flaps beside my cheeks bend back the insolent apple branches like heralds clearing the lesser mob from the path of a powerful ruler. Apple branches crack and fall, or bend and sweep back lowly behind the turret like courtiers doffing plumed hats and cloaks as the royal chariot passes.

Yes, until ... like a riot of peasants in revolt, the massed apples on a tough, resilient branch suddenly plunge up over the restraining flaps. They leap, slashing at my face, crashing home with the brain-stunning, explosive force of a hand-grenade! Blackness ... Echoes of distant chariots ... blood ...

The white, worried face of Johnny Martin our gunner, thinking me shot by a sniper, bending over me. 'Thought you'd got your bloody head blown off! Blood and gore all mixed with apples over our nice clean turret floor.'

Robin squints up into the turret. 'What a bloomin' indignity,' he complains, 'if we had to report on the wireless our Sunray killed in action by ten pounds of apples. Never live it down. And you'll be picking splinters out of your face in ten years' time.'

'Can't traverse the turret for flaming apples,' curses Johnny. 'We'll have to bail them out. Seriously!'

Harold joins the commiseration, 'Can always tell your kids it was shrapnel not apple pips. More heroic, like. Hey, Johnny. If you could get the old turret traversing and mash all that lot up we'd have a few pints of scrumpy slopping around there by evening.'

The jollity does not last long. We enter a village where someone brings a kitchen chair out onto a green apron of land in front of a farm. Two men come from the barn dragging a thickset farm girl with pale face and red eyes. Sit her roughly on the chair. The sparse population of the minuscule village gathers. One of the men grabs the girl's hair and the other wields a pair of sheep-shears, chopping through the long locks and ripping strands from the scalp. The tiny crowd jeers and shouts 'Collaboratrice! Traitresse! Prostituée Nazie!'

'That's ruddy cruel,' says Harold from below. 'Can't we stop them, skipper?'

'Not as long as they are not interfering with us or blocking the road. It's their France.'

'Serves the filthy bitch right if she's been sleeping around with Jerries,' observes Johnny. 'Can't blame the locals taking it out of her hide. Me, I'd be shoving a red-hot poker right up where she wouldn't misbehave any more.'

Beyond the village a farmer leans on a five-barred gate. I go over and question him. He says the Germans are clearing out fast. Asks if I am British or Canadian. Where do I come from? I say, 'A small city you might never have heard of: Hereford.'

His surprising rejoinder. 'Do you know Bulmers' cider works?'

'I was born and brought up within the smell of Bulmers.'

He laughs, 'Before the war I exported all my cider apples to Bulmers.' He was wounded in 1940 and repatriated. He invites us to stay for supper and champagne, a special bottle which he has been saving to greet the Liberators. But only Bill Fox knows where we shall be by supper time. 'Driver, advance.'

26 AUGUST 1944:

No champagne. We bedded down in another anonymous orchard. This morning the medical corporal looks at my apple scratches, and 'oo's' and 'aa's' and says cheerfully, 'Doesn't quite qualify as a Blighty wound,' dabbing on raw iodine.

Our objective is St-Leger, and on this road the orchards are thinning out into cattle and horse country. I sit on the turret top in bright sunshine and Harold rolls the tank gently in Bill Fox's wake.

'Hullo, Xray 4 Baker. Hullo, Xray 4 Baker. Sunray injured. We are halted awaiting medic. Xray 4 Baker, over.'

'That's Corporal Brown bought it,' comments Robin. 'He was up in the lead. Haven't heard any great sounds of battle though.'

'Aha ... Hallo, Xray Baker ...' (Bill to me.) 'Ah, Baker, get up there in the jeep and take over 4 Baker, that's a good lad. Off.' Not exactly purist wireless procedure, but endearing in its way.

Robin comes up to command as I climb into the squadron leader's jeep and we go buzzing along a fine, white road, through country like Newmarket Heath. Holiday country. Holiday weather. Holiday speed. Xray 4 Baker stands all on its own behind a low tree which offers no cover at all. But although the tank rests at the extreme point of advance, there seems to be no enemy reaction. In fact, the driver, Cliff Cuthbertson, is standing outside the tank, looking disconsolate but unafraid.

'The lad chopped's fingers off, then, didn'a,' explains Geordie Cliff. 'The blinking flap fell on 's fingers and chopped 'em right off, see. The lad's awa' wi' th' ambulance already.'

'Aren't there any Jerries over there in those woods, Cliff?'

'Aye, there's Jerries over there but they're taking no notice of us, like.'

Suddenly we are surrounded by French people emerging from holes and folds in the ground. Instead of the usual Calvados or cheeses or apples their arms are full of flowers. It is as though all the florists were arriving for an expensive funeral. They strew flowers across the front plates of the tank, and stick flowers under the ugly steel projections of the hull, and lob bunches of flowers onto the turret. One comedian even sticks a bunch of roses, stalks first, up the muzzle of the 75. I pick up a handful of roses and lay them over the roseate mess where a steel trap clashed down on a human hand only minutes ago.

Now the French people dance a kind of maypole jig around our floral, multicoloured Sherman. ('The buggers'll see us a mile off,' says Cliff scratching his head.) Inevitably a batch of Moaning Minnies splashes dirt across the field not far away. The continued explosions cause the civilians to retreat, liberated not cowed, waving as they go. We are the spearhead on target with nothing to do but watch. So, rather ungraciously we consign the outrageous floral decorations to the ditch and sit in our usual drab livery.

Evening, back with Harold and co., Johnny Howell comes running past us, brandishing a spade. 'This old French goat buried his wine store before the Jerries invaded. Wants us to dig it up for him. Free booze for all.' Kempy, Bruce, Harold and others follow. I don't drink so I do the washing up.

Johnny Howell's 'old French goat' is indeed an elderly man with a luxuriant grey goatee beard. He fusses like a hissing goose, fearing that we who handle fulminating explosives may damage his precious bottles, dark with ageing Burgundy and dim with dust and soil. He brings a bottle to the door and mutters something.

'What the hell!' Kempy's voice. 'One bottle between all of us? Bloody hell, that's not a ferking sip each. Come on, lads. Help yourselves.' The hissing goose is helpless as a mass of baying troopers push past and begin extracting bottles, but very responsibly taking only one each, plus some for absent comrades, of course. The wine-owner rages around the orchard in the gloom sending up high-pitched cackles of '*Scandaleux … brigandage … abominable … penitentiaire …*'

He accosts Bill Fox whose voice rumbles on in specious prevarications. 'Damn dark, you know. Difficult to play detective this time of night. Have a full investigation tomorrow. Come back tomorrow, afternoon, old chap. Full investigation. Run along home, *mon ami*, and get some kip.'

The owner retreats, still muttering seditious, uncordial sentiments. Dick Bates whispers to Bill, 'Will you also be investigating that bottle that's hiding under your camp stool, sir?'

28 AUGUST 1944:

Our pre-dawn start eliminated the possibility of Bill Fox's investigation into the wine riot. Perfidious Albion once again!

Our lead tanks hurry on into the sizeable town of Bourg Achard, rounding a bend into the main square and coming face to face with … a Panther tank! Each commander in turn lets out a gasp of instant apprehension. Not since La Taille have we bumped into a Panther at 10 yards' range. This Panther is, in fact, 'dead', and we are told the story by jolly drinkers from the local underground.

The Panther had gone to ground in the square during the night, the crew apparently exhausted by the retreat but safe enough inside the locked 45-ton vehicle. The local blacksmith then crept up to the tank and deftly knocked out one of the track retaining pins, so that the entire track sprang loose. Resistance fighters, invisible in the darkness, sniped every time the Germans opened the turret. Their huge gun was useless. The crew eventually took the sensible decision of waving a white cloth and surrendering their vehicle inviolate.

We advance north of Bourg Achard. In a long, narrow wood the enemy has established a resistance line defending the River Seine. We sit on opposite sides of a vast field and blast off expensive ammunition which will make taxpayers at home poorer but munition workers richer. The Germans are probably firing off all their remaining ammunition on this side of the big river. The stationary battle rages on, more than anything else like a children's firework display on bonfire night.

An elderly, bowed civilian appears in the middle of the battlefield. At a typical ploughman's pace he plods out into the field, undeterred by the pyrotechnics. The blazing patterns of tracer in front of him fall away. The old man trudges on, looking towards neither ally nor enemy. He approaches a ramshackle, partly destroyed shack in the middle of the field. Reaches the ruin and goes in. Guns stay silent.

'Must want to pee bloody bad,' says gunner Johnny, 'if he goes all that way in all this lot just to relieve his bladder.'

'More likely got his girl friend there,' suggests Harold. 'Calls on her every day at this time. While his wife's washing up the dinner pots.'

'It wasn't a girl, Harold,' I observe from my higher point of vision. 'It was a cow.' And the old farmer leads from the hut a single cow at the end of a rope. Begins his slow walk back the way he came. I imagine I can hear a tidal wave of laughter rolling through our serried ranks; someone is laughing over an open mike; I'm laughing myself; maybe Jerrry across there is laughing too. And as the man with his beast turns into a lane, a machine-gun begins to stutter apologetically. Another and another. German Spandaus and Yeomanry Brownings and Highland Brens. Spitting fire and noise but lacking the true heroism of the old Norman farmer.

The enemy fire falters and dies away. Presently a furtive Sherman edges along the lane in the steps of the farmer and the cow. Now bold, we all charge over our hedgerow, like huntsmen chasing a fox, trundle across the intervening field, past the broken-down hut and into the opposite wood. Nothing moves in front of us. But one, two, three field-grey bodies, lying sprawled at the foremost edge of the trees, witness that, for some of the enemy, it was not just a show of fireworks this afternoon.

29 AUGUST 1944:

Bill Fox thinks this might be the last advance before the River Seine. With its bridges destroyed, the river presents an impassable barrier across our line of advance. A great expanse of forest, the Forêt de Brotonne, fills a vast U-bend in the river. And it is into this forest that we advance in one last mopping-up operation before we rest from the battles (we hope).

As we bounce and sway over an open space, a grassy mound like a bald pate rising out of the surrounding woods, Bill Fox's voice calls to me. 'Ah, hullo, Roger Baker. Lead tanks are taking prisoners. Stay put and round up prisoners as they come. Talk nicely to them, the buggers. Baker, over.'

Three Germans come walking hopefully down one of the rides. One man, a major, is a medical officer, the other two medical orderlies. The major has studied medicine in Edinburgh and we sit on the grass for a pow-wow. They are hungry. Starving. Ravenous. Three days since they have seen supplies and then little. Robin climbs into the tank and lobs out tins of corned beef, cheese, packets of biscuits. They devour the food but have no news in exchange of Tigers or Panthers lurking in these woods. Several other prisoners appear through the trees, hesitantly as they see our tank then more confidently as they see the major.

A single prisoner emerges from the woods to our right rear. Claims his biscuit and corned beef. 'Are there any more troops in those woods?' I ask. The doctor translates. Listens. Smiles wanly. 'He says two friends are still there. In a gun-pit. With a gun. Arguing. Whether to shoot you or to come in and be taken prisoner.'

My crew and I duck behind the tank. Stalemate. Nobody inside the tank. If we try to climb into the turret or one of the driving hatches the enemy gunner will have us in his sights. But he cannot do much harm to us whilst we hide behind two thick walls of armour plate.

Robin says, 'we don't have any weapons in the outside storage boxes. Not even hand-grenades. Too far anyway.'

'Might as well try chucking a corned beef tin at him,' grunts Johnny. 'Might bounce on his ruddy nut and knock him out.'

I slap Johnny on the back. 'Genius! Corned beef!' I turn to the major.

'Ask him to go back to his trench. Take them a biscuit each. Tell them if they surrender there is a whole tin of corned beef between the two of them. They haven't eaten for days, right?'

The soldier, a boy of eighteen, shrugs his shoulders, nods, stands up. He ploughs through the bracken. After 20 yards he drops out of sight. So near? We wait. 'Pity we haven't got any sauerkraut. That would bring the bugger running,' mutters Johnny, lying flat.

Still we wait. Movement in the woods. Our emissary rises out of the invisible trench in the bracken. Waves. Another man with him. Waves a white rag. Two men only. 'Keep down, lads,' says Harold. 'It may be a trick.' Another head appears surmounted by a long object. It wobbles and tips. Becomes a man holding a Spandau high above his head. Suddenly we are brave. Johnny vaults into the turret to fetch a Sten gun.

'*Kamerad*! Corned beef!' says the German with the gun. Welcome words. 'Three days not eat. Three days bloody Hitler army not eat. Now join Tommy army and eat.'

Is there a distant German commander watching the tableau? Into our tiny, green sanctuary of peace and goodwill scream the familiar insults of descending shells. Flashes leap up on all sides. Vicious ghosts of smoke, dirt, clods, fire dance around the glade. Devilish tom-toms thrash out their persistent beat. Germans and British, Jerry and Tommy, we dive cursing into a large ditch. One and then another shell clangs horribly on the steel deck of the tank. Disintegrating steel venting its rage on unmoveable alien armour. A clangour as of a thousand charging knights-at-arms in one combined collision.

Silence! Listen! The Spandau gunner is beckoning frantically from his part of the ditch. The German doctor lies there, face as field-grey as his uniform. Eyes half-closed. Breathing rapidly and stertorously. Body rigid. I look for blood. None evident. The Spandau gunner clasps his heart, says 'Ughhh! *Herz*!' and pretends to collapse.

'Heart attack!' snaps Robin, dropping on his knees and wrenching at the major's collar, slapping his face, and banging his chest. 'Do you know what you are doing?' Harold asks anxiously. 'Where are his own ruddy order-lies?'

One of the orderlies is bandaging the leg of the other. The only blooded casualty it seems. The elderly major fights his way back to consciousness. I shout at him, 'You must tell us what to do to make you better.' Behind me Harold chuckles, 'We've been trying to kill the beggar for two months. Now we're trying to save his blinking life.'

Our laager is in just one more orchard. The air-filters at the back of the tank are shot through and through like sieves. I unroll my bedding. The blankets fall in tatters and patches between my fingers. Harold wraps a rag of blanket around his waist like a kilt. We gather up the remnants and make our way to where the quartermaster's truck has just arrived. Tall, peace-time farmer SQMS Pete Mapley looks at the damage with tears in his eyes.

'Was you so hungry, you lot? Got to chewing your blimmin' blankets? Real negligence I calls it. Negligence in the face of the enemy. No respect for WD property. What's wrong with this blanket, Corporal Hoult? Can't you wrap bits of it round your fingers, and bits of it round your toes and bits of it round your ...'

'Bollocks!' says Harold irreverently to the SQMS.

'Yes, them too,' says Pete, busily sorting through his piles of stores for replacements, chattering on, 'Now, don't go near no bombs with them new 'ns, look!'

30 AUGUST 1944:

We have now advanced from the outskirts of Caen to the Seine, covering 90 miles in fifteen days. We could have done this journey in our tanks in four hours if unimpeded. But our advance of about 6 miles a day has to be considered almost precipitate in comparison with the 500-yards-a-day average for the better days in the *bocage*. Compared with Great War advances it is hares compared with tortoises. It even betters the Germans' own progress through Belgium to Dunkirk during the 1940 *Blitzkrieg*.

There are many loose horses roaming the forest and some Yeomen have been huntsmen or stablemen to one or other of the officers. Bill Fox comes trotting through the squadron harbour on a frisky chestnut horse. 'Safer in a tank, sir!' yells Tommy Tucker. 'Damn sight more comfortable to ride,' Bill retorts as he gallops bareback through the trees.

'O Great God Montgomery!' cries one of our humorists, clasping his hands in mock prayer and turning his eyes to the skies, 'leave us here in Heaven for a few ferkin' days at least.'

2 SEPTEMBER 1944:

The Great God Montgomery did not heed our prayer. He or his minions scheduled us to cross the Seine today. The Royal Engineers have worked their usual miracles with Bailey sections and pontoons to provide a crossing.

We hurtle along open roads in our fastest advance to date. The roads are dusty and the holiday atmosphere is spoiled by the mash of dust, stones, smoke and fumes churned up by our long column of vehicles. Evening finds us in a narrow wood near Doudeville. In my progress from tank to tank I have failed to carry goggles. My eyelids feel as though they are packed with grit and dust and splinters. My worry is *closing* my eyes. I hobble off to find the quack corporal.

As usual he exudes total lack of sympathy. 'Looking for your third wound stripe?' he laughs as he delicately directs drops into my eyes. 'Wasp sting at St-Aignan. Apple scars from Lisieux. Now granulated eyeballs at Doudeville. What's next: haemorrhoids at Le Havre? Bus-driver's balls at Boulogne?'

5 SEPTEMBER 1944:

We move a few miles to the smaller village of Gonneville. Rumour has it that we are to attack Le Havre. Street fighting! The ultimate terror of the tank man. Here in the Channel ports the Germans are defying us to storm their coastal fortresses. By comparison Caen seems a picnic.

We are lodged in another of Normandy's million orchards. The farm labourer's family at the nearest cottage regale us with presents of fresh farm food. They cannot adequately express their joy at being liberated. We offer them chocolate and cigarettes and soap and tinned peaches.

7 SEPTEMBER 1944:

The old colonel is back. Doug Forster, wounded at St-Aignan, is to hold a conference of all commanders. We sit on a grassy slope as he delivers his glad-to-be-back speech.

Our 'second line' (2nd Northamptonshire Yeomanry) has been broken up after massive casualties, and a number of them have joined us, including Lord George Scott, who becomes 2 i/c of the regiment. David Bevan comes back to command our squadron with Bill Fox back to 2 i/c. Captain Todd moves back to squadron captain's tank. *My* tank! There is no mention of the fate of one Lance-Corporal (acting, unpaid, temporary, unwanted, as they say) 147 Tout.

Bill Fox is sympathetic. 'You go back and sit with the echelon for a few days until we need you again. You've had some damned nasty moments. Forget about the war for a day or two, that's a good lad.' So I again collect my belongings and depart in the squadron leader's jeep. Back to a quiet barn piled with deep and cosy hay. Paradise for weary soldiers!

10 SEPTEMBER 1944:

The famous 51st Highland Division has decided that our efforts during the Normandy campaign merit the honour of our Englishmen wearing their divisional sign on one arm. So it's needle and thread and a favourite book from my pack.

11 SEPTEMBER 1944:

Someone shakes my shoulder as I lie on my imperial couch of downy hay. 'Get up, Ken. *Tout de suite*, Mr *Tout*. Hank wants you. Dress as you ride. It's that urgent,' says Lowe, the jeep driver, in the pre-dawn darkness.

'What's all the hurry?' fumbling in the hay for shoes and pistol holster.

'Don't know. Wireless message "Bring spare Sunray most urgent". Up where the regiment's been doing a night mass shoot imitating the ruddy artillery who haven't arrived yet.'

As we swerve and skid along the narrow lanes, I manage to insert myself roughly into clothes. In the dark we almost crash into our tanks halted by the roadside. Tail to tail, the huge Shermans bulk like castle battlements against the grey-black sky. Bill Fox's face emerges out of the gloom, his rasping voice calling, 'This way, lad. At the double!' Behind him are Hank, tall, slim and cool, and Bobby McColl, and Ken Snowdon. I am back in 3 Troop.

'Ah, right, take over troop sergeant's tank. Damned bad accident. Poor man smashed his arm falling behind the 75 recoil. Nasty thing to do. Ah, yes. Lead tank. Damned inconvenient. Take over Sarn't Wilkins's hot seat.' I see that the troop sergeant's tank is indeed at the head of the column – a condemned cell, a prime target, an unwanted seat of honour.

'Off in five minutes,' says Bobby. 'Here's the map. We are at this point, here—'

'No, this isn't sensible,' interrupts Hank. 'No time for briefing. Corporal Snowdon will have to lead. He knows the plan. You follow and conform.' I glance at Ken Snowdon, whose face reveals what I was thinking a moment ago, but he smiles grimly and says gallantly, 'That's quite correct. I know the route. I'll do it.'

Bobby says to me, 'You keep troop sergeant's call-sign, Sugar 3 Able.' I give a brief early dawn salute and turn to Snowie, 'Thanks, pal.' I swing up into the turret, switch to I/C. I do not know this crew, knocked out several times and now mainly reinforcements. 'Driver, advance behind 3 Baker.'

We come to a very sharp right bend in the country road. Corporal

Snowdon halts until our tank has nosed right up to his tail. Round the bend we are in an urban area, familiar desolation. Hickie in 3 Baker chooses a way through the rubble, a scrabbling climb over featureless rubbish, like an immense grey lobster crawling over a rocky sea-bed. A new stretch of road widens into a kind of small circus some 100 yards or so ahead. Sugar 3 Baker moves a few yards. Stops. Waits. Moves. Stops. Waits. We wait partly hidden at the bend behind him.

No anti-tank gun flash ... but puff! Puff! Puff! A familiar clutch of Moaning Minnies right at the crossroads. Then around 3 Baker. Then in front of us. I yank the hatches closed, remembering someone else's mashed fingers. Black Watch men snuggle into the bases of walls or cuddle up behind our tank. More Minnies at the crossroads.

'Hullo Sugar 3 Baker to Able. Cover me. I'm going across. 3 Baker to Able. Over.'

As Hickie revs up and launches the Sherman forward under full power, 3 Baker squats back on its haunches. The tank hurtles across the intersection and into a continuation of our street. Halts. A split-second afterwards a massive rose of flame blooms off the wall of a building at the corner, flames like a huge climbing plant, sprouting leaves of soot-black smoke and red brick dust.

My turn. 'Gunner, traverse left. Something shooting up the left-hand road. Be ready to shoot back AP. Driver, slowly forward until we get a view down that side road.' And we roll forward into the vacant crossroads. Wait for obliterating flame to erupt from our front plates or left-hand track. The side road, a wider street than ours, unwinds to reveal ... nothing ... and nothing ... and still nothing ... 'Loader, HE. Gunner, right a bit. That alley. Scare any nasties. On! Fire!'

Red fires, like visible lions' roars, rage back at us from the house at the focus of the far street corner as our gunner (whose name I do not yet know) stamps twice on his 75 firing button. The world has again become a dead place. Sugar 3 Baker ahead. A group of Black Watch behind us lying in gutters or crouching in doorways. Farther behind Bobby McColl's tank watching. The new bright sun darkens doorways and alleyways. Its blazing light mists the walls with veils of incandescent dust. Only the *pavé* of the road lies clear, open, bleached and desolate.

But my mind supplies visions of Tiger tanks moving just beyond the street corner, their omnipotent 88mm guns already loaded with the immense, lethal missiles which will destroy us. Resolute panzer grenadiers crouching behind windows and loading their bazookas. Invisible, tank-shattering mines dug into our road and neatly covered over. And I remember the men in tanks who travelled at the arrow-point of earlier advances: four Germans cooked to a cinder in the tank above Creully; the headless co-driver still watching along the bridlepath before Lisieux; the Sherman alongside us boiling up into a 50-foot column of fire at St-Aignan. As I analyse the sinister signals sent out by the ominously silent street, these spectres crawl up out of the cellar of the subconscious. Hammer at the mind's door. Demand relief from their mortal agonies. I sense rather than see Black Watch infantrymen shuffling up beside us. Running quickly across the intersection.

A door in a house to my right opens and a teen-aged girl looks out cautiously. Runs into the street, waves a box camera at me, motions me to smile. From my lofty perch I assume a smile which is only lip deep. The girl snaps for posterity her photo of the liberating hero! We roll forward and I peel off my thin smile, replacing it with the sour scowl more appropriate to those silent streets still ahead.

Occasionally an enemy machine-gun chatters abruptly and we swing our guns in that general direction, dousing the houses with high explosive and Browning tracer. Sometimes weary dying fingers seem to tap on the turret or scratch in the road ahead. Way behind us Randy Ginns announces that the crowds of celebrating civilians are so great that he is going to fire a burst of machine-gun fire over their heads to clear the way for the advance.

After an hour, or several hours, for time is motionless, Ken Snowdon waves me past him and I take the lead. The street rises steeply towards the naval barracks and I begin to believe that our fears about street battles were as insubstantial as this morning's thin sea mist. A gaggle of Black Watch walks serenely behind us. Ken Snowdon back there, leaning on his elbows out of the turret, not a care in the—

The whole spinning world jolts, halts, shudders. The hillside leaps at us. Gravity thrust upwards. Centrifugal force lashes outwards. The gates of Hell open and all the infernos of earth's primeval belly gush towards us. Choirs, millions of lost souls scream damnation over our heads. A force like an invisible aeroplane smashes into the turret. Leopard's claws dig and drag at the folds of my checks and the joins of my eyelids. A solid giant fist of air crashes into my face. The Sherman shrieks in agony of oppressed springs as it wrenches back against its sprockets and fights against its striving pistons.

I am inside a resounding black drum the size of the universe, and Thor's eternal hammer is beating upon the reverberant drum-head. The noise comes from inside my skull and tries to explode my eardrums outwards. My eyeballs and nostrils bulge with the expanding ferocity of solid darkness. The world shudders once more and then begins to spin again. The darkness in front of my eyes thins into shapes of houses and streets. The battering monsters of noise power away into the distance.

Bobby McColl recovers first. 'Hullo, Sugar 3. Naval gun firing point blank from fort. Very large calibre. 3, over.' To which the deliberate voice of Hank is reassuring as ever, 'Sugar 3, I believe I may possibly have heard it. Stand where you are ...'

Fourteen-inch guns against my 75mm, barely 3-inch, pea-shooter. Guns intended to sink 30,000-ton battleships at 20 miles range shooting at our 30-ton Sherman at 200 *yards* range. We tuck ourselves into a side street. That first shell soared over our heads. Maybe the naval gun high up will not be able to depress sufficiently to do us harm. Maybe!

The gun fires again but the huge shell churns through the injured air above our heads, creating for itself a howling wind-tunnel through which it whirls away towards some far, random point of fiery disintegration. Silence again. Idling tank engines.

Eventually the colonels and brigadiers decide to send the infantry crawling in under the vast but clumsy barrels of the naval guns at the top of the hill. But soon afterwards God himself decides to send an army of black, glowering clouds from the sea, with his own barrage of thunder and lightning, and the rain pelting the earth like machine-gun bullets to curtail the tankers' day. We withdraw to rendezvous on a local football field in laagers of four tanks nose to tail. Two sides of the football field are occupied by the Black Watch. The other two sides are still possessed by German defenders, fortunately quiescent. We sit in the middle. Undaunted by the spectator enemy ranged somewhere along the touchline, we light our Primus stoves, make tea, boil our usual mess of mixed tinned meat and vegetables. Jerry over there, undoubtedy hungrier than us, observes in silence.

We all take turns at guard duties. At 03.00 hours I am prowling around the outside of our tiny laager, savouring all the disquieting thrills of this ultimate frontier. The night is black under dense cloud. Now and again someone emits a snore, a grumble or a curse.

Then: '*Wilhelm, warum konnen Sie nicht schlaffen?*'

'*Wilhelm! Konnen Sie ...*'

'O, shut your pissing face,' (voice from under a tank) 'you great Teutonic squarehead! Go home to Heidi.'

'*Ach, so*! Very sorry, Tommy.'

In the silent night the words of Wilhelm's anonymous companion come with startling clarity. And the tired German voice obviously has no wish for middle-of-the-night conflict or controversy.

12 SEPTEMBER 1944:

Again we head up the hill. I find myself in a street of quiet, respectable houses. I might be a tradesman plying my peacetime van along a street like this. The two or three Black Watch privates standing beside the tank might be simply waiting to buy my wares.

Surprisingly we hear the ripping sound of a Spandau machine-gun, unmistakable in the velocity with which it pours out bullets. I climb down to enquire what is happening of a Black Watch sergeant, a very placid, self-controlled man, older than most of his company. 'What is it, sergeant? Can I help?'

'Not unless you knock those bloody houses over first. Bloody Huns! Up the back of these houses in an open space. In a trench. Waving a white flag. Our lads got up off their bellies and walked up openly to accept the surrender. Then the Spandau opened up. Mowed them down. My lads. Bloody SS! Must be. Ordinary Jerry soldiers don't do that.'

'Can I get the tank in somewhere?'

'No room. Don't worry. Our lads are going in. Bloody mad they are. Taking off their tin hats and putting on their bonnets with the old red hackle. Going for revenge. No survivors.' And the infantrymen run up the road, burst through front doors. The morning pleasance is disrupted by a gale of battle echoes from behind the houses, bomb blasts, Sten gun volleys, rifle shots, shouts, screams. Silence.

The sergeant emerges from a front door, waves us past him, nods his head savagely. Takes off his bonnet with the red hackle. Stuffs it in his pack. Puts on his tin hat again. Bloody mad they were.

At the hill-top there is a sudden view to the cape and a row of fortress buildings, the last defence of the German garrison. Over to my right is 2 Troop and I see the face of little Sergeant Warren, fierce moustache visibly bristling in the morning sun. His tank fires. The tracer of the shell seems to slide lazily in a slight arc from the gun to the main door of the buildings. As the tracer hits the door, fire and smoke shoot upwards. The door swings open. A large white sheet pokes through the doorway and waves vigorously.

'Gunner, try that double door straight in front of us,' I say. 'One round 75 HE. Fire!'

We fire, the door opens and a white shirt tied to a broom handle waves at us. Opposite Sergeant Warren's tank where the white flag waves, a tall, elegant German naval officer emerges. He marches resolutely out into the road, about 200 yards away from our lines. Behind him more officers, ranks of seamen, in full uniform. No weapons. All in step. Arms swinging.

Lines correctly formed and dressed. From our own gate several ambulances with white rags on their aerials drive out followed by more ranks of soldiers in more ragged formation than the sailors.

'There's hundreds and hundreds of the buggers,' crows Sergeant Warren, his voice coming unexpectedly over the external radio waves. (Presumably, in his astonishment, he had forgotten that his set was on 'A'.) Then he switches to formal talk, 'Hullo, Nan 2, I say again, hundreds of the buggers. Have put one shot into main barracks. Doors open. White flag up. Prisoners marching out to surrender. Hundreds of 'em. Bloody admiral leading. Please send more little friends. Too many for us to look after. Nan 2, over.'

As the great procession continues I join in with my reports: 'Hullo, Nan 3 Able. Barracks opposite us apparently surrendering. Considerable numbers of prisoners emerging. Troop Sunray forward interrogating prisoners. Nan 3 Able, over.'

'Nan 3 Able, bloody good show. Keep an alert watch in case of last-minute tricks.' And from our door still the soldiers emerge, each one holding a white rag. Hosts of them. Not marching. Simply trudging across the open space. The Black Watch in force trot up to us, lining the road astonished, rifles and Sten guns at the ready. Bobby McColl intercepts one enemy sailor sporting a considerable array of gold braid and badges and questions him rapidly. The battle degenerates into a farce. Wireless reports sound like a bingo game as tank after tank comes on the air to quote numbers now surrendering.

It feels as though we might have won the war?

13 SEPTEMBER 1944:

For reasons of the kind evident only to higher strategists, we pulled back to our football field – now abandoned by Wilhelm and his comrades – and waited in reserve for any eventuality. What eventuality might be expected when the garrison had completely surrendered was beyond our comprehension.

14 SEPTEMBER 1944:

Back to our little orchard in Gonneville-le-Malet. A number of tank commanders jostle for parking space near the big, central farm buildings, but I direct our driver to a far corner, a row of modest cottages, where lives the very friendly farm labourer, a repatriated prisoner of war from 1940. His wife, teen daughter and small son form a delightful family. We knock on their door and announce our return. They dash for the coffee cups and the Calvados bottle. We are only too happy just to sit on civilized chairs with a roof over our heads.

8 No Dutch Holiday

15 SEPTEMBER 1944:

All our wheeled transport has been called away. The advance through France has been so precipitate that the supply columns cannot keep up with the forward tanks. So a number of regiments like ours have been left sitting in the orchards whilst our lorries join the almost continuous conveyor-belt convoy from the Normandy beaches to the Belgian border.

Meanwhile our old friends the Black Watch startle and then amuse the inhabitants of Gonneville by marching into the village square with bagpipes groaning and shrilling and drums beating. 'Sounds like the end of the war,' says my co-driver Fred. The gunner, Eddie Bollens, answers. 'Now we've won the Normandy campaign, perhaps they'll let us go home.'

16 SEPTEMBER 1944:

'*Le Boche a pris tout*' is the watchword of our friendly farm labourer. 'The *Boche* has taken everything.' He took this man's elderly horse. He took all the horses from the farm. In his haste and anxiety to retreat, the German soldier was pressured into grabbing any and every primitive means to escape the oncoming Allied hordes. So we inherit the gratitude of these people whose orchards we are desecrating and whose towns we have razed to the ground. This Frenchman tells us haltingly that he was afraid for his girl, that she would come to a certain age before the Liberators arrived. Now he feels that she is safe.

'He doesn't realize,' say driver 'Mackle' Pryde, 'that his girl might be safer with disciplined German troops, anxious to get a good name with the Frogs, than with some of the drunken buggers on our side.'

18 SEPTEMBER 1944:

The farm labourer's little boy plays in our turret and fancies himself a soldier, wearing my beret. Today he picked up my belt, lying on the front of the tank, pulled the always loaded revolver out of the holster, pointed it at me and said something that must have been 'Stick 'em up!' He tried to pull the trigger. His aim was good but his finger was not strong enough. So I live on. And we hide our personal weapons.

22 SEPTEMBER 1944:

Today we assemble in the big hay barn for a concert given by the lads of the squadron, several of us concocting a version of the popular *ITMA* show. We sit on the straw and hay with Bill Fox and RSM George Jelley at the front. George jumps to hear his own voice bark from the rear (Harry Graham being the impersonator) 'What-do-you-think-you're-bloody-well-doing, then? Stand up! H'officer present!' – launching into an hour of bawdy jokes, sentimental songs and tunes on the clarinet by Lowe. Norman Plant and friends sing a negro spiritual.

The audience roars with laughter at jokes about our local personalities. 'Why does the colonel go to see the brigadier?' ask one. 'Because he's *Forster!*' says another. Showers of straw descend from the listeners upon the jokers and scriptwriters who perpetrated the pun. The idiotic behaviour releases the turbulent and persistent tensions of war.

26 SEPTEMBER 1944:

Some under-employed staff wallah has had the bright idea of removing us from our sheltered orchards at Gonneville, where we lolled in luxury like lotus eaters, and setting us down on the edge of dank, sodden ploughed fields somewhere near Criquetot.

28 SEPTEMBER 1944:

We battle-worn warriors had thought we were now immune to shocks. We had underestimated our new ex-infantry SSM, promoted on Sid Turton's death. He has ordered us out for first parade on the ploughed field with chins shaven, boots clean, brasses shining and carrying personal arms. 'My God,' grumbles Tommy, 'these days I only shave when a piece of shrapnel passes me close enough. What does the bugger think he is playing at?'

'Right! Less-ave-a-marker from each troop! Brighten yoursel's up! Itsaluvlymornin', can chew see?' cries the SSM, as perky as an early blackbird and the only grinning face in the whole wide, ploughed world.

'Go on, Ken, you're tallest,' says Tommy to me, exercising his democratic right as a British Yeoman and giving me a push so that I stagger from the top of a ploughed rut into the bottom of a ploughed furrow, while the SSM crows, 'C'mon, lad, at the double. It's nearly sunset. Juggle your balls a bit.'

In his wisdom he lines us up diagonally to the furrows so that forming a straight line across the undulating field become a physical impossibility. I hear some of the sergeants enter into the party spirit. 'Kemp, you're out of kilter ... Try balancing on that cow turd ... Graham, pull your belly in. It's out of line with your skull ... Somebody rescue Bollen from that hole he's fallen into ...' The SSM's smile begins to falter. But he is willing to leave us to it. There is nothing else to do anyway.

29 SEPTEMBER 1944:

Don Pateman whispers that when Hank came back from brigade conference yesterday he took the SSM to task. 'We don't want any of your damn infantry ideas here. These are tank crews. I don't care if their brasses are not polished as long as the breeches of their guns are clean and oiled, and their tank engines are running smoothly.'

Today for the first time since Aldershot we are served with real bread after months of 'dog biscuits'. We dance a jig and wave our slices of bread to a benevolent God in the skies and his servant on earth, the gentle Pete Mapley, SQMS. And Fred has been to a brothel. Well, not exactly ...

'You see, I heard that this Frenchwoman was, like, inviting people in. The old mother was at the door in a filthy black dress, collecting the subscriptions. There were all these blokes, see, on the stairs – infantry, artillery, ordnance, even bloody pioneers. Anyway I went up just to see what was happening. There was just this farm wife on her own, with a bloke if you know what I mean. But muck! The place stank like a midden in the middle of a sewage farm. I slung my hook pretty quick. Never know what you might pick up just walking up them stairs. But old Tommy's still there. Waiting patiently, like.'

Returning from the house of subscriptions Tommy is unwise enough to boast of his doings. So the lads decide that he needs an FFI. (Freedom From Infection, an inspection normally the province of the MO.) Tommy is mobbed and debagged. He leaps up like a startled stag on the Highland moors and gallops away across the field, stark naked. A howling, baying pack of two-legged staghounds chases him over plough and thistle and grassland. One by one the hounds sink exhausted whereas the indefatigable Tommy bolts for refuge into a discreet and distant patch of woodland.

Bill Fox has been watching the performance. He catches my eye. 'That'll damn well larn him,' he laughs.

Later, snuggled into rough blankets, head on my small pack, I chew on a scrap of white bread, raw, soft, untarnished by butter or cheese or honey or lesser staples. Gourmet stuff. But, as the stars go blind with approaching sleep, my subconscious mind prepares to stage another of its midnight improvements on Shakespeare's ghost scene from *Macbeth*.

4 OCTOBER 1944:

We are to move at last. Possibly to Begium. Possibly to the Netherlands. The distance which we must cover is vast for tanks with their limited track life. So we shall be lifted by huge tank-transporters. And we shall be coming once again within the sound of the guns.

7 OCTOBER 1944:

At dawn we set off, the transporters wriggling with great difficulty through the narrow lanes between Criquetot and Goderville. We sit perched on our tanks upon the slow, grinding transporters. By afternoon we reach the Somme battlefield where, during the 'first lot', my father and uncles and schoolmasters endured sufferings far beyond anything we shall ever know in this more mobile war. I spread my map and look right and left for the places: Mametz and Thiepval, Montalmaison and the tiny River Aisne, places made sacred by father's tales at the supper table. And by the serried regiments of white gravestones dimly visible to us today across this corn-gilded landscape.

At evening we come to one of the most evocative names of all: Mons. We are delighted when we are told to unload off the great Scammels and Diamond Ts and park tanks along the boulevards of Mons because, as long as we leave one crew member on guard, we can go off to the *estaminets* and the streets where the red lights glow (but not from the rear of tanks). A small crowd of Belgians stands watching the tanks. A little nine-year-old girl and her father approach me.

'My daughter wants to know if you sleep underneath the tanks?'

They both clamber over the tanks and poke about in the turret with avid interest. Then, 'Corporal, little Monique insists that you cannot sleep out here when we have a bed to spare.' Co-driver Fred is on guard, so I can go with Monique and her father, while other crew go to other homes. My Belgian friend was, until the Germans came, a commercial traveller for a British firm, Port Sunlight soap. So they squeal with delight when I hand to them a gaily wrapped cake of genuine, softly scented Erasmic soap, sent by my mother, after years of the loathsome local soap substitute.

My first night in a house since May! Paradise! After savouring a huge supper I advance on a vast flock bed. Climb in perilously. Roll about in ecstasy. After a minute or two begin searching for the familiar hard lumps of earth and stone. Toss and turn. Groan and argue with myself. Get out of bed. Doss down on the floor. Sleep the sleep of the Elysian Fields where, no doubt, the souls of departed soldiers lie down with lion and lamb, rather than tolerate the heavenly mattresses of cast-off angel-wing feathers.

8 OCTOBER 1944:

As daylight filters through the unfamiliar curtain shapes, I hear the rattle of a cup and a footstep on a stair tread. With the urgency of a tank man baling out of a burning Sherman, I gather my pillows and quilt, fling myself back into the great bed and pretend to sleep.

The door opens gently and a female voice says, '*Bonjour monsieur! Sept heures! Du café? Avez-vous bien dormi?*'

'*Oui, madame. J'ai dormi … toute la nuit dans le Paradis.*' (Liar!)

Eating breakfast I help little Monique with her Latin homework, ignored last evening. She gazes devotedly at my strange Liberator's uniform and I think it will be a very bold school teacher who will dare correct any of my Latin translations. Monique, clutching her satchel, has special permission to tarry and wave us on our way.

Our route takes us through wonderful Brussels whose citizens halt and turn and wave and cheer just another tank on the endless conveyor-belt advance. Then Malines – grey buildings in seeping rain, like Southampton so long ago, but sunshine smiles on war-worn faces. Gierle village where we are to sleep in the school tonight.

After a long day's drive, the objective of every man in the squadron is the school latrine. War conditions have wreaked havoc with waterworks. The single latrine is mounded high with paper. A trooper strikes a match in order to aim better. The match slips from numb fingers, falls, and flares up into an inferno like a brewing Sherman. 'Fire!' shouts somebody. 'Water!' yells somebody else. There is no water. There are no hoses. There is no fire brigade. 'There's only one way,' cries a third trooper. 'Make your own, lads.' A circle of long-travelling troopers assails the blaze with accurate if insignificant jets of innovative fire-fighting equipment. Numbers prevail.

'Saved ourselves a bloody court-martial there,' says Alf Rushton.

9 OCTOBER 1944:

Only a mile or two today, to the tiny hamlet of Poederlee where our first surprise is to see Flemish wives scrubbing their doorsteps at reveille time and then scrubbing the entire pavement and street outside their house frontage.

'God, my wife would drop dead at the thought,' says Fred.

12 OCTOBER 1944:

We go to Turnhout for our first bath since leaving Aldershot, in an old factory rigged up with lines of skin-scalding showers. Our towels and thick, rough underclothes are taken away for laundering and will be reissued to later bathers, whilst we are to be issued with rehabilitated towels, pants and vests bequeathed by earlier bathers.

Unfortunately the staff sergeant (baths) is away on NAAFI break and nobody has a key to the stores. Naked, we double up and down in the early winter frost as the great God Pneumonia stalks through our ranks. When the staff sergeant returns we curse and shout mutinous slogans. He calls us to attention in our nude. We respond by giving the Hitler salute and shouting '*Sieg Heil.*'

Troopers cannot win. The staff sergeant has endless problems opening the lock of the door. And my 'new' towel and underclothes appear to be First War relics dragged through the Ypres mud.

15 OCTOBER 1944:

Football match between the village and the squadron. With the score at eleven to nil in our favour, full back Pete Pedder says to the goalkeeper (me), 'You've got to let one in, Ken. Eleven-nil looks bad after taking their wine and their gin and their meat and their eggs. And these poor buggers weak from Jerry rationing.'

No need for me to act. The Flemish wing lashes in a drive of First Division ferocity. It almost amputates my hand. It crashes through the goal like an 88mm anti-tank solid shot. 'Good acting,' whispers Pete. 'Goal!' shout the villagers in the Esperanto of football. The Flemish players leap about as if they have won the FA Cup. Pride is restored. Honour justified. Alliances cemented.

17 OCTOBER 1944:

Suddenly we move. Evening finds us in a suburb of Eindhoven. We park in the main street in Meerveldhoven. A slim, undernourished youth invites us to his house. He is a radio technician employed by Phillips. He shows us a thick book. Opens it to reveal a cigarette tin nestling in a cut-out square.

Inside the tin is a mass of intertwining wires and terminals. Another tin contains miniature headphones. He connects up. Fiddles with coils. Clearly over the war-tormented ether comes the music of the BBC. This boy was the local Resistance radio operator, risking his life during the Gestapo house searches. He and his colleagues are the real heroes, unsupported by big guns and tank armour and marching battalions of infantry.

I wonder, 'How would I have reacted had *my* parents raised me under the Nazi occupation of Meerveldhoven?'

18 OCTOBER 1944:

Solemnly through the avenues of Eindhoven. We see our first Dutch canal. We laager in a farm beyond St-Oedenrode with the single road towards Arnhem riding away straight in front of us.

We are told that in those woods over on the left, there, and in those other woods, away on the horizon, there, the German infantry are still entrenched. Allied troops are spaced along this road and defending the fields on either side. We are in a military vice, a trap narrower than that near St-Julien-le-Faucon where SSM Turton was killed.

19-20 OCTOBER 1944:

All ranks share night patrols and static guards. Tonight I am paired with Sergeant Ted Prentice who sports fierce moustaches like a Uhlan of the Great War or an RAF squadron leader of this war. He seems immeasurably older and more mature than me though our birth certificates would show only a five-year age gap.

Last night, we are told, enemy infiltrators from those woods, there, crept across those fields, through our pickets, and cut the throats of several Scottish Highlanders lying asleep in their blankets. We are ordered to patrol in pairs. And back to back!

This is an inclement, hostile world of bewitched darkness. Upon a dense backcloth of moonless black skies, river mists move like Hell-tormented ghosts, seeking a resting place but never able to alight upon the moisture-brimming sod. We place ourselves back to back. Ted advances, Sten gun at the ready. I step backwards, close against him. My fingers frozen. The Celtic depths of my subconscious conjure up invisible blood-sucking vampires and hideous ghosts to inhabit this haunted wilderness.

We cross a tiny footbridge. As we plough into the mists beyond the steaming rivulet, the footbridge creaks with stealthy footsteps. Both Ted and I halt, arrested by our mutual terror. We listen to the dripping silence.

Our hearts almost stand still when a sinister, mausoleum-shaped Sherman dome appears out of the overhanging fog.

We retrace our circuit. Again, the footbridge. Again, the footsteps. Again the sodden inhuman silence.

It seems unlikely that a squadron of our mates lies sleeping around us. They could not be so silent. They are all dead. It cannot be that a battalion of Black Watch lies snoring along the road. They too are pale corpses with throats slit and eyes staring. But there *are* Things of the unholy night, whose horses we see galloping in the mists, whose wings beat suddenly out of the darkness, whose low moans sough on the chill wind, and whose cloven feet snuffle through the muddy grasses. And their footsteps!

I shrink back into Ted's rough khaki as we approach the footbridge again. Whisper, 'You go on. I'll duck behind that bush and find out who's following us.' We tread softly over the bridge. Under our feet the malevolent rivulet boils and hisses though its water is near freezing. I step to the left and crouch behind a thick bush as Ted shuffles off into a lost eternity. I wait.

The footbridge crackles. Eases. Moves. Footsteps tread over the bridge, and nothing is there. Nothing is visible. Nothing materializes. Only the white-sheeted ghouls of moisture wavering around the bridge.

Somewhere a trooper snores and breaks the spell. The old footbridge creaks and eases and adjusts itself, sighing throughout the length of its sodden, elastic timbers. Easing itself back into shape. I hurry after Ted. Hurry to the warmth of his human body and movement.

22 OCTOBER 1944:

Find a field and you find troopers playing football, surrounded by enemy or not. We play one troop against another. Dear old Ralph Hill, wit and amateur actor, careers down the wing, lashes the ball with one foot and puts the other foot in a rabbit hole. Scores the winning goal. Crashes to the ground in mortal agonies. A dislocated cartilage. The half-track with the Red Cross on the canopy tears across the field. They load Ralph into the ambulance and rattle him away down the enemy-infested road.

'I bet that was a Blighty one,' says Pete Pedder, torn between laughter, sympathy and envy.

Tomorrow we go into action again. Reveille an hour before dawn.

23 OCTOBER 1944:

The fateful roulette wheel of war fortune continues to spin in its own haphazard manner. Bill Fox appears by my tank to announce that Sergeant

Cliff Thompson has returned from hospital and will take over my tank in its true role as troop sergeant's tank. I am to 'ride shotgun', as Bill puts it, in the squadron leader's jeep.

I am loading my kit on to Hank's jeep when Captain Bill again taps me on the shoulder. 'Come along, my lad. We have two cases of flu. It's a wonder it isn't double-bloody-pneumonia in these God-blasted fields. Come and gun in 4 Troop. Only for today. Attacking one of these outlandish Dutch villages. Unpronounceable name. St Miggles Giggles or some such thing.'

An unfamiliar reinforcement corporal stares down at me from the turret. 'Panter's the name, kid,' he says. 'Who are you? Climb aboard quick. It's draughty with the front door open. All ashore that's going ashore!'

We have to make a 4- or 5-mile advance to Bill's unpronounceable village, Sint-Michielsgestel. Not far for an enthusiastic hiker. But almost a month has passed without our forces being able to move more than a mile off that fatal Arnhem road. And the enemy has barricaded the main road with fallen trees, so we move to the left and outflank his position. Soon the tall church tower of Sint-Michielsgestel comes into view. We follow Sergeant Warren and Corporal Dwight.

Out of the pleasant, peaceful day there bursts the familiar slamming sound of a German 88mm gun, a vicious noise we have not heard at close quarters since Normandy. As we look feverishly ahead for significant smoke or flash or movement or square shapes, a geyser of fire gushes from the front of Sergeant Warren's tank. Another double crash. Another flare rebounding from the sergeant's tank tracks. Men bale out of the turret. Len Moore leaps from the driver's compartment helping his mate who stumbles, runs, and then disintegrates into a shapeless bundle of clothes. A Black Watch medic comes running.

'Gunner, traverse right,' shouts Panter. 'On! Right of the church tower. Between those two houses. Now! Fire!'

I fire three or four shots in succession although I myself can see no shape or movement. Out of the corner of the periscope I see Arthur Dwight climb from his turret. The field slopes down so sharply to a narrow, hidden stream that the muzzle of his immensely protruding seventeen-pounder has struck into the muddy bank on the other side of the stream. Arthur walks forward to look at the gun. Huge, flaring, bulging flame springs out of the ground at his feet. As he reels, flung to the ground, a cloud of smoke wraps itself round the scene. Someone else jumps from the tank. Another Black Watch medic appears.

'Bloody SP!' Panter screams with rage. 'Put some more rounds into that same area. Fire! Can't see the bugger but he must still be there.'

I pump shot after shot at an invisible target. My flying tracers blossom into blinding flame amid the houses. Then Panter breaks in, 'They suspect observers in the church tower. Gunner, give us five rounds HE into the openings in that tower.' We halt, traverse and desecrate the church tower. No response. We roll on. The street bends into a tiny square at the foot of the desecrated tower. A miniature town hall opposite us.

To the left, along 100 yards of cobbled street, the tank of RSM impersonator, Harry Graham, roars triumphantly on to capture our target, the bridge over the Dommel river. As the tank reaches the bridge, the wooden timbers and cobblestones all disintegrate and are transmuted into a rising, writhing column of fire, smoke, dust, detritus and shattered rubble. A hundred feet high the erupting column rises. Hovers. Begins to descend. Then the flailing, paralysing physical noise lashes our tank.

Harry's normal Scouse voice breaks in (unaware that his tank radio is on 'A' set) 'That was a ferking Fritz ran out and set that one off by hand. Saw him. Their electrics must have failed.' Panter comments, within our own I/C system, 'Bloody Jerry's blown the bridge. Now we're stuck for the night. Old Bill says it's a deep river. Can't wade over.'

Now leading tank, throughout the afternoon we edge forward through the village. Small groups of Black Watch follow us. Each corner and bend is yet another dying time: time to savour all the imagined agonies of wounding, ripping of flesh, mangling of bone, shredding of muscles, laceration of nerves … The village is 100 miles long and the day lasts 100 years.

At last a road junction diagonally to the left. A vast ditch alongside us. The objective! Job done! That 88mm gun chased away. Sint-Michielsgestel liberated. 'That's it, then,' exclaims Panter. And, as though he has given some weird order, the Sherman begins to slide and tip. To the left. Swinging. I glimpse through the telescope that deep, deep ditch. And we are toppling into it. The tarmac street collapsing under our weight. Falling. Spinning. I crash out of my seat against the solid, unyielding gun breech. Cruel iron objects rain on me. Something heavy and brutal smashes into my knee.

Then the final crash: a spine-battering halt, almost upside down. In the silence, as the engine stalls, somebody begins to laugh hysterically. 'Shit!' shouts somebody else. And I am jammed *on top* of the gun and therefore now underneath it as the tank lies!

I hear Panter put out a distress signal as we disentangle ourselves gingerly, careful lest the tank should entirely turn turtle and seal us off in a tomb flooding with the petrol which could so easily ignite. No frantic bale out now, but a gentle worming up to the surface. Sergeant Shadlow and the ARV arrive and unleash their massive towing rope. The ARV tugs the Sherman back into the horizontal whilst we sit and massage aching limbs.

Meanwhile no 88mm shots crash at us from the unliberated road ahead. Shadlow and his rescue crew stand and smoke in the road oblivious to the war.

Darkness approaches. Our tank is withdrawn to the miniature town hall. Over the doorway is a coat of arms with St Michael himself bearing a flaming sword. Harry Graham's tank and ours will stay 'sentry-go' to support the infantry through the night.Our night is not to be undisturbed. Whilst the Black Watch search for a boat to put an advance party across the river, crashing shells vomit fire at us. Either the Germans are aware that the engineers will be moving up with a Bailey bridge, or else their artillery commander is suffering from dyspepsia and is determined that, if he cannot sleep, nobody else shall rest.

The clashing of shattered roof slates mixes with the tinkling of broken glass and the crunch of fractured brickwork. Smoke from exploding shells and dust from shattered bricks permeate the tank, mixing with the animal odours within our mobile iron cistern. Our driver has 'Gypo tummy' and at our advanced battle station will not open his hatch to empty the tin ammunition box which he uses frequently as a chamber pot. He moans, 'Bugger this for an all-night picture show.'

Then, in the middle hours of the interminable night of torture for all the senses – blinded eyes, battered ears, offended nostrils, aching, cramped limbs – there is a scratching and tapping on the back of the tank. Panter, who has been closed down, pulls out his revolver, opens his flaps and thrusts the gun over the edge of the cuppola, to be confronted by ...

A Dutch civilian carrying a tray of coffee. 'Goot evening, my friends,' he says, smiling at our surprise, 'or may it be not a goot evening. You would like some coffee, please? This is not the very goot coffee. There is a war. Maybe you know there is a war. This is very bad coffee. But you are *welkom* in Sint-Michielsgestel.' And the coffee is served by the Dutch doctor, for such he proves to be, in tiny blue-and-white china cups which contrast oddly with the grim brutality of our cell.

The wireless is silent, unresponsive. Tonight everybody seems to have gone home except two Shermans, a Dutch doctor and an insomniac German artillery commander. And, of course, the invisible but ubiquitous Black Watch.

I sit and stare through the periscope at the fitful world which flickers between total black obscurity and rending lightning not of God's creating. In the red glare the Dutch street stands solid under the continual pounding of high explosive. Rain, the colour of blood, streams over the cobbles and grins back at us amid the lunatic fire flashes, mirroring the dead waxen grins of so many we have seen along the way. We all carry the scars of death, of comrades and enemies, struck and struck again, like white-hot iron, into the soul.

I sit, still tasting the bad but *welkom* coffee, and wonder about Arthur Dwight, enveloped in flame, with a Black Watch medic bending over him.

24 OCTOBER 1944:

Dawn breaks sullen, damp and smoke-blackened. The engineers have erected a Bailey bridge over the river and B Squadron tanks file past us, their commanders looking curiously up and down the village street and making obscene gestures at us. Then platoons of relaxed Highlanders. Then familiar faces above turrets, Ken Snowdon, Bobby McColl, Hughie McGranahan, Percy Sumner, Bill Fox, Hank.

Lieutenant Skipper comes aboard and briefs Panter. 'Esch, Hal and Halder are our objectives today,' he says, 'Esch, Hal and Halder: sounds like a Dutch music hall act.' We plead for scraps of news. 'Old Bunny Warren is OK, a bit battered but cussin' even more than usual. Young Moore got his driver out but the lad was dead. Corporal Dwight lost a leg. Right, tag on. Reserve role.'

If given any other role today we would be of little use, battle-weary, noise-crazed, body-sullied. More than twenty-four hours since we trod on firm steady ground, washed, or cleaned out our mouths; and any natural functions have been negotiated from a cramped position into an empty brass shell case; and we have not stretched our limbs (except for that moment after exiting the overturned tank) beyond the strait-jacket limits of our noisome den. The morning drags slowly by, with sluggish progress, 10 yards at a time. We wriggle and jerk about in our tight coops, like battery hens.

In the afternoon we progress along a straight, tree-lined road that ends in a railway crossing. Our tank is suddenly in the lead down this isolated road. (In Normandy the entire regiment would attack along one road. Here we advance like ten fingers poking out at the enemy.) We bump on to the railway track and halt there. Fortunately there are no trains running today. The ruler-straight track runs away into misty invisibility both northwards and southwards.

A solitary German stands up 300 yards away. Races across the track. I sit in amazement and fail to tread on my trigger button. 'Where there's one bloody Jerry there's bound to be fifty,' growls Panter. 'Keep your eyes and bowels moving, mate. Get your ferkin' foot ready on that button. Give 'em a few extra creases in the arses of their trousers.'

Far to the right I see movement. Traverse the turret. 'Not that way, mate.

Those are Jocks advancing.' Yes, the Highland gamekeepers and poachers and deerstalkers, disguised in khaki, beating the bushes as though driving grouse.

A bunch of field-grey figures detaches from the right-hand bushes. Both my feet stamp without deliberate command from my brain. Distant running figures shudder, freeze, stagger, are flung upwards, catch fire, disintegrate, collapse, roll writhing on the railway lines, lie still. Others sprint, jump, duck, crawl prostrate. 'Bloody murder,' grunts Panter. 'Say alert. Keep it going. We're winning.'

I sit in my tiny judgement seat and tread on buttons. As the grisly game of man-hunting fizzles out, I gaze along the railway lines, empty of movement now, except where a contorted body still twitches as its spirit takes a darker and more distant journey. The Scots dig in. We are released. Back to a grassy field at a crossroads. 'Unload all guns. Driver and operator, switch off,' quotes Panter and then shouts down inside the soundless tank, 'All right, lads! Get out! That is, if you're not shat solid to your seats.'

We haul ourselves up by reluctant arms. Roll off the turret. Slide to the ground. My left leg folds and I fall flat on my face. Strong arms pick me up. Cooks and lorry drivers. Jack Aris and the rest.

'Had yer legs shot off, then?' laughs cook Scotty.

'No, he's bin out all night boozing that Jong Genever that they calls drink,' suggests Harry Claridge.

'Aw, come on. Can't you see the poor lad's tired out,' argues kindly Jack Aris. 'All that time in the tank! No wonder your legs come out feeling like bloody corned beef. Give him a nice old cuppa.'

Fortune's wheel gives yet another jerk. Panter's gunner is waiting to resume his place on the tank. I gather my few belongings and limp to HQ(F). Slump on my blankets. Share rations with old mates – Pete Pedder, Don Pateman, Robin, Harold, Troop Sergeant 'Basher' Bates. 'Basher' passes round ready-worded field postcards on which we strike out inapplicable sentences. There is no sentence which says 'My left leg is aching like blazes.'

'Hey, you guys,' quips Bruce Dickson, 'Why is there no message that says, "Dear Mother, I'm dead"?'

'Because,' says Don, 'for you it would have to add "from the neck upwards".'

The remark triggers off an all-in wrestling match, with more and more people involved, cheering and booing, ridding tortured minds of the horrors of battle. I evade the rough and tumble and soon slide into my blankets. Explosions of smoke-black sleep kill the day and drive me down into instant unconsciousness.

25 OCTOBER 1944:

As I sit on my blankets in the cold, grey morning light and pull on my trousers, the leg of the garment jams around my left knee. I look down with bleary eyes and see something reminiscent of an elephant's leg, huge, distended, shapeless and mottled purple-brown.

Dick Bates is sitting on his blankets a foot or two away. He looks at my leg with disbelief. 'You wants to get that attended to, young Ken. Go and see the quack corporal. I'll tell Hank.'

Everything blurs ... becomes unreal ... time becomes compressed ... is it sheer bodily weariness, or delayed shock from the crash, or months of compounded horror? With Hank's permission Lowe drives me to where the MO works in a tent beside an ambulance. 'Let's have a look at the leg,' he demands. He and the quack corporal watch with undisguised interest as I struggle to wrench the tightened trouser leg from the even more swollen elephantine limb. 'Oh, my word,' he whistles. 'Get your driver to run along to the brigade MO. He is an orthopaedic specialist. A bone man. Now if you had come to me with lungs ...'

A marginally more auspicious gathering of vehicles. The brigade MO's examination is long, detailed and painful. 'Two days ago? Bursitis obviously. But what's underneath? It's hospital for you, my lad. There's bone damage. Dismiss your driver. I'll send you in the ambulance. Lucky you came to me. Could have been bad if you had landed with some under-qualified pill-and-ointment man. Don't bother putting those damn trousers on ...'

I am the only passenger in the ambulance which trundles along down the Helmond road. To a real hospital. Occupied by the army. Waiting outside the X-ray room a nurse in starched, pure white apron offers me tea and a queen cake, a delicate bun after all our dog biscuits and sawdust bread. I remember that I didn't say goodbye to the lads ...

Today or tomorrow a nurse brings labels which are pinned to each patient's pyjamas or shirt. Khaki-coloured cardboard labels. On these the doctors write either 'BX [Brussels]' or 'UK'. The doctor holds my label and writes: 'UK', the top prize in this final spin of the roulette wheel of war ...

Today or yesterday we were pushed in wheelchairs or carried on stretchers to a number of ambulances waiting to take us to Eindhoven aerodrome. 'Lucky bugger,' says my orderly, 'you'll be home in time for tea.'

But today or yesterday the fog came down enveloping the runway. The RAF say they can't take off. The ambulances have dispersed. 'We'll see if we can get some char and chow. And more blankets,' says my orderly. We sleep on stretchers beside the runway through the chill, damp night. In the darkness I feel a vital spirit divorcing itself from my body and returning to the regiment where it belongs ...

Morning: the mists are still with us but we are lifted into the long, cavernous box of aeroplane with double-tier beds slung from the walls. As a 'walking wounded' I am asked to watch the plasma bottle mounted above a badly mutilated Durham Light Infantryman. The fuselage walls shudder and stretch as we begin to move. The plane lifts off with all the resilience of an old bucket with a hole in the bottom.

Now in the sky an unspoken hierarchy of suffering takes effect. Those of us with plebeian ailments minister to the real aristocracy of pain – the engineer with two legs missing, the Highlander with shot lungs, the artilleryman with half a face blown away, my own light infantryman with blood still staining his bandages. They have come so far. Death leaped upon them, savaged them, raked them tooth and claw. Almost drank the life blood out of their veins. But they fought back. On the bumping stretcher as their clumsy pals carried them delicately back to the aid post; in the churning, clashing medical half-track, blundering across country; through the hospital bed and the surgeon's kind but torturing fingers; finally bundled awkwardly into this chilly, thundering plane.

Now there is the altitude, the cold, the diabolical noise, the smell of other men's decay, the vast distances, the ease with which the spirit might lift from this height into the farthest skies, through the clouds to peace – beyond the pain and beyond the noise and beyond the terror of war.

So we, who sense the inferiority of our suffering and the hypocrisy of our flight back to Blighty, we serve them and encourage them and woo them towards the place where the surgeons may again impose their healing will. We watch them and we touch them and we breathe the very breath for them, holding them close in the ongoing rhythm of life.

Then the cold grey sea is behind us. The golden towers of Oxford send up their ancient radiant greetings. The clumsy flying box becomes a graceful, gliding bird, flattening along a lush, green unending meadow as though the soft, spinning tyres hesitate to bruise those butter-rich wild flowers across our triumphal path. Down! Thump. Rattle. Squeal. And all our aristocracy of pain are alive and lifting themselves painfully to look with misting eyes at the soil, the bracken, the greenwood of Blighty.

Another ambulance. The plain, stubby country girl in khaki, the driver, is an inexpressibly beautiful welcoming angel. A railway station sign says 'SHRIVENHAM'. A GWR train is drawn up there. Solicitous Women's Voluntary Service (WVS) workers hold sandwiches to the mouths of those too ill to raise a hand. Endless cups of tea slop on the carriage floors. I ask a St John sergeant where the train will be headed.

'Us don' know, do us, son. They don' tell us. P'raps all the ways to Scotland. Manchister. Wales. But us be pointed westwards so't won' be Lon'on. Anyway, it's war secrets, en' it, like? Ol' 'itler might find out where you was 'eaded. Then where would we be?'

In the low glow of tiny war lamps I see familiar, quiet, rural stations. A callow, home-loving youth, the civilian me, begins to take control, and my *doppelganger*, the hardened military Yeoman, drifts away into the distances behind the chugging train ...

Worcester! Familiar sights, the cathedral, the cricket ground, the known streets. 'All change! Walking wounded proceed in buses. Stretcher cases stay put for now. Watch your step in the dark, lads.'

Beyond Malvern, destination still unknown (Hitler might find out!), I hazard a question to the orderly sergeant coming round the bus with a clipboard. 'Are we, by any remote chance, heading for Hereford, sarge?'

'Know it?'

'Born and bred there.'

'Then you effing-well drew the ace in today's shuffle, boyo. Most of the wounded on this convoy are Geordies or Jocks.'

01.00 hours: Ledbury Road, St. James's Road, Green Street. Open gates. Dimly lit courtyard. People. And a silvery moon glints on the river down the garden slopes. Extended, eager hands! Excited, babbling 'Ereefut' voices! I stand at the top of the bus steps, tired, dirty, hungry, battle-shocked, alien, frightened of these solicitous civilians. My battle-dress collar still scorched from a turret fire. My trousers stained with oil from a Sherman's guns. My socks matted with dirt. My face scored deep with fear furrows. A deflated, juvenile St Michael with extinguished sword and shoddy armour. Two campaign ribbons on my chest, one stripe on my sleeve, a tiny red-and-blue HD (Highland Division) sign on one arm, and six revolver bullets in my pocket.

A civilian takes me by one arm and a St John Ambulance man by the other, while nurses hover. The St John man stares at me. 'Yer, don't I know you? You gotta be Jack Tout's boy. I'm Mr Phillips from down Portland Street, just round the corner from you. Hey! *Hereford Times*! There's one of our own boys yer.' The dark hour blurs into a barrage of words like machine-gun bullets, and laughter like bomb-bursts, and back-slapping like the battering of gun blasts. And the weariness.

Almost like Hank's voice speaking coolly over the air in the fury of battle, I hear a sister order 'Come along and let that boy get to bed. He's ill. He needs to sleep. This is not a victory parade. Clear the ward. Quickly now.'

THIS IS NOT A VICTORY PARADE. This is not a victory parade. This-is-not-a-victory-thisisnota ...

The sister and the St John man from Portland Street pull off my shoes and socks and trousers and battle-dress blouse and roll me into bed partially clothed as I am, for this is not a ... not a ... not a ...

The St John Mr Portland Street Phillips leans over my bed and whispers, 'I'll go roun' now to your 'ouse. Wake your folk. Throw stones at their blimmin' window. Tell 'em you're 'ome. Tell 'em you blimmin' well finished with that there war ... tell 'em ...' this not a ...

In the dim doorway a still dimmer and dimming figure in oily denims and black beret seems to beckon ... blowing a silver trumpet ... sounding the 'Rally!' ...

But I shake my head ... my denial is complete. I want to go home.

9 Those Blasted Bridges

Meanwhile, the colonel, Doug Forster, has said, 'It's going to be a different battle now. Long Dutch villages, wide canals and rivers, dozens of bridges. Squadrons will diverge to capture bridges and shut off the enemy's main retreat routes. The Hun will try to blow the bridges. So, gentlemen, let's go capture those blasted bridges … before they are truly blasted in front of our own eyes.'

In 3 Baker, fourth in an inevitable advancing queue, Rex and Hickie surveyed the work of the artillery. A huge building, a convent of sorts, was spouting flames and smoke from windows. Monks or priests in long robes were rushing out carrying precious bundles, then fetching tiny buckets of unavailing water from a nearby well. Some cottages also blazed, setting off their own unmilitary smoke screen. Rex saw a large Dutch woman, arms waving, legs pounding, lips opening, words unheard amid the scream and blast of mortar bombs. Inspiring small groups of peasantry to dash into burning buildings, rescuing here household possessions, there animals and poultry trapped in out-houses.

Rex pressed his mike switch. 'Ken, that woman will get killed. Can't you shout her to get under cover until it's all over?'

'No chance,' replied Snowie. 'She's saving her household and that's more important to her than a shell splinter up her backside.'

'Makes you think,' added Stan Hicken, 'Us sitting here, frigging frozen to our seats inside inches of armoured steel, when that poor woman's running around bareheaded and barefoot, without a thought for Moaning Minnies.'

In the lead, recce Sergeant Jack and Sherman Sergeant Bamford had found another great tree felled across the road. Rifles, machine-guns, mortars, howitzers were beating out fortissimo sound with orchestral precision. Everyone was so intent on the pyrotechnics that Jack and Bamford were able to crawl up the middle of the road. No response came from behind the tree. Bamford unhitched a tow rope from his Sherman, and crawled forward.

'My backside feels as high as the summit of Ben Nevis,' muttered Bamford.

'Keep your voice down. Jerry might hear,' grunted Jack, though noise like a thousand blacksmiths' forges would have made it impossible for 10,000 Welsh male voice singers to have made themselves heard.

A wave of Bamford's arms to the Sherman. A jerk from the tank. The tree slid wide enough open for Kenny Jack to squeeze his narrower Honey tank through. Another bend. Another tree. 'Once bitten ...!' Kenny got down from his turret and stalked, crouching, around a farm building. He spotted an enemy group behind the tree, invisible from the road but exposed to the farmyard. He also noticed an old cartwheel lying in the farm yard. He beckoned to driver Ovens.

'Get that clumsy anti-aircraft machine-gun we've never used off the turret. I've found a use for it at bloody last,' he whispered.

Some old rope lying about enabled Kenny to lash the gun to the wheel, forming a perfect traversing table. The 0.5 was a large gun, slow in rate of fire but delivering large bullets with impressive fury at a few yards range. Ovens pressed the trigger. Field-grey figures toppled over, catapulted backwards, turned in dismay, ducked into ditches. A few moments and a piece of white rag waved above a ditch.

'Come out, you buggers,' shouted young Ovens jumping up and waving arms, '*Heraus! Kamerads!* Surrender!'

'Get down, you bloody idiot,' yelled the sergeant. But Fritzes were already waving bits of white rag, handkerchiefs, pieces of paper.

Lieutenant Vaughan Green, a troop leader, reported, 'Hullo, Queen 4. Approaching Daffodil ...' That being his target bridge. Alongside his tank Captain Charlie Robertson of 7th Black Watch was trudging with his men at the steady pace designed to walk the thousand miles from El Alamein to Berlin. Now they hastened the step towards bridge Daffodil. A field-grey figure was visible for a moment in the far bushes, and ...

UP WENT THE BRIDGE! Rising as an entire structure, then twisting, disintegrating into wood and tarmac and mortar. And leaving that vital gaping hole over the next stream to cross. 'Send up the Pioneer Platoon, bugger it!' Charlie called into his radio.

Ex-schoolmaster Captain 'Ratters' Rathbone was leading another half-squadron towards the Dommel river at Hal. Stan Hilton, gunner on Sergeant Huitson's tank, could see already, through his magnified telescope sights, bridge Marigold. Objective! Victory! Success! 'Driver, speed up!' snapped Huitson. 'Gunner, two hundred.'

But Stan's sights blinked red, clouded black, whirled grey, brown, silver, red again. The tank halted, rocked, shuddered. Smoke filled the turret. Huitson ducked down behind Stan.

'Blast!'

'You can say that again!'

'Hullo, 2 Able. You can see … bridge is blown … bang on time …'

'Yeah, BANG is right, too,' thought Stan.

'Gunner, hose down those houses on the far bank.'

Towards Esch Harry Graham turned his telescope on bridge Sunflower, his second vital bridge in two days. Still that damnable river which turned and twisted across country. 'Sarge! Bridge! Suggest you creep up on this one unawares, sort of …'

Randy Ginns broke in, 'God! There! Man lighting fuses. Gunner, on! Fire! Fire.' Harry stamped on both buttons at once but did not cause what happened. Slowly at first the bridge took off in helicopter flight. Spun a little. Then a second explosion reached up flaming claws and tore the soaring bridge apart. A red-hot, dagger-sharp hail of shards began to fall. Ginns dived for cover and slammed the flaps closed.

'Damn, damn, damn!' he shouted into the continuing echoes.

25 OCTOBER 1944:

Sergeant Bamford, called urgently to attack another roadblock, informed his crew, 'No crawling about today. Normal tank tactics. Brass up that roadblock.' Then, as Highland infantry spread out to either side, on 'A' set, 'Hullo, Mike 3 Able. Am now in sight of—'

Saw the pin-prick of red flash in faraway trees, and, before thought could grapple with the sight, saw the tornado of fire which billowed up from the turret in front of him, saw a lightning flash, a sudden brief sunset and then black darkness. Sudden. Swift. Total. Eternal darkness.

Behind him Sergeant Lloyd saw and heard and felt the blast and knew. 'Driver, reverse. Left hand down. Quick! Move!' The Sherman slipping sideways, cocked over into a ditch. Another great 88mm shot howled through the air where Lloyd's head had been a fraction of a second before, hit the artillery observation tank, slewing it right across the road leaving all retreat blocked.

Young 'Reb' Reboles (lance-corporal but commanding a tank), also caught in the storm of destruction, noticed that the tank in front of Bamford's burning one had crashed into the next, becoming locked together, blocking escape hatches. 'Only one thing,' thought Reboles, 'Move the front tank. Simple!'

He ran across the road, jumped into the driver's seat of the abandoned tank. Found the engine still running. Engaged gear. Frightening grinding noises came from the engine. Reb accelerated. Crashed forward a few yards. Ran to the other tank and freed the driver's hatch. Wreathed in smoke like a black phantom the driver rose up. Behind him the co-driver, gasping, coughing and groaning also pulled himself up. Fell over the side. Rolled into the welcome ditch.

A Gordon Highlander captain watching called to Reboles, 'Good show that, corporal. But you could have had your balls blown off.'

'Thank you, sir. But if Jerry couldn't hit me that time, he won't have a better chance again. I'll see to that.'

Stuck in the ditch Lloyd called to his driver, Wally Tarrant, 'Let's go and look at Bamford's lot, then, Wally.' Bamford's tank stood high above the ditch, which made a safe approach through the trembling, burning earth. Bamford's crew lay underneath the tank where they had taken refuge. 'God damn and curse bloody Hitler!' snarled Lloyd. Bamford's crew had been hit by a shell improbably bouncing *under* the tank and lay shredded, indistinguishable as to who was who, in the ultimate comradeship of sudden, brutal death. 'We can't do a ruddy, sodding, ferking thing,' groaned the sergeant.

Bobby McColl, listening to the battle reports, checked his map, calculated that the offending gun must be somewhere to his right. About 600 yards away. He ordered driver Don Foxley to swing right, slowly and carefully. A squat, square outline appeared among the woods, beam end on to 3 Troop. 'Gunner, traverse right. On! 600 yards. AP. Fire!' A single AP sufficed to breed explosive fire and thick smoke at 600 yards.

'How's that then, sir?' asked the elated gunner, Norman Plant.

'Too good too late!' snapped McColl. 'Yon bastard got an entire troop of ours before ye ended him.'

Stan Hilton saw some Dutch people searching in the ruins of their cottage. He called a Dutchman to commiserate. 'Sorry about your house, friends.'

The man smiled wanly, 'No go! We are enthusiast. All Dutchmen enthusiast. Yesterday we have house and Germans. Now, no house and no Germans. Better no house. *Ja*? We are all enthusiast. *Welkom*! How are you?'

Big avuncular RSM George Jelley ran his scout car into a town which must be Vught. Dutch people ran out of their houses to embrace him. A pallid, hungry-looking man lifted his little boy up to kiss the burly RSM. George searched in the scout car, found a bar of chocolate, offered it to the child. The boy winced and shrugged away as though from a venomous reptile. 'Good chocolate. *Shokola. Cocooolat-ee*,' soothed George.

'Not understand,' responded the father. 'Never see chocolate all his knowing time. No chocolate from Huns. Look! *Kijk!*' He took the bar, bit off a tiny corner and chewed. A glorious look of contentment spread over his face. The son understood and tasted the chocolate nervously. George handed out more bars to more children.

Geordie Johnny Byrne was discontented as he eased his tank up to the captured river-bank. He had been delighted to see a white cloth waving on the far bank. Several Germans began to climb out of a ditch or peer fearfully towards the British tanks. Then a machine-gun opened up from the British side. Immediately the evening came alive and alight with frenetic firing from both sides. Several Germans fell. A Highlander collapsed. Later Johnny counted up to forty bodies strewn like the proverbial rag-dolls across that tiny battle patch.

Johnny turned to a Gordon Highlander lieutenant standing nearby, growling 'The man who pulled the trigger of that bloody gun when they were surrendering ought to be shot himself.'

'Itchy fingers,' replied the officer. 'It happens in war.'

If Johnny Byrne was discontented his emotions were less complex and infinitely less sad than those of a small group of Cameron Highlanders and Northants Yeomanry. Military police were debussing at the gates of a large camp near Vught. Two of them barred the way against the Camerons and tankers.

'Now, lads, you can't go in there. You don't need to go in there,' said the MP sergeant, gruffly but more kindly than the normal MP response. 'Fact, you ain't going in there!'

'Christ almighty, what a stink!' uttered a Yeomanry corporal. 'Is that the local slaughterhouse, sarge?'

'You might call it that, corporal. I'm not supposed to say anything. You'll find out anyway. The whole world has got to bloody-well know. It's … it's monstrous. Concentration camp, it was. Dutch. And Belgians. Civilians. Thousands of them. SS guards tried to shoot the lot of 'em before we arrived. Shot thousands. Against that wall there. You can still see bodies. Still some live ones hiding. Afraid to come out.'

A slow, hesitant group emerged from behind dark trees, an erect Dutchman wearing the orange armband, a dishevelled British MP and between them a bowed, slight, shuffling figure in rags. 'One of 'em,' grunted the MP sergeant.

'Dutch?' asked a Highlander. The escorting MP shook his head.

'*Belge?*' asked the Yeomanry corporal.

The central figure looked up. A face haggard, wasted and scarred, '*Vous êtes Belge?*' he asked in a cracked voice as of an old gramophone record.

'*Non. Nous sommes anglais.*'

The man shook himself free from his escort and stumbled forward, croaking, '*Anglais? Anglais? Les libérateurs? Mes amis! Ah, Dieu vous benisse! Dieu vous ...*' and he threw himself down, kneeling, trying to kiss the Yeoman's muddy boots.

28 OCTOBER 1944:

Tommy Tucker, with his gift for perverting any name, had seen the map markings pointing to Loon-op-Zand and immediately christened it 'Lunacy on the Sands'. Indeed the battle was reaching across an area of inland sand dunes, a freakish place that would become ghoulish.

Because little Bobby McColl was such a good troop leader his troop caught quite a lot of sticky tasks. And, as Bobby's troop corporal, Snowie naturally inherited more than a fair share of lead tank jobs. Now Holland, and Rex Jackson was wondering if Snowie might suddenly go bomb happy like some other commanders back in Normandy. But in his calm voice Snowie ordered 'Driver, slowly left through that opening in the trees. Gunner, alert when we break into the open.'

As the Sherman thrust through the trees a howl, and a crash, and a screaming of metal splinters, and boiling flame, and a hardly-heard far-off thud, paralysed the crew for a moment. Blast ripped and ricocheted round the confined space like a screeching, whirling dervish trying to escape. Flame slithered through the turret ring. Periscopes were wrenched out of their sockets. Tommy threw himself over the gun and out through the impossibly restricted space even as Snowie shouted into the microphone, 'Bale out! Bale out!'

Rex, leaping and sliding, vaguely saw others jumping and running. He threw himself down under the trees. Then realized he was on the wrong, the enemy side of tank 3 Baker. He crawled frantically but it seemed whichever way he moved it was always towards the German gunfire. He had a vision of one tiny British soldier crawling hopelessly about between the two armies under the storm of battle and never arriving.

No. 4 Troop of C Squadron were trying to find gaps in the same barricade of sand banks and trees. Ron West, operator on 4 Charlie, watched Lieutenant Skipper trying to work his tank across sandy slopes at awkward angles. The tank appeared to jolt, slither, spin and circle on the moving sands. 'Right! Our turn, lads,' ordered Percy Sumner, Ron's commander. 'Advance, Larry.'

A brief, bright flash beyond the trees, Percy ducking instinctively. The space where his head had been crashed and roared with impact, explosion, flame and shattered fittings. It was like dwelling within the midst of a thunderhead. The mounting of the anti-aircraft machine-gun took the full force of the shock, blue lightning flared from it, ball-bearings and splinters of metal from it peppered the tank top and shattered into the turret. Again the crew members were stunned for a moment.

Driver Larry was first to recover. 'Is there anybody alive upstairs? Percy? Are you OK? Shouldn't we bale out? Who's in charge up there?'

'I am,' came Percy's voice at last. Ron peered over the gun to where Percy had collapsed behind the gunner's seat. The commander looked as though a grizzly bear had ravaged his face with dirty claws.

'Yes, better bale out. You ought to have gone already. Without me. All out,' initiating a wild scramble from the confined dangers of the smouldering tank into the more widely spread calamities of the sand dunes. As co-driver Les Carr measured his leap to the ground another explosion buffeted the tank which swayed, causing Les to tumble, his ankle cracking on impact. Stumbling, shuffling and cursing, the group sought shelter in the nearest angle of trees.

Still disorientated Rex Jackson trudged on. Saw a Sherman. Smoke, thin smoke issued from the turret. Engine still running. He moved closer. It was his own tank. Stan or somebody else might still be inside. And that scarred old Sherman was a friend too, a veteran of battles, 3 Baker.

Nobody in the driver's compartment. Nobody in the turret. A fire extinguisher hanging there suggested sensible precautions. Rex squirted foam lavishly. Now for the final call of the cards. If that 88mm gunner is still watching, and if he is a psychotic arsonist from Berlin, then look out, Rex! Into the driver's seat. Reverse gear … gentle pedal … sundry bangs and shakings … 'Lunacy-on-the-Sands,' Tommy says … 'Come on, then, old girl … right hand down … and home, James!'

'Stat me,' exclaimed Ron West from their hideout where he had been wiping the blood from Percy's face. 'Rex has got his tank moving.' The excited group jumped up and cheered, until a random shell threw sand house-high a few yards away.

Another Stan, Hilton in reserve, lay enjoying a luxurious bed of soft grass beyond the dunes under a pleasant sun. 'Many happy returns, Stan,' said a sergeant passing by. 'Is it the bugger's birthday?' asked Hughie McGranahan as they lay looking up into the sky. Long, pure white vapour trails, like flowing scarves of wool, pointed from east to west against the clean blue sky. 'What's that?'

'Rockets. German V2 rockets. Aimed at Antwerp,' said Hughie. 'Pity the poor Belgies and Dutchies those fall on. They say fifty per cent cut out and come straight down en route to target. So keep looking, lads.' Stan groaned, 'You've just spoiled my twenty-first birthday party.'

Spud Taylor out in the dunes saw his commander, Mike Tansley busy digging a hole. 'What's that for?' he asked. 'I'm digging a hole to bury you in, Spud,' laughed Tansley. Spud shivered. 'Don't say that, Mike. It's tempting fate.' The corporal grinned 'Don't worry, lad. I'll see all you lot safely to Berlin.' He was burying ration packets and tins in keeping with strict orders to bury all rubbish, even amid the ruins of the battlefield.

Later, called to advance, Spud, in the co-driver's seat, was brassing up ditches and woods with his machine-gun. Then, 'Misfire. Co-ax!' The chill words sounded over the intercom. Tank crews hated misfires in the close quarters of the turret. Norman Sidwell started to clear the hot gun in its mounting. Having failed he loosened the gun from its fixture, handling it more delicately than a nurse with a premature baby. 'Steady, the Buffs!' he intoned the traditional army watchword.

The bullet, cooked in the hot barrel, exploded. Shot out of the gun. Hit the curving turret wall. Screamed through a pattern of ricochets, the crew ducking pointlessly as the fatal busy bee buzzed around the tiny turret, pinged through the cage and subsided exhausted beside Spud. 'God, I'm hit,' yelped Norman, pulling up his trouser leg to reveal a slight weal. 'Fatal, that!' scoffed the driver. 'Up yours, too, mate!' gritted Norman. 'I knew something would happen,' thought Spud. 'Pray God that's all for today.'

29 OCTOBER 1944:

Second behind the lead tank, Spud had a good view of the road ahead. A clear view of a flash at 500 yards. A clear view of a red spark coming straight at him. Time frozen. A clear, precise, indisputable view. An armour-piercing shot. Sparking off shreds of crimson fire. Growing larger. Bang on target.

CLANG! Like a mighty hammer clanging on Wayland's smithy, the shot crashed into the moulded steel beside Spud's ear and gouged its way along the side of the tank, whining, grinding and spattering fire. The impact plunged Spud into silence and darkness.

'Spud! Spud! Are you there? Are you all right?' Mike Tansley's anxious voice. Spud shook his head and decided that it was still on his shoulders. The tank smelled too foul for it to be Heaven. His limbs were too frozen for it to be Hell.

'Good news: that shot only grazed us,' explained their always cheerful commander. 'Bill Higham up front has knocked out that gun. Bad news: snipers reported. Nasty people. Hose down those trees, Spud, right, two o'clock.'

Tank commanders hated reports of snipers when it was so much more efficient to keep one's head out of the turret rather than closing down the flaps. Spud set to work again. So simple. The motion of hosing. The flare of tracers. The almost musical drumming of the stout Browning gun. It became a rhythm. A ballet of fire. An art. A fascination. Spud became a mechanical extension of his gun and then, in that marriage, the gun became a joyous, obedient, throbbing extension of his flesh. A longer arm. A more powerful fist. A strident, dictating voice.

'Good shooting, Spud,' chirped Corporal Mike Tansley. And died.

Spud turned from the fun-filled shooting gallery in front of him to the ghastly carousel spinning behind him. The commander's body had collapsed and fallen across gunner Titch Crawshaw, forcing the little man down into the tiny space in front of his seat. His arms were jammed against the power traverse and the turret was caused to spin round and round with no way of stopping it. At each revolution the mangled and still bleeding face of the corporal glared unseeing at Spud. Only inches, through the thin metal grille of the turret cage, separated the petrified, static co-driver and his mate from the spinning obscenity of cheerful life transformed in an instant by a bullet in the brain.

Reporting feverishly, reversing down the road, the crew tried to lift the fallen body from the turret. The corporal, a cold mortal, habitually wore a greatcoat. As the crew strained to lever the heavy load up through the narrow turret opening the sagging body slid down inside the greatcoat and back to the turret floor. Sweating, swearing, daring God to blast them with lightning, the slight youths struggled on with bloodstained hands.

Mortality exerted itself in another way for Bill Higham on Sergeant Ray Eley's tank moving into the objective village of Waspik. At the first house an unexpected infantry officer appeared and waved to Eley, motioning him to descend. The sergeant waved the second tank past him, vaulted down and gave the officer a sketchy salute. Bill climbed on to the turret to keep watch. The second commander gave him a rude 'V' sign. Bill watched that tank swing into a bend. He saw flame belch out of its turret. He saw black objects spinning into the air. He saw the entire Sherman crunch backwards. He saw milling figures on the turret top. He saw one pause to jump and go cartwheeling back across the tank. He saw another hit the ground and run for, it seemed, seconds, after his head had been smashed like pulp. And he saw the infernal furnace-pillaring of fire that only the Sherman, the roaster, the griller of Tommys to black charcoal shapes, could produce.

Bill, phlegmatic Scouse though he was, gulped and swallowed as his bile-filled stomach revolted. He gripped the turret flaps until they cut into the palms of his hands. 'Bloody hell,' said Eley, coming back on board, 'if it hadn't been for that officer ... who shouldn't have been anywhere near ... THAT would have been US.'

Captain Bill Fox encountered Michael Hunt and asked 'What's that blood on your head,' to which Mike replied 'I'll be alright, sir. It's nothing,' causing Bill typically to snort, 'Boloney, man! Silly twaddle! You've damn well been hit. You need at least to take a standing count. Get back and see the MO. That's an order, or I'll knock your head off myself.'

The brief interview with the MO gave Mike the opportunity to catch up on news – about Arthur Dwight: 'Bad case, that. Lost one leg. Eyes affected. But he's a big lad. Should win through' ... about Harry Brown: 'Now that *will* be a long job. Extreme multiple burns. Have to lie in a cradle' ... about Ken Tout: 'Severe case of elephant's leg. But I'm no vet so he's off to hospital' ... about Sergeant Warren: 'Oh, him! Hopping around and cursing all quacks. We'll be letting him loose on the unfortunate Fritzes in a day or two. Now hold still!'

30 OCTOBER 1944:

Colonel Doug explaining again. 'Just one more push. We've circled right behind the German army in North Brabant. Now we must capture Raamsdonk, from where we shall dominate that last bridge over the Maas. The trap will have snapped shut.'

'That sounds just a little too easy, sir,' commented someone.

'I agree. Intelligence believe that large enemy reinforcements, infantry and tanks, are moving in to prevent us. All the roads around Raamsdonk are exposed. No question of us outflanking it. So straight up direct roads into the hornet's nest. We've done it before.'

Which meant that Lieutenant Wall was forming up 1 Troop of B accompanied by Argyll and Sutherland Highlanders. Because of casualties 1 Troop was down to using two lance-corporals as commanders. Reboles's tank would be followed by Wall, then Sergeant Falconer and, bringing up the rear, Lance-Corporal Knoth who was so new to the task that he had not yet been issued with binoculars.

Seen from the distance Raamsdonk was just another small gathering of modest but substantial houses strung along the elevated road that ran through marshy ground, much of it actually waterlogged. It appeared innocuous, peaceful, too insignificant to be the focus of desperate strife. But Reb Reboles, the Northants Yeomanry's only Argentine soldier, knew that the enemy would let them come on, perhaps to the very heart of the trap, without giving the slightest hint of his existence.

Some commanders dealt with this moment by counting up all the eventualities of catastrophe and then working back towards reassurance, as a purge for fear. Others slammed the door on predictive thought, driving fear back down into the subconscious where he, frustrated demon, would await his day. A few commanders considered the permutations of chance to be an essential element in the great heroic adventure in which they considered themselves to be engaged. A few older time-serving veterans had insufficient imagination to see beyond the next bend.

Into that blank, silent, empty bend in the road where the first ominous houses began, Reboles, Wall, Falconer and Knoth and their crews and their infantry escort advanced. The first tank, churning on its near track, the outside track accelerating, slithered into the bend. Round the bend. Out of sight of its followers. And the second tank moving into the bend. Supporting the first. Hurrying to keep in sight. To watch. To see. In time to see ...

'God, get me!'

The whole street seemed to burst into flames and noise and smoke. The first tank was out of sight but the second tank, speeding on, was engulfed in the same torrential outburst of explosions, from enemy guns, from random bursts, and from the funeral pyre tanks themselves as they were pulverized from without and within.

To the following tanks the entire scene looked like a forbidding Turner seascape: an outline of dark, rolling, menacing clouds, behind and within which lightning played: below the clouds a wild, fiery torment which no mind could understand; at the central point a focus of ruddy, oscillating anger; and into this inferno the two stark, brilliant fireships sail. Indeed, although destroyed, the two tanks continued slowly to advance in mechanical momentum as though trying, without human aid, to seek out their unseen destroyer.

Back from the angle Stan Hilton and other gunners launched into a mad fury of firing without sighting. Suddenly a haystack, set blazing by tank guns, seemed to lift off and climb skywards like a misshapen aircraft with jet flames streaming from it. In mid-flight, mid-extinction it glowed even more fiercely, exploded, exploded and exploded again, sending the tanks rocking as on a typhoon-swept sea.

'Loving Jesus!' said a voice, 'what in hell or earth was that?' The commander, trying vainly to sound calm, replied, 'Those haystacks were obviously ammunition dumps camouflaged by straw.'

Behind them Paul Knoth's tank could see some distance in spite of the smoke. Gunner Bert Moreland called that there was what appeared to be an anti-tank gun at the far extent of vision. Having no binoculars the young commander screwed up his eyes, stared and pronounced 'It's only civvies with a pram,' causing Bert to mutter, 'Ferk that! If I was a civvy in this, I'd be twelve feet down the nearest cellar. Under a load of coal.'

Dutch farm lad, Piet de Bont, was worried about the animals which had been shut up. But guns were firing, haystacks exploding, houses burning, barns tumbling. Piet hoisted himself up and went to inspect. He was scared but intrigued by the sound of metallic jangling, guttural voices and thudding boots around the corner of the farmyard. A German crew was hauling a massive gun on its mounting to point towards a Sherman tank about 200 yards away. In the tank Sergeant Falconer snapped out an order to Stan Hilton.

Piet de Bont stood in an agony of indecision as the two guns, the German gun here and the Sherman gun distantly, vectored in towards each other like long-lost lovers reaching out to embrace. The Sherman gun swifter but overshooting the mark. The German gun almost on. The Sherman halting, traversing back. Fire! from the Sherman. A black spot in the centre of the red flower at the Sherman gun's mouth. A black spot, blob, bolt, howling missile, straight, true, smashing into the German gun, splaying it, flinging its undercarriage like a child's toy away across the farmyard. And the gun crew: some of them falling, writhing, crawling, dragging comrades with them. Piet dived into a ditch thinking, 'Let the animals take their chance!'

Falconer and Knoth urged their tanks tentatively forward with their consoling groups of Argylls beside them. Sight was virtually impossible. Hearing had been battered and ravished. Smell became the dominant sense gathering all the obscene messages of battle. Both tanks continued to fire precautionary shots, machine-guns hosing down buildings, big guns blasting out high-explosive warnings. Highlandmen threw grenades and added slighter sounds of Bren and Sten bursts into the dark, mid-afternoon void.

'Hold fire,' gabbled Stan Hilton. 'Somebody out there in the smoke. Khaki. Black beret. Corporal Hammond. Alive, moving, wounded, legs not working properly.'

'German medical orderly,' reported another voice. 'Helping Hammond. Christ, no he ain't. The bugger's trying to drag Hammond away, sarge,' and Falconer himself could now see the orderly wildly trying to drag the injured corporal back into nether smoke as though with some unmedical idea of taking him prisoner. 'Fire over his head!' Falconer barked.

Stan urgently, mistakenly, providentially, trod the wrong button. The 75mm cannon, massive to a non-tank man at close range, belched fire, bellowed sound and propelled a shrieking shot over the orderly's head. Incensed, Falconer leaped 9 feet down from the turret. Saw Argyll people holding the medical orderly. He waved his revolver furiously, finger on trigger.

'You bloody unscrupulous bastard. I'll kill you. Get back, corporal' (to the Argyll NCO).

'*Kamerad*!' cried the orderly. 'Me medic. Me no combat. Me Red Cross. See!' tapping his armband.

'You yellow bastard. You combat, see! You try to take Corporal Hammond prisoner. That not no combat, see! Me firing squad. This revolver. So say your bloody prayers.'

'Can't do that, sarge,' intervened the Argyll. 'We're not ferkin' SS. Leave him to us. A nice soft Highland boot up his balls, cure him of any rape ideas. Come on, sarge. Get back in your tank. We haven't won the war yet.'

Falconer grinned sheepishly. 'Lost my temper, Jock ... Thanks, corp. Look after Hammond, will you?'

Soon the dark blankets of torrid, stench-ridden, all-pervading smoke intervened between German and Britisher as effectively as a military umpire. And down came night to reinforce the darkness. Dutch civilians crouched lower into ditches or cellars. Highland infantry sought demarcation pits in which to set up Bren guns at the new, most forward line of Liberation. And Major Wykeham's voice ordered B Squadron back for replenishment, cleaning of guns and binding of wounds.

31 OCTOBER 1944:

'Just a seven-furlong sprint down the straight. Then we're home and dry,' said Captain Bill Fox to C Squadron commanders. 'But it won't be Epsom or Ascot. B Squadron found Raamsdonk thick with nasties. No reason why today should be any easier. So not so much a gallop, lads, as a good day's stalking.'

Bobby McColl's batman, MacGregor was surprised to hear little Bobby thank him as superfluous kit was packed away. 'Not easy, trying to keep kit decent in this filth. Anyway, may not need it again.'

'Don't say that, sir. It's tempting fate.'

'Ye're a betting man, Mac. Ye know about odds. How many times has 3 Troop taken the lead role into terrifying towns and nasty little villages?'

'You can bet the odds on the gee-gees, sir. But you can't live by them. Every day is a new day.'

Along the road, inspired for the moment by the mighty momentum of this full tide of tumultuous, booming tanks, 3 Troop advanced, Sergeant Thompson, just returned from hospital, now insisting on the lead position. McColl next, then Jack Ginns in the Firefly and Ossie Porter, a tall, gangling youth, fourth. Ossie's tank had been co-opted into 3 because Snowie, Rex and Hickie were away fetching a replacement tank. Behind the tanks, two Black Watch Kangaroo carriers with Lieutenant Donaldson commanding the infantry.

Round a bend and into the narrow straight that led to the church, which would mean victory, and relief, and another day to live. Flash! Thompson saw, ordered: 'Gunner, fire.' Self-propelled gun by church. Flash again. SP garlanded with flames. 'Another AP. Fire.' Panzer bites the dust. McColl still prying through dust and smoke to see. See. See! So important to be able to see.

'Hello, Jig 3 Able. SP by church. Now brewing nicely ...' then on I/C 'Driver, squeeze past that SP. Careful, big ditch. A big—'

Dick Oborn, closed down, stared through the tiny oblong of periscope at the vast, looming SP, a destroyed house, a yawning ditch; Dick twitching the hand-held steering sticks, swerving, reversing, judging, peering; something crumbling under the track; the tank tilting, yawing, sliding into the ditch. Angled sideways. A ship blown over by the hurricane. Turret almost level with pavement. Gun pointing hopefully forward.

'Damn!' said Thompson without emphasis, 'Have to get a tow. Driver, see if ... SP!!! Gunner, another! Two o'clock. Fire if you can.'

Bowden traversed, sighting while swinging, saw massive steel slopes of armour, great gun moving towards them, feet away. Trod. Waited to be blown to hell. By our own gun. Fired at such an angle. From a ditch. Flaming round might cook inside the gun. Blow us all to ... Gun belches. Outwards! Answering belching flame from SP. Two wraiths of fire and smoke meeting, kissing, embracing, dancing together, a mad barbarous fling, encircling the two vehicles. Killer and killed.

Thompson's quiet voice. 'Hello, Able. Second SP brewed. Am ditched but OK.'

Bobby McColl switched to intercom. 'Steady forward, driver. See if ye can get through. Everybody eyes peeled. Bloody smoke!' Don Foxley driving, muttered another prayer. All mind, eyes, hands, feet concentrated on the road, the ruins, the burning tanks. Then the sensation of the road crumbling underneath, the tank slipping, falling, foot pedals impotent. Into the vast ditch.

Black Watch Donaldson saw the second SP loom through the black haze. Knew the Kangaroo to be the eunuch of armoured warfare, a gunless, empty Sherman body. Saw the imperious 88mm projecting in the gloom. Gave driver the order to charge. A Kangaroo tilting at a rampant rhinoceros. Charged. Smashed into the great enemy vehicle. Two wrecked leviathans slaughtered together. Did not know the SP had already brewed.

Turmoil raged all around. Calamity, cacophony and chaos.

Tides of smoke and floating embers lashing and swirling between the tanks, smothering and suffocating commanders in the turrets. Brewed SPs blazing and spewing forth more carbon fog. Shermans ditched, Shermans prowling, seeking passage. Infantry splashing in flooded ditches. Germans in that house. Black Watch in this. Germans *and* Black Watch in others. Supporting artillery pumping more death into the street. Machine-guns casting random nets of sparkling danger across the scene. And always the hanging veils of blackening smog, the repulsive vapours of cordite fumes and rotting flesh. The steady, dogmatic side-drum beat of the Brownings, the faster irritated rattle of the Brens, and the sinister, ripping-calico crackle of the Spandaus.

Bobby McColl surveyed the chaos about him. Reported back to Hank. Lithe, athletic, bounding with energy, he pushed himself out of the turret. Went down the front of the tank past Don Foxley's periscope. Hit the road running. Aiming himself through the blind oblivion, premature night, towards where the infantry might be.

It was an unaimed, careless, probing burst of Spandau fire which took him. Killed him as he was folded, flayed, flung backwards by the succession, the torrent, the Mach speed of bullets.

Ossie Porter's tank weaved in and out of the maze of vehicles. Ossie, exceptionally tall, was first to see three enemy vehicles. Not 88s but fatal at 10 yards range. 'Gunner, right! Right, right, right. On! SP! Fire!' Double deafening blasts. Boom-crash! 'Gunner, gunner, right again. On! Fire!' Boom-crash. 'Right again ...' Boom-crash. Three SPs alight, above them incendiary red mouths bellowing echoing curses. Hydra-headed armoured serpents, three springing when one was amputated. Death-dealing traffic jammed into a narrow street between high, crumbling houses.

Don Foxley peered over his shoulder into the turret and saw glowing, ruddy fury. Reached up. Pushed open the hatch. Climbed out. Roasting heat from the oven where the turret had been. Hurled himself into the sooty darkness ahead. Headed for the church, the only object higher than the prevailing holocaust. To the church. Crawled under a pew. Don Foxley, strict Baptist not seeking divine protection but simply the refuge of solid walls. Wounded Black Watch men stretched out on pews. Germans in their field grey, stooping and scowling. Civilians huddling tight here, while others, down in cellars, were showered with shrapnel, broken bricks, glass shards, smoke and the gruesome almost tangible smells. Sanctuary!

Sergeant Thompson, up front, tank jammed stuck, but amazingly immune from brewing, kept wireless control. In Ossie's tank, Alf Rushton, star footballer, saw it and exclaimed 'SP! Behind us! Behind us!' No time to traverse, but McKenzie in Ginns's tank behind also saw it. Fired. The muzzle blast from his gun almost blinded Ossie, brazing his cheeks.

Between the two Shermans Hell again opened up its bright red fountains, and the stark, square intruding SP quickly became a white-hot beacon of devilish glory.

No. 3 Troop of C squadron holding the last bottle-neck before the last bridge, but itself equally stuck in that bottle-neck.

No. 3 Troop of B to support, with the doughty Sergeant Lloyd to lead but his operator down with a severe fever. 'Take this new lad, Williams I think his name is,' said the troop leader. 'Over here, boy,' shouted Lloyd, 'How old are you, boy? Look as though you should still be at school.' Driver Wally Tarrant laughed, 'Say that to me and I'll bugger off straight back to school now.'

Lloyd's tank, Nan 3 Able, bowled boisterously along the road to Raamsdonk. 'Nineteen years old, then, what's his name – Williams?' Round a bend into battle murk. And round a bend. And ... blast wrenching at Lloyd's face. A bright whirring projectile boring through the turret wall, smashing the homelite, setting its petrol on fire, spraying young what's-his-name eighteen or nineteen years old with flame, splinters, blast, axe-blow death. And silence.

Lloyd and Stan Hilton levered themselves up past the rising flames, jumped, bounced on engine covers, went to earth. Drivers Wally and Les lifted their flaps, catapulted themselves on to the tank front. 'That door's open over there, Les. At the double!' They plunged across the street. A German stick-grenade, mallet-shaped, hand thrown, planed through the smoke. Hit Les on the head. Tapped Wally on the shoulder. Did not explode. Seemed to follow in their footsteps like a friendly dog. 'Who flung dung?' gasped Les hurtling through the house doorway.

But Sergeant Thompson was going home, ordered out by Hank, Ossie continuing traffic policeman role, back and forwards, Charlie Robertson's Highlanders wading through their ditches and establishing a new tidemark of advance. The enemy had been unable to save Raamsdonk. Other British troops were now safely bypassing the village, bereft of its 88s; and the bridge, the last bolthole from the south, was in sight.

A German commander beyond the bridge saw the approaching tanks and Kangaroos, ordered the blowing of the great bridge, consigned his comrades in North Brabant to British prisoner-of-war cages. Or common graves.

Sergeant Thompson was going back on the rear deck of Ossie Porter's tank. Don Foxley, Wally Tarrant, Stan Hilton, Sergeant Lloyd, Lance-Corporal Knoth would also be going back. Nineteen-year-old-first battle Williams would not, nor would Wall nor Reboles nor some others who would never be recognized as human bodies.

Four hundred Fritzes would surrender around the perimeter of Raamsdonk. Later Hughie McGranahan and his crew sat at ease on their turret, guns vaguely pointing at the mass of prisoners marching past, with half a dozen Highlanders to shepherd them. 'The price of victory,' sighed Hughie. 'See those smiling beggars. They're off to demob. Their war is ended. Nice comfortable billets in England. Plenty of grub. Routine duties. No more killing or dying for them. No more wondering what's round the next bend.'

'I suppose you're right. Put it like that!'

'The price of victory. What do *we* get? A rise of pay? An early release from this man's army? Like hell we do. What I shall get is "Right now, corporal. Stand up nice and straight in the turret so that the *Boche* can see clearly to shoot your bloody head off."'

'You're right. I wouldn't be a commander if they paid me.'

'That's just it. They don't pay you. I'd get a bigger bonus for making the tea in an aircraft factory. Roll on demob. What's for dinner?'

3 NOVEMBER 1944:

Tom Boardman, now wearing the ribbon of the Military Cross, jumped from the jeep which had brought him back from hospital. Colonel Doug greeted him warmly but with a glint in his eye that spelled sinister intentions. 'We are scheduled for another indirect shoot. Line up all fifty tanks by the compass. Range them one by one. Your job! Then fire two hundred rounds each at a large island in the Maas.'

'When is this barrage due, sir?'

'When *could* it happen, but November 5th? "Operation Guy Fawkes", of course. Get those fireworks lined up, Tom.'

5 NOVEMBER 1944:

Troop by troop, some forty-eight available tanks of 1st Northamptonshire Yeomanry lined up near Helvoirt to range on an area where German units were making a last stand on a long island in the Maas. The big Firefly seventeen pounders would be ranging up to 3,500 yards in unseen firing. It was astonishing how silent forty-eight waiting tanks and some four hundred men could be. A family of badgers might have passed along the regimental lines without being frightened off. Then the colonel's voice. 'Hullo, all stations William. Ready? All stations William ... Two hundred rounds ... FIRE!'

If silence had been total, noise was an overwhelming sensation. Noise, a living, moving thing that hammered at the eardrums and thudded on skulls so that, within seconds of the colonel's abrupt 'Fire!', stunned ears were again listening to what seemed total silence. Ears deafened. Giving reason to the order not to give orders. After that 'Fire!' no other orders would have been heard until the long-suffering flesh had adjusted its sensitive organs to distinguish between the thunder-beyond-thunder of the guns and the quiet radio-borne words of commanders.

And the heat from the gun muzzles. The temperature of the open air in front of the tanks rose several degrees within seconds. And smoke there was, the usual terror-bearing, cumulo-nimbus clouds of black, semi-solid particles. Yet the firing was so intense that the flame bore through the smoke which could not dull the stupefying, blinding light of the ultimate day created by the guns. Something like a cabaret of living fire danced back and forward here and there as gun muzzles poured out flash upon flash. Gunners moved like automatons, firing, staring at an empty world, adjusting, aligning, firing again, hands tight on controls, most like coxswains of embattled ships, dashed and wrapped about by fearful tropical storms. Operators slammed huge rounds into narrow breeches, breathed foul smoke from the reopening breeches and loaded again, developing what Ken Squires had forecast as 'the strongest right arms in the West, and not from drinking Guinness'.

'Misfire, 75!'

Rex Jackson heard Tommy Tucker say the word that chilled a tank man more than the advent of a Tiger tank. The operator, failing a second attempt by gunner Butch Burrows to fire the thing, would be drawing the misfire out of the breech, through the turret, to the commander. 'For what we are about to receive ...' Regulations prescribed a period of waiting to see if the round cooked within the barrel. Today there was no time for that. So hand it up to the commander. And down to Rex, who with Stan, was continually lifting up more shells from outside to replace those fired. But what to do? Suicide to leave the misfire amid a stack of more than a hundred live shells. Like a rugby player Stan ran with it to a small depression in the ground and gently laid the misfire there.

And returned to hear on his headset hanging from the hatch: 'Misfire!' And Snowie's voice, irritated, 'You can't be cocking properly.'

Tommy's voice, exasperated, 'Don't tell *me* about cocking. I'm an expert at that.'

And Stan's retort from down below, 'You're the regimental ferking expert on that.' But the bawdy humour was a weak straw of human effort in the face of the human danger, being cuddled in the crew's arms, of *nine* misfires in an unprecedented failure of the gun on their recent replacement tank.

When the barrage eventually died away, with a few irregular bangs from tardy guns, nobody spoke, nobody moved, nobody reported by wireless for an indefinite period which nobody recorded.

Ray Ager, offering his commander, Vaughan Green, a cup of tea noticed that the lieutenant, mainly unoccupied during the shoot like most commanders, had been scribbling some of his poetry on a page of his note-book: 'For we saw the bridges we'd broken ... where the leaf-green river bends, and our tracks raised the dust of our ... passing? ... shelling? ... bombing? ... from the shattered houses of ... FRIENDS!!!'

Later, after Hank Bevan's squadron officers' briefing, old, loveable Dick Bates, senior sergeant and inveterate eavesdropper, whispered urgently to crews, 'We're on the move. We're going to bombard again. But this time it's Germany. Going to bombard blinking Hitler's own perishing Bocheland!'

9–12 NOVEMBER 1944:

It wasn't actually Germany yet.

Dick Bates had not listened closely enough. It was indeed a long-distance move. From a river site close to the North Sea, to an area of Limburg on the opposite side of Holland. As near to Germany as British troops could yet attain. But still ground to be won, villages to be liberated, 88mm guns and mines to be suffered.

And the ground was sodden, swamped, awash from incessant rains. A vast sump of mud across the entire region of the regiment's ordained plan of advance. November was damp. November was dark. November was deadly.

14 NOVEMBER 1944:

At Nederweert B Squadron leader, Philip Wykeham, was discussing with a colonel of the Argyll and Sutherland Highlanders a move to recce lock gates in the mist-wreathed village of Hulzen. 'I'll push Huitson up. He's a cool customer.'

So Sergeant Huitson directed his tank towards the lock with troop leader Vaughan Green in close support. The engineers had appeared on the scene with emergency bridging equipment. Beyond the damaged lock, ¼ mile away, was another dike with a small bridge over it, apparently undamaged. Huitson clambered across the lock on foot and began to stroll towards the second bridge for all the world like a casual hiker crossing by a public footpath.

'Careful of Schu mines,' shouted Vaughan Green. 'Mines, Huitson!

Watch your feet.' Pausing only to wave, Huitson continued on through the mists in his rather spectral adventure.

'Damn me if I'd want to be out there walking,' said Ray Ager to Ken Lyke in the driver's compartment of Green's tank. 'Mines. And Jerry guns behind that bank. And all these dikes and swamps to fall into. Catch me out there?' But Ray's presentiments were unfounded. Huitson walked to the second bridge. Waved encouragement to infantry and engineers. Walked back.

In the gathering dusk in the village street, Ray and Ken slung a large tank sheet from the side of the vehicle to form the customary bivouac. Shorty Coleman lit a stub of candle to give a comforting glow to the tiny shelter. 'Get some tea now, sir?' he called to Vaughan Green. 'At least Jerry has gone home for the day.'

'I must be off to the conference now. Squadron HQ is in the school building over there. Keep a mug of tea for me, Shorty.' An ex-schoolmaster, he picked up his map case and began to walk across the school yard. In the schoolroom hefty Captain Sandy Saunders looked through the window to see if Vaughan Green was coming. He heard the whoosh, as of a high speed railway train.

Shorty Coleman, in the bivouac, saw the candle flicker and go out.

Vaughan Green saw something drop between his feet, as a football might. The world turned red. Unbearable light. A massive sledgehammer shape of flame, edged with hard, sharp daggers, thrashed up from the ground, hewed and bludgeoned through the soft flesh, and smashed the delicate brain.

Shorty looked out of the bivouac. Saw a torso flung to the ground. Screamed. 'Ken, get out there. Vaughan's had it ... bugger the bloody *Boche*', and he himself was running without thinking, bending down without comprehending, recoiling without wishing to. Ken Lyke, a fast mover, was inches behind him. 'Stay here, Ken. See what you can do. I'll go find somebody ...' 'Much good will it do,' exclaimed Ken, limbs suddenly totally refusing to move.

Sandy Saunders came at the gallop, shouting, 'Oh, my God! Oh, my God! Get a blanket somebody and cover him. Cover what you can. Why Vaughan? I must go find Captain Rathbone. They were schoolmasters together. He'll be devastated. They are almost like brothers ... *were* ...!'

15 NOVEMBER 1944:

Dawn, next day, shed tears. But they were the ethereal tears of mist and rain which seemed to have been dampening and flooding this land for an eternity. Landmarks merged into an inconstant murk. Measured advances might have been impossible but for the aid of the local Dutch Resistance.

Bill Fox, renowned for his interpretation of foreign names, looked at the map, looked up at David Bevan and grinned. 'Heitheuzen! How does one pronounce such damnable words. But next it's Neer. Not far, hey? Near! And Sergeant Warren is back. Chafing at the bit.'

Warren's troop motored at top speed, all guns blazing, like some rein-carnated Wild West posse. And the Germans, ever elusive, decided that honour was satisfied. Retreated to somewhere 'not so near', as Bill Fox reported. Concentrated on dropping odd shells and clusters of bombs on places where troops might be in bivouac or lieutenants might be walking to conferences.

As the sodden days continued, and the Northants Yeomanry forced a route through towards Helden, everyone from colonel down made frequent efforts to raise morale by the use of wireless witticisms when the entire regiment might be listening in. Sergeant Jack, again up front, one of his tasks being to contact the Dutch Resistance, radioed, 'Hullo, Sugar 6. I have made contact with the chief of the Underground.'

'Good!' replied the HQ voice, 'take a ticket for Victoria on the Circle Line', so helping to cheer another weary mile through the rain.

18 NOVEMBER 1944:

Wally Tarrant and Les Redgrove were still nursing bumps they had received from flying hand-grenades in Raamsdonk, still thanking their lucky stars. Sergeant Lloyd was an efficient commander so when they found themselves in lead position, and creeping along the edge of a wood in thick mist and driving rain, they were not unduly worried. 'If we can't see the buggers, odds are they can't see us,' commented Wally.

Each periscope turning and probing they scanned the line of trees, and the fields beyond, looking always for the shape or movement which did not belong to nature. Where they did *not* look, could not look, was where the infantry always *did* look: at the ground men must tread on.

The tank seemed to jump in the air and something like a huge wave of fire and smoke gushed up from the ground even before the mighty grumble of explosion assaulted their ears. Wally and Les were, as they put it, 'kicked solidly up the ass'. The 30-ton tank shivered and shuddered so that the crew were flung about as though in a cocktail shaker. Sharp steel edges acted as scalpels and rounded iron corners served for bludgeons. With a crunch that almost turned the body to jelly the tank settled back on solid earth.

'What in hell … ?' shouted someone in the sudden quiet.

Wally looked down. Two wide fissures had appeared as though someone with a power saw had been trying to saw a way through the floor beneath his seat. Multicoloured snakes of flame and smuts slithered through the cracks. Wally opened his hatch and took a sudden, violent fit of shaking as he saw vicious-looking, squat, round mines spread all along the edge of the trees. 'How are we going to walk through that lot? It'll be like those Indian magicians that walk on hot coals or jagged glass.'

'Be far hotter than that if this tank brews. Let's go. And watch where you're treading,' said Lloyd.

21 NOVEMBER 1944:

Vaughan Green's discouraged crew had inherited a new commander. Corporal Dave Bucke had served through much of the desert fighting against Rommel. Now through the jolting processes of the reinforcement system he had moved in six months from Cairo to England to Holland, to army, to corps, to divisional reserve, and now to regiment. 'You'll find us a helpful lot,' said Shorty Coleman as they briefly shook hands all round.

Ray Ager started up and the Sherman moved off. Five minutes along the road and it was evident that this day was to be no walk-over as they assaulted Helden. Mortar bombs began to fall on the infantry. Shells roared overhead.

Ten minutes along the road, a black, sharp missile rushed across the fields, slammed into the tank and brewed the usual blast furnace out of the front armour. 'Bale out!' and Dave Bucke was crouching with the others behind the tank. Until the conflagration sent out grilling heat which drove them into a convenient ditch.

'Bugger that,' complained Dave. 'Six bloody months to get here. One sodding day in command. Ten flaming minutes of battle. And then it really is a flaming, blasted-open Sherman. Would you credit it?'

23 NOVEMBER 1944:

Tall, even-tempered Jack Pentelow of A Squadron had been 'unhorsed' by a hand-held bazooka which had blown up his tank, causing the crew to scurry for the nearest ditch. They were at the sharp end of a salient 3 miles deep into the German lines and on this misty day it was difficult to know which way was north and which way south. The battle had gone silent for a moment and, taking advantage of every bit of cover, they trudged back with no clear sense of direction.

Pushing through trees they almost bumped into two men walking towards them. Germans! Before Jack could draw his Smith and Wesson revolver, the Germans had casually raised their hands, turned around and fallen into step with the tank men. No words spoken. Almost without breaking step. Surrendered. 'Cripes!' muttered Jack to his lads, 'have you ever seen two such scarecrows in uniform? Plenty of medals too.'

Without warning the two Fritzes jumped into the nearest ditch. Jack jerked up his revolver but tearing, shrieking bombs, horrid Moaning Minnies, hurtled out of the rain clouds and spewed up mud, splinters, flame. Jack and the others jumped on top of the Germans. Jack muttered again, 'They heard what we didn't ... and long before us. Old soldiers.'

Twice more the Germans precipitately went to earth. And the tank lads went with them, Jack shouting 'Dive!' after they were all down. The 'Germans' were gabbling away in some tongue afflicted by the curse of Babel. Jack had an idea. 'Ruskies? Russia? You? *Wehrmacht*? You Ruskieland. Stalin – boom-boom?'

The 'Germans' nodded, faces wizened, gaunt, filthy, expressionless. One held up three fingers. '*Ja! Russland! Drei! Drei Jahren! Hitler kaput!*'

'*Ja*, old boy. Hitler will be. Hitler *kaput*.'

24 NOVEMBER 1944:

Lieutenant-Colonel Doug Forster was momentarily deaf. The intelligence officer, Lieutenant A.J.Owen, was temporarily bereft of his senses. In a frail scout car they had driven over a German mine charged to destroy a 30-ton tank. The car was hurled into the air, a ruin of scrap metal. Colonel and lieutenant were flung bodily away, arms flailing, to land on sodden earth. The regiment paused in awe at the news that the colonel had been hit again, remembering that awful day, 8 August 1944.

But here in Holland the regiment suddenly, for the first time, blessed the rain. The swilling, seeping, saddening, insistent rain synonymous with Limburg. For the colonel had landed at jet speed, with full force of his big-muscled body – on soft, swampy ground. Owen too.

The MO, Captain MacIntyre, himself experienced in suffering wounds, tried to persuade the colonel to go back down the line. 'No, Mac, I'll be all right. Don't send me down. I'll obey doctor's orders. Lord George can carry on.'

What bothered the colonel most was: he had lost his pipe.

25 NOVEMBER 1944:

Ken Ward, driving a leading tank just as he had done up the solid main street of Helden, surveyed the sea of brown paste ahead. Nobody, no tank man particularly, liked driving into an enemy town with all the perils of street fighting. But Ken wished he was back in Helden, oh, and with those Dutch citizens venturing out with flowers, wine, cheese and kisses. Not in this limitless, directionless, uninhabited wilderness where the tank continually dipped and swayed as though about to tip and sink into bottomless depths. Tanks had been known to sink into unstable soil.

Flail tanks, the sure deliverers from mines, were ahead, sunk into the earth, their great rusty chains still beating unsuccessfully at the yielding ground, their tracks churning and driving the heavy vehicles deeper and deeper into clinging, all-conquering mud. The squadron recovery tank had come up to tow another Sherman out of a bad slough. Now the recovery tank itself was slowly sinking.

'Halt!' said Ken's commander. Unnecessarily. More potent conditions had already enforced the halt. Engines switched off to listen for any enemy sounds. There were none. Only the wireless crackled and whispered. A loud voice came from HQ suddenly, critically, jovially.

'Hullo, all stations Yoke. Your guns are now pointing into Germany. Anywhere beyond two thousand yards is Deutschland. You are welcome to fire at random ten rounds 75 each. At Hitler's country. Give 'em hell!'

27 NOVEMBER 1944:

A move back to West Holland. 'Hope to God it has stopped raining over there!' Tanks had been driven onto long, sturdy railway 'flats' near Helden. Crews sat on turrets and watched the countryside go by.

Now everybody switched radios to Lord Haw-Haw, the British turncoat broadcasting Nazi propaganda, and sat back for the comedy of obvious lies. 'Jar-meny calling,' pealed the snide voice. 'On the borders of Jar-meny, the famous Highland Division' – tank men now sitting bolt upright on turrets – 'have gained a few thousand yards, with the aid of a fanatical armoured division.'

'Fanatical armoured division? Oh, my God, listen to that!' All along the train tank men clung to turret flaps, rolling about in agonies of laughter, tears welling from their eyes. 'O, my God! Fanatical? Colonel Doug and RSM George? Hank and old Bill Fox? Fanatics? And Spud and Wally and Sergeant Jack and Rex? This Yeomanry shower? Oh, my God! Give him a medal. Good old Lord Haw-Haw, OBE.'

10 White Hell Christmas

29 NOVEMBER 1944:

Gusts of hilarity had seemed to propel the train all the way to Roosendaal. Hilarity subsided somewhat when the arrival of the grounded tanks at appointed billets coincided with the advent of lorries bringing gallons of paint for refurbishing unmilitary-looking battle tanks. Troops were located in Leur or Hoeven or Rucphen. And as local children, learning the meaning of liberty, thronged around the fascinating Shermans, the news came through, 'We're here for Christmas. A month's rest. Go on leave to Antwerp. Arrange Christmas parties for the kids. The quartermaster is dressing up as Santa Claus. Extra rum ration all round.'

Still unpacking, Spud Taylor looked up and saw a shape speeding past the village church spire. 'Look, chaps! What kind of plane is that? It nearly hit the church steeple.'

'Plane?' guffawed Sergeant Danny Danson. 'That was a buzz bomb. A V1. Flying bomb. The Jerries are still up north, loosing off those things. And V2s. Pity the poor buggers in London on the receiving end. Here they're just part of the scenery.'

1 DECEMBER 1944:

Hank's operator, Ken Squires was reclining on the ground with kindred spirits like Harry Graham and Hughie McGranahan, planning to resurrect the concert party. They were already scribbling notes about funny acts which would be comprehensible only to troopers. The regimental Christmas concert for local kids would have to be of a different variety.

Ken was making a list of candidates for a squadron orchestra. 'I've always got my accordion on the SQMS truck. Harry Swift will play the pye-anner, pupil of Charlie Kunz and all that. Locke on his clarinet. Bunny Hare keeps a trumpet in his scout car. All we want now is somebody that knows the National Anthem.'

3 DECEMBER 1944:

Leave! For the first time since landing on the beaches just after D-Day leave was available to all. For some it would be a week back in Britain. For the majority a brief but wonderful forty-eight hours pass to Brussels or Antwerp. Rotas would be determined not by who was on the squadron leader's most favoured list but by fair drawing of lots. Staying in Roosendaal area until after Christmas there would be time for everybody to go.

Spud Taylor's name came up for Antwerp. So did Shorty Coleman's. And Danny Danson's. And, among the officers, Sandy Saunders. A 'liberty truck' was available, a euphemism for a slow, doddering lorry from the echelon for troopers to travel uncomfortably on its bare boards. But bare boards could not dampen the enthusiasm, delight and frivolity of the selected first few.

7 DECEMBER 1944:

Captain Sandy Saunders was aware that, with his strong build, light curly hair, and pink cheeks, he had an advantage with the girls. The officer's tunic was no drawback either. At the reception desk in the hotel, reserved for officers, he encountered a chattery, middle-aged, not unattractive woman who impressed him as rather a delightful old stick. Later, walking past Sandy's table, she stopped, smiled. 'Alone?'

'Yes. And glad to be. Seen too many people lately. Dead friends. Live bloody *Boche*.'

'I thought you might like to escort me. You're a big man. I have several visits to make and they involve cash. Terrible things happen on the streets of Brussels now. Especially to women. I always like a guard if I can get one.'

'Why not?' thought Sandy. 'Seems a decent old Dutch.' And aloud, 'One Northamptonshire Yeoman at your service, Madam!'

They marched off down the street. She paused at a club door. Spoke to an attendant. Collected a small parcel. Dropped it into her large bag. On again. Another club. Another parcel. Several British infantrymen were brutally punching and stamping on two American soldiers while military police came running, blowing whistles. Sandy strolled gallantly on with his companion. At the next stop the girl on the door was scantily dressed and excessively painted. But she had a packet of cash ready. Drunken soldiers slept in doorways, or staggered along bumping into people, or stood in alleyways urinating.

Sandy escorted the woman back into the hotel, he always an officer and a gentleman, she always a strict lady. Her bag bulged with packages. She thanked him, smiled and departed. Sandy turned to the man at the reception desk. 'Strange lady that. What does she do? Collect insurance?'

'You could call it that,' said the receptionist. 'Actually she is the madam of all the local brothels. Goes round every night collecting her percentage. Nice person. Of course, she never does it herself.'

9–11 DECEMBER 1944:

The liberty truck was spilling Yeomen off in the centre of Antwerp. A flurry of plans ensued. 'Anybody for the flicks? What's on? Is the local beer any good? Where do we go for girls? Is there a Sally Anne canteen?'

Time passed quickly. Tommy T. had asked a policeman and headed straight for a house of girls. Danny Danson was going to a cinema. 'Chance to sit down in comfort. A film. A soft seat. A choc-ice. And plenty of fags.'

'What's showing?' asked Shorty Coleman. 'A cowboy film and an Al Capone gangster feature? I've seen enough gangsters in field-grey uniforms these last few weeks. And done enough range riding to last me for life. For me, a nice quiet bar – no bangs or wireless messages or shouting sergeants – lead me there and lean me up.'

Two nights passed. Propped against the now familiar bar Shorty thought that somebody had slammed him against the bar. Unused to the extremely strong Belgian beer he turned and demanded, 'Did one of you beggars just punch me?' A trooper beside him responded, 'I thought *you* punched *me*.'

Danson and a young trooper were again in the Rex cinema. Sit well back on the cushions! Let the music flow! This was heaven after so many weeks and days and minutes and seconds of sheer hell. The Broadway musical strummed on. Elegant chorus-girls danced across the screen. Then something interrupted. Something foreign. A sound high-pitched and fearsome. A new radiant whirling on the screen which was not dancing. And the screen rending, like the veil of the Temple, allowing furies to speed and scream out of Broadway and down into the audience, stabbing with red-hot skewers and coughing flame. Brief, sudden, dying impressions. Then the darkness.

The V2 missile had plummeted down directly behind the screen and burst its fuse on the stage floor, sending its tremendous force of steel splinters and blast and seething heat, down through the auditorium, lacerating, asphyxiating, roasting open-mouthed watchers by the hundred. Then the roof fell in.

To Shorty Coleman the imperative thought was that forty-seven hours fifty minutes had transpired. As he and Tommy T. and other Yeomen hurried to where the liberty truck must be waiting they saw a commotion of people, a pyre of blazing buildings, running policemen, sirens in the distance. A bomb? Or a V2?

The unlucky corporal in charge of the truck scratched names off his list. 'Did any of you sods bring back a bottle of decent beer for us workers? Or some fags? Now, that's only two people missing. Sergeant Danson. Anybody know him? And ... can't read my own writing ... Trooper Blakiston? Any bugger seen 'em? Sorry! Strict orders not to wait. Driver, advance!'

'Danson?' said Shorty. 'Danny Danson? Didn't he go to the cinema? And wasn't that the cinema that was on fire. Must have been a V2 ... that slammed me against that bar too.'

16 DECEMBER 1944:

For days Danson was missing. And Blakiston. Days to dig and scrabble in the ashes of the cinema and find identity discs. Days before the regiment could, with certainty, add to the Roll of Honour two Yeomen done to death in the innocent peace of an Antwerp cinema.

Doug Gardner was, however, back from his travels, an ingrowing toenail finally rectified. 'You won't believe it,' he told his story again and again. 'At the aid post they said "Want your leg chopped off we can do it here and now. But not ingrowing toenails. Too complicated." So back to Brussels. A label for UK. Loaded into a 1930 vintage bomber. To Scotland. I reckon they took me two thousand miles past hundreds of hospitals. In civvy street I could have walked down the street to the hospital. Out with the nail. A day or two's rest. I bet our own MO could have done it himself here outside the tank. No wonder we're so long winning the blooming war.'

19 DECEMBER 1944:

Brian Carpenter was also back from hospital. And looking forward to an ENSA concert. But the sergeant-major called him, 'Time you did a guard, lad, now you're fit and well.' So Brian disconsolately watched the ENSA group arrive, two males and two lovely girls. He and his mate prowled their route, passing and re-passing the little hall where voices crackled in laughter and a girl's voice soared like a skylark.

A flashing of lights, a burst of frenzied activity, and a corporal from HQ Squadron was running towards them. 'Report to the guard commander. We're moving. The regiment's moving.'

'But we're supposed to be here till Christmas. What's the matter? Has Jerry invaded England at last?'

'Worse than that. The American front line has collapsed. Von Runstedt's broken through. It's crisis ... crisis ... crisis ...' and shouting these words he burst into the hall where the comedian was capering about.

At RHQ things were near to panic. Hank Bevan and Tom Boardman had gone to Paris with the brigadier himself. Lesser fry were indulging in the delights of Antwerp, or sitting in local Dutch houses, promising the kids a Christmas such as none of them had ever seen. But now, whoever was left, it was pack up, load, test gun controls, start engines. And face SOUTH. The war had gone into reverse gear.

20 DECEMBER 1944:

Dawn. Target hour. Yeomen arriving back, befuddled, full of the joys of life, Belgian beer and Brussels brothels. Enough tanks lined up but not enough crews to be fully operational yet. And the regiment knowing that German armour had punched through a weak American line in the Ardennes: 'just about level with our strategic backsides', as one of the Yeomanry officers put it, 'and von Runstedt has got a red-hot poker ready to shove up our arses.'

21 DECEMBER 1944:

'Let's make a book on the mileage,' said someone as the regiment started out, along narrow, twisting roads, and bumping into other convoys, and suffering the concertina effect of halting and starting. At dusk Brian Carpenter's speedo said 86 miles, and the trooper who had bet on 50 miles had the nearest guess.

Sergeant-Major Farnham boisterously hurried over to Rex Jackson as he was climbing stiffly out of 3 Baker. 'You speak French, laddo? Come with me. You can say "Mercy" and "San Fairy Ann" and all that twaddle.'

'Ça ne fait rien! What do you want me to do?'

'Trans-a-bleeding-late, laddo. For your uncle SSM who's going to find us all nice comfy billets.' Farnham knocked like a policeman at doors, and Rex repeated the phrase he had worked out. 'Nous sommes anglais. Nous demandons un lieu pour dormir. Peut-etre le garage.'

'Mercy buckets,' chirped the SSM and allocated Rex, Hickie and Snowie a large house. But when they hoisted bedding rolls and made to go into the garage, their hosts barred the way. 'No, no! In the house. You are our guests. To the bedrooms.'

After a superficial wash, but feeling unbearably filthy, they descended to find a dining-table laid with gleaming silver and sparkling cut glass. As they ate, their hosts explained, 'Only yesterday we dug up from the garden boxes of china and cutlery hidden when the Germans came. And we are glad to provide you a good dinner table because, for the past years, we have had to entertain you poor English with bad food, cheap china and hurried meals.'

'How do you mean?' asked Snowie, pausing in his enjoyment of delicious soup. 'Past years? Entertaining English? There weren't any English here?'

'Ah! Many English. Some Americans. Polish. French. Escaping after their planes shot down. We had safe houses. A shot-down airman was brought here. Stayed one day, two days. Then away, we never knew where or when. To Spain, we think.'

23 DECEMBER 1944:

Hank Bevan roused Bill Fox in their billet. 'Word just come through. We are forming the final line between von Runstedt and Brussels. And where? On the Field of Waterloo, no less! Even Monty cannot better Wellington's ideas.'

Soon Yeomanry officers were strolling across the old battlefield, flicking their riding crops and tracing Wellington's movements. 'Did you know that our regimental badge, the White Horse of Hanover, was worn at Waterloo by the 17th Regiment of German Hussars?'

Other troopers were less romantic on that field, where the snow was now bringing its warning of further icy sufferings to come, when the tanks would convert from summer ovens into winter refrigerators. 'What the hell were the Yanks doing, letting the Jerries through the Ardennes, anyway? Jerry came through that way in 1940, didn't he?'

'I blame the American generals,' commented Tommy Tucker, confounding the conversation with his usual piece of non-logic. 'Some of those five star generals couldn't play a trombone in Glenn Miller's band!'

24 DECEMBER 1944:

Von Runstedt, Montgomery and others did not share the vision of a second Waterloo, so it was on and on endlessly through the worsening snow, towards Namur in a total vacuum of defences. But the mail had come up and Alf Rushton had a parcel. Always popular, he was now THE most popular person as he opened up a pie, biscuits, chocolate, a thousand cigarettes, sent by a girlfriend of one of the lads now in hospital in Blighty; and a Christmas cake!

He laughed, 'Happy Christmas and "When the snow lay round about" and all that!'

To which Hughie McGranahan added, 'Bugger me, yes, it's Christmas Eve, ain't it?'

25 DECEMBER 1945:

Christmas Day, at the traditional hour of banquet, the 1st Northants Yeomanry were moving on. Don Foxley, on the replacement Helmdon tank since Bobby McColl's death, sat on the outside while the snow continued to fall, Christmas card fashion; his midday meal a doorstep slice of bread spread with jam, his drink a mug of cold, thick unsweetened cocoa. He thought, 'Well, at least I can whistle a carol. How about "In the Bleak Midwinter"?'

Spud Taylor thought of the children back near Roosendaal who would not get that Christmas party for which he and others had been plotting. Now, as the tank rolled at an average 10 miles an hour, he noticed that civilians were no longer waving but were looking apprehensively up the road to Namur, wondering if the blitz of panzers would again roll along this road as in 1940.

Jack Pentelow, 'rehorsed', leading the advance, halted at the entrance to Florennes aerodrome, his objective. The American Air Force commander came running to the gate, jumped on the tank, and shouted, 'Jeez! Am I glad to see you guys. If I had a million dollars I'd give it you.'

'What's happening here, sir? Where are your own troops?'

'They ain't no troops, brother. Zero! Zilch! I've sent my Black Widows away, mounted their guns around the perimeter, and put air crew in foxholes as infantry. I've got enough ammunition for two minutes pree-cisely. One hundred and twenty seconds pree-cisely. Any wonder I'm pleased to see you guys? Come and let's celebrate with Jack Daniels.'

'Jack Daniels, sir? Who's he?'

'Oh, you wouldn't know. That's our Tennessee whisky. Sour mash. Good stuff. Better than this local "gin-eever".'

As often happened, RSM George Jelley, officially rear echelon, was up front ready to take charge of any action that did not involve direct tank shooting. Florennes village was deserted, except for an elderly man crossing the street. George halted his scout car. 'Are you English? Or who?' stuttered the man.

'English as they make 'em.'

'Thank God for that. We didn't know who to expect.' And insisted that George billet at *his* house that night. Later George noticed the man quietly unpacking a case and explaining, 'We didn't know if the Germans would come back. I was a Resistance leader and if they had come back, well ...' and he drew his finger across his throat.

Michael Rathbone was also looking for billets. As he trudged in deep snow towards a chateau he overtook a stately woman, well dressed, wearing a veil, and carrying a small, black religious book, obviously returning from Christmas Mass. Hearing his mission she said, 'You can stay with us.'

'Seven officers, nineteen tanks, about a hundred tank crew. Plus fitters, medics, and so on?'

'Oh, yes. Large house. Rows of empty loose-boxes. No horses now. Large courtyard. Barns. And as many logs as you like to warm you. Come in and we'll talk to my husband, the count, who will, no doubt, want to invite you to a wild boar hunt.'

The cooks had reacted quickly to the general panic to find quarters. The Jack Arises and Harry Claridges lit huge log fires, unpacked what stores they had been able to bring from their Christmas hoarding and, by midnight, were serving Christmas dinner. No crackers, no decorations, no bands, no dancing, no girls. But FOOD. And SNOW.

Later, having shaken snow from boots and got bedded on clean straw, Roy Clarke was awakened by local girls, smiling but shy, bringing jugs of hot milk, fresh, creamy, warming. Roy saw them through faltering eyelids. War, travel, cold had reduced lusty troopers to a state of bedraggled weariness, where they could hardly rouse to drink the welcome milk, let alone indulge in any other activity which might be suggested by the appearance of girls!

26 DECEMBER 1944:

Ploughing on, literally, through deep snow at the pace of a slow plough-horse.

27 DECEMBER 1944:

Rex Jackson was summoned to the squadron leader's tank, wondering what he had done wrong. 'Ah, *Corporal* Jackson,' said Hank, grinning, 'Good man! I wanted you to be first to know: you've been awarded the Military Medal and promoted for your action at Loon-op-Zand. You can put the ribbon up straight away. The QM has a stock of ribbons.'

The way ahead was now a potential battlefield. Almost a no-man's-land. But Corporal Jackson, MM, did not fire at the first thing he saw moving. It was a very aged Belgian man, pushing a loaded pram and trying to cross the road between tanks. Even well-designed Shermans were sometimes clumsy vehicles and, trying to swivel on snow and ice to avoid the old man, one of the tanks caught the pram, flung it across the road into a ditch, emptying its contents, leaving the wizened Belgian standing as though unseeing, unfeeling, frozen solid physically and mentally.

RSM Jelley leading a small convoy was halted by a hunched figure in a hooded sheepskin coat and scarf standing in deep snow. Using his best parade-ground voice, he bawled 'Get out of the bloody way there. Who do you think you are?'

'You cannot go through. The road is cut ahead. Turn around.'

'I'll find my own way, roads cut or not,' roared George.

At that moment a captain came running along the road, pointing meaningfully at the man arrayed like an Eskimo, who responded mildly, 'What are you? 1NY? RSM? You must be Jelley. Heard of you. Dismount, please. I want you to stop everything. Everything, d'you hear? Turn 'em round. Good man. Hold the fort.'

As the Eskimo figure turned and headed for a jeep, George caught the sleeve of the staff captain. 'Who on earth is he, sir? I must know in case people question my orders. Can't see his badges. Major? Colonel?'

'General! GOC 51st Highland Division himself. General Rennie. Cock of the walk for miles around here. Day you've waited for all your life, sarn't-major. You can order them all. Colonels. Even brigadiers if they appear. Not to mention piddling little staff captains,' he laughed, running after the jeep.

31 DECEMBER 1944:

Ever onward, through an empty world of billowing snow and thickening ice, Wally Tarrant was weary of constant low-gear advance, but commented, 'You know, Les, at least it's better than Raamsdonk. No hand grenades hitting you on the head.'

The column halted as lead tanks viewed suspicious corners. Moved on. Wally automatically followed but there was a shuddering and grinding as of a monstrous mincing machine chewing up iron bars. The tank slewed in the snow. Then sank rather wearily on one side. 'Blast! We've shed a bloody track!'

To the derisory cheers of other crews churning past, Wally, Les and mates clambered out, sinking deep into the treacherous Christmas snows, and began the heavy, perilous, time-consuming task of re-linking the viciously sprung track, the nightmare of every tank driver even when not a recipe for frost-bitten fingers as well as frozen, broken toes.

1 JANUARY 1945:

Celebrations? The regiment was moving into a land of delirium. A place of frozen suffering compared with which the gentle rains of Limburg seemed positively benign. A region where blankets of hanging snow and sheets of frozen fog hampered vision. A terrain for which tanks had never been designed. A purgatory of bitter cold which, intensified by living in unheated iron containers, could have been thought intolerable to human flesh, even without the fear and rage of battles ahead.

2 JANUARY 1945:

Johnny Taylor had driven his Honey tank up a long icy slope with Wilf Mylan commanding it in the brigadier's absence. Snow had become hard packed under pressure of tracks and in places had turned to solid slides of ice.

'Hold on,' yelled Johnny, 'We're going down!' The tank whirled around, almost in its own length, adjusted itself and went weaving down the slope. Faster. Faster. Too fast. Becoming a toboggan, ice screeching under locked tracks, chill air shrilling around Wilf's ears, child's play of sleighs and sledges. Fun?

A lorry, caught in the same ice trap, began to skid straight across in front of the tank, now bearing down on it like a dive bomber. Hitting the truck at incalculable speed. Smashing through it. Crushing the back of it. Reaching the bottom of the slope. Crashing into trees and deep impeding snowdrifts.

Back up the slope, behind the cab of the truck looked like a large collapsed tent. The cab still stood intact with the shocked driver vacuously holding the steering wheel.

Harboured for the night in arctic open country, Bill Higham and George Smith had removed frozen boots and were sitting on the tank toasting their toes over the hot rear exhaust vent. Swayed by weariness and welcome warmth Bill was nodding to sleep. Until an agonized squeal woke him from his opium state. George had roused to find his socks on fire.

3 JANUARY 1945:

Phil Wilkinson was one of the echelon sergeants with the gruesome task of loading up trucks with metal ammunition boxes like blocks of ice, then trying to find a way, in total night, to a cross on a map. Even wireless messages were unable to identify the precise locations of forward troops in a desert of unidentifiable snowdrifts. The only hope was to find an inhabited hole in the snow at which to enquire from infantry who might point a blunt, gloved mitt to where the tanks would most likely be.

And, on arrival at last at some God-forsaken spot in the wilds, their only thanks would likely be, 'Where have you buggers been all night? We're sitting here freezing, while you cushy lot are back there smoking all the spare fags.' And then the journey back to a spot almost as unidentifiable as the tank lines.

4 JANUARY 1945:

The Shermans were now meeting the foremost feelers of the Germans' dramatic life or death drive for the North Sea. Orders were to 'brass up' all suspicious cover where enemy reconnaissance might be sheltering. In Normandy the skilful handling of their cumbersome charges had enabled crews to evade many an anti-tank shot. But not here.

On frozen downhill stretches the machines chose their own route, their own speed, their own destiny, skidding, swerving, sliding, speeding. Drivers hung on to controls and hoped. Commanders prepared to jump. The rest of the crew ran alongside, often in peril from the swaying hulk, throwing logs, rocks, and any old objects in front of the churning tracks, trying to get some kind of grip on the ice. And then crash, halt, shudder, adjust and blast the visible countryside with cannon fire.

6 JANUARY 1945:

'I'll never go to another blinking fairground or the dodgems, however long I live,' moaned George Smith as they helter-skeltered downwards somewhere in the forest near Waritzy. 'Who would pay when we've got all the thrills of an aeroplane crashing or a racing car going over the banking at Brooklands?'

'I think we've seen it all,' agreed Bill Higham. But they hadn't. A tremendous thud under the driver's seat stopped the huge machine dead, throwing them all around the tiny space. A tower of flame merged into a vast red-tinted cloud of soft snow, rising as on the wings of a gale and hovering like a gargantuan ghost over the tank. 'Let us out,' yelled George, 'we're trapped down here. The gun is over the hatch. Traverse for God's sake.'

Bill Higham found that the power had died out of the traverse system. Desperately he flung himself on the hand traverse handle, slow, so slow to move, expecting the tank to go up in cremation fire any moment. Then the gun came level. Hatches opened. Bodies leaped out. Bill followed commander and operator out through crackling flames.

'A mine,' said George. 'Right underneath me. I expected to find me sliced in half.'

'Wireless has gone phut. Can't call for help. It's coming on a blizzard that will cover our tracks. We'll freeze to death. Better get back in, use extinguishers and hope the fire doesn't spread. But then we might be a sitting duck for any Jerries with 88s.'

George was decisive, 'Let's get in. Me, I'd rather be a sitting duck than a frozen turkey.'

8 JANUARY 1945:

Thirty-seven degrees of frost and 20 feet of snow made fighting or any movement difficult.

Sergeant Huitson was now commanding a troop, owing to the constant drain of officers killed or wounded. One of his tanks had plunged into a snowdrift amid intermittent German firing. Huitson had his own tank driven near to the ditched tank. With his own co-driver he unhitched their tow rope, dragged it to the sunk tank and linked it on.

'Now go back to our tank,' he ordered. 'Tell the driver when I raise my arm, to take the strain. If I drop my arm, stop. OK?' The co-driver waded back through flurries of snow, in that grim murk a figure like Captain Oates going out into polar oblivion. Sergant Huitson raised his arm.

Two things happened. His own tank revved up into a thunder of acceleration prior to taking the strain of the other tank's weight. But over that noise there soared first the sudden demonic shrieking of falling mortar bombs. Then the group of thudding explosions. One batch. Two batches. Three batches right among the tanks.

His arm still raised Sergeant Huitson performed what looked like a classic gymnastic backward roll. He did not get up. The pure snow around his body was spattered with even purer red blood, and then sullied by the fall of smoking splinters, carbonized shards and charred rags of clothing.

That night guards were instructed to start up every tank at each two-hour change of guard to prevent engines from freezing. Stan Hilton was on radio watch in the early hours at what seemed the peak of the Ice Age. His mother had sent him some wax night-lights to enable him to read in his bivouac. Now Stan lit them to warm his feet in the glacial turret. Not funny, for next morning he heard that three night operators were being evacuated in an ambulance with severely frostbitten feet.

9 JANUARY 1945:

Percy Sumner, his face still speckled with tiny black splinters, bent down in the snow, with frozen fingers, to lace up ice-solid boots. The laces disintegrated into tiny brittle shreds.

Captain Sandy Saunders was approached near Lignieres by a Resistance man with a strange look of horror on his face, and seemingly broken in spirit. 'Thirty-four,' the man was repeating. 'Thirty-four.'

'Thirty-four what?' enquired Sandy, to be greeted by repetition, 'Thirty-four, thirty-four ...' as the man led him down into a cellar. Sandy came fully alert because of the smell. Sweet, putrefying, all-pervading stench. He covered his nose. He wished he could have decently covered his eyes.

Bodies lay in the cellar. Civilians. In ordinary clothes. All pitched into a great, untidy obscene heap. All only recently dead. All bearing the burning and ripping marks of machine-gunning. Difficult to count. A dozen? Twenty? Then Sandy understood. THIRTY-FOUR.

Unable to walk away, though repelled, the big captain looked closer. Each man had also been shot cleanly through the head by a pistol, as well as being machine-gunned. Sandy was too physically shocked, petrified, even to be sick.

10 JANUARY 1945:

At least one Yeoman, favoured by the destinies of war, was celebrating his twenty-first birthday in the warm, surrounded by loved ones in a hospital in England. Spud Taylor was soldiering on and had left his tank for purposes to which all Yeomen yielded sooner or later. Hearing the ominous sound of Moaning Minnies Spud tried to hitch up his trousers quickly, then heard the familiar sound of a freak, jagged chunk of self-propelled shrapnel, adequate to amputate exposed oddments of the body, speeding towards him. He threw himself over a mound in the snow.

He had landed in a tiny infantry trench and speared himself on a Black Watch bayonet. Strangely he felt no pain. The Highlander and Spud cautiously effected a separation of bayonet and leg. To find that the knife-sharp point had lodged in the big front leg pocket of his thermal overalls.

Joe Watkinson, driving Bill Fox's tank, had a moustache like two tiny golden bayonets projecting one on either side of his stubby nose, giving him a look of fierceness only justified if the regiment's fame was impugned in some rowdy pub. He turned to co-driver Kemp and said, 'I've seen them at last. What I've always been looking for. A pair of German officer's boots. Over there. By that body.'

Captain Fox being elsewhere and Harry Swift commanding for the moment, Joe jumped out of the tank. Kemp watched him stride through the snow, pick up the boots, stroke them. Then come back to the tank. Lean over Kemp's hatch. Drop the boots in. Kemp stroked the boots. Admired them. Stared. Stood up, head out of the hatch. And was sick.

'Joe, you rotten so-and-so. Didn't you look inside these boots? They've still got feet in them. Blown-off feet. And frozen solid.'

11 JANUARY 1945:

Tanks were moving through touristic scenery into the pretty, central town of La Roche. Much of the town was in ruins, having been liberated, reoccupied and liberated again. Sergeant Lloyd's tank was ordered to halt outside the Hotel de Liège, only to find a war photographer already there waiting for a picture of tanks.

The hotel was unoccupied and so Wally Tarrant had the idea of borrowing some bed sheets. 'Sheets no good this weather. What we need is blankets,' interrupted Les. 'Will you shut up and listen. The white paint they gave us to camouflage the tanks wasn't enough for more than a smear or two. But hotel means beds means sheets, lovely white sheets, means camouflage.' So they borrowed some sheets, swathed the tank and, in the mid-distance, were the best disguised tank in the squadron.

Lieutenant Tony Faulkner, prospecting a farm for possible fresh milk, found and released a local Resistance girl heroine, a priest and sixteen others from a barn where they had been locked up previous to being shot by the retreating enemy. Tony's tanks had arrived so unexpectedly that the SS had no time to carry out the intended execution.

The centre of La Roche was so jumbled with ruins that there was no place for a 30-ton Sherman to pass through. So Lloyd's tank and others stood firm and fired over the heads of the Black Watch as the infantry climbed and stumbled over the obstacles. The enemy, as usual, was making his discreet but not unbloody retreat, to avoid being caught between the Highlanders and the now advancing Americans.

Beyond La Roche Bill Robertson, with his platoon of Gordon Highlanders, found a dozen or more enemy soldiers sitting frozen solid in a wheeled troop carrier. Civilians related that overnight the men, including the driver, had been sitting dozing, apparently waiting for orders. Then seemed to have been lulled into a deep sleep by the cold. And eventually had lapsed into the deepest sleep of all.

12 JANUARY 1945:

As C Squadron moved down towards Hives, Bill Fox quipped, 'Ah, I can pronounce this one. Hives. Like Beehives. But why do the Belgians say "Heaves"?'

Fingers, feet, brains working less swiftly at 30 degrees below freezing, turret crews were numb, drivers less able to control the wayward tracks on ever deeper ice and snow. Commanders saw blurred figures through frost-misted binoculars. And the Germans had had time to dig in amid concealing woods, provide minimum heating in dug outs, know the ranges, defending this last pincer junction of the British with the resurgent Americans.

Amid the revealing snows, Sergeant Warren's tank came in sight over that deep and crisp and even field of fire. Old Bunny back in the turret, hopping to go on the quickest route to Berlin. A Panther tank, superb German creation, fired at nearly a mile's range. Giving Warren time to see the flash. Time to see the shot. Time to curse the Hun. Direct hit! Iron shards ripping off the inside of the turret acted as flying bullets, mashing the sergeant's legs. The little man was no great burden to be dragged out as the crew hastily evacuated the blazing tank and signalled for medics.

That popular joker, McKenzie, now commanding the next tank in line, looked along those blurred woods for signs of the Panther. Another unseen Panther hurled its armour-piercing shot at McKenzie, smashing the tank, causing the crew to debus frantically, though without major injury. Other troops paused for the artillery to put down a retaliatory 'stonk'.

While they waited turret crews were ordered to dismount and stamp around to keep themselves active. 'Bugger this,' mumbled Harry Graham. 'Why did we bother?' Even McGranahan, usually so cheerful, looked grim. 'After this lot, mate, I shall get up in church and disagree with the parsons. Hell is not burning in hot eternal fires. Hell is living in damn, unsheltered, freezing cold, shut up for ever in blocks of ice.' To which Tommy Tucker responded, 'Send me a message when you get there, Mac. I'd even give up whoring to get to somewhere warm.'

No. 3 Troop, meaning Snowie, Rex, Stan and Co, were sent to find a way through the thick trees to outflank the two (at least) Panthers. The artillery sent up a wall of fire where the Panthers had been, while 3 Troop joined in through the murk with their seventeen-pounder and 75s. As the barrage died down the Shermans moved forward, crashing through trees and crunching over ice. No sound or shot came now from the Panthers.

The German artillery commander changed to firing shells high into the trees above the advancing Shermans' heads. Showered with dead twigs and leaves, and menaced by more lethal fall-out, some commanders closed down. Corporal McGranahan did not. He and his crew were seething with anger about Warren. They disliked the man but admired him as a soldier. It was not the Panther commander's fault. He was doing his duty. But, in war, anger must surge, human kindness must shrivel, animal instincts must growl, vengeance must be sought. McGranahan was seeking it.

But the battle died down. The pincer was closing. One final shell burst in the trees over Hughie McGranahan's head. It slashed down with red claws of death, showering into the turret, and over the gunner's head, leaves, twigs, grit, shell particles, sharp icicles, pieces of bone, spouts of blood, spools of brain.

'Hullo, 4 Baker.' (The operator's voice.) 'Hit by HE high in trees. Vehicle OK. Regret Sunray killed …' And away through the trees, Tommy's eyes were wet: 'My God! And me, silly bugger, just asked him to send me back a message when he gets to Hell.'

13 JANUARY 1945:

McGranahan's demise was what is often termed 'a parting shot'. The regiment was bewildered by the news that, as the American front was now safe, the 1st Northants Yeomanry were losing their association with the Highlanders, and moving to Major-General Hobart's 79th Armoured Division with its 'funnies', peculiar vehicles designed for peculiar purposes and not normal fighting tanks.

Michael Rathbone headed a column of tanks clanking through Ciney towards the railway sidings to be loaded up. He noticed none of the normal jubilation of the first liberation occasion, which could only have been a few weeks ago. He could not understand it. The Northants Yeomanry had fought a good battle. The Yanks had compensated for the first unfortunate error. The Battle of that awful Bulge had been a shock and a bloodletting but it had left the German army weaker.

Then he saw pale Belgian faces peeping out through windows at the retreating Shermans. RETREATING! 'Ah!' thought Ratters, 'Are they thinking that maybe the Germans will come yet again?' A Belgian was waving, running by the tank, jumping on, apologizing for the sullen looks, the lack of welcome. The SS, there for only a few hours, had dragged out and shot all the local Resistance men. And then left. Might come again?

A woman at a window shook her fist at Captain Michael Rathbone.

11 One More River to Cross

Dick Bates, prime eavesdropper, was again the first to hear the news. He also heard Hank's little joke about it, made to Bill Fox. Dick immediately appointed himself town crier, but a town crier passing on news in an awed whisper.

'We've got to change from C Squadron,' said Dick, tracing a letter 'C' in the dust on the plating of a Sherman. 'We're now going to be "Sea" Squadron', tracing 'Sea' in the dust. '"Sea"! See?'

'You been drinking, Dick, you silly old sausage,' queried Kempy. 'Explain what you ferkin' well mean.'

'We're going to hand in our Shermans and we're going to man ... Buffaloes. BUFFALOES!' To which somebody responded, 'You mean they're sending us to work in a zoo?'

'Listen, I'm serious. We're now in 79th which invents all these peculiar vehicles. And the Buffalo is a tank that floats on water. An amphi-bilious tank.'

'Me, I'm always bilious when I'm sailing on water,' said Johnny Howell, who had just rejoined after a bout of appendicitis.

2 FEBRUARY 1945:

The regiment found itself by the quiet Willemsvaart Canal (which name Bill Fox quickly and joyfully anglicized), launching the queer-shaped tanks that walked on water. Half-boat, half-Kangaroo infantry carrier, they looked like iron shoe-boxes with tractor fittings, and outboard motors. But they floated serenely on the still, chill canal waters.

The weather was bitterly cold and the canal frozen over. Brian Carpenter immediately found a new use for the Buffalo. Testing the driving system he blithely cruised around, smashing up sheets of ice into smaller floes and then into tiny pieces like broken crockery. He guffawed, 'Hey, chaps. This talk of crossing rivers is to deceive Hitler. We're going to invade Iceland. And these contraptions are really ice-breakers.'

8 FEBRUARY 1945:

Partly because it was raining and partly because the road was a sea of mud, Roy Beer had climbed into his driver's cab to read letters from home. A sudden stream of bullets sent a row of splashes up from the mud in front of his workshop truck. Multiple machine-gun fire rattled and a plane screamed low overhead. 'Don't worry. It's a Spitfire. He's made a mistake,' shouted somebody, waving fists.

But the flight of Spitfires swooped again and again, criss-crossing the convoy with tracer. Roy thought, 'These must be some of the captured RAF planes which, rumour has it, are being flown, still with RAF markings, by German pilots.' But he did not stay to reason it out. He opened the cab door and slid down under the lorry. More howling engines produced more tracer, flicking up a long row of mud splashes within inches of Roy's left leg. He hurriedly withdrew his leg under the lorry. The raid did not last long, but Roy's fury did. Especially when he found his tyres shot flat. In 18 inches of prime mud.

28 FEBRUARY 1945:

Blizzards, gales and frozen canals disrupted training. When the weather cleared it was a repeat of Limburg mud. Having handed in his beloved Sherman, Don Foxley was trying to lavish the same kind of mechanical care on his clumsy iron floating box. He seemed to go through tons of cotton waste as the odd vehicle churned through seas of mud. A Buffalo had no dignity on land. It was a crawling, craven, clumsy thing, responding brusquely to its master. And, as Don steered it into the fast-flowing Meuse for the first time, it wallowed like an ancient collier in a storm at sea. Being under-powered, it would go into a spin like a dead leaf in a gush of filthy water swilling down a drain. 'Horrible beast!' thought Don.

2 MARCH 1945:

A regimental proving run of the Buffaloes on the river. The river-bank looked as though it was bathed in sunset, so many red-tabbed, scarlet-hatted generals had gathered to watch: Dempsey, the top man; Ritchie of Africa, and Barker, corps commanders; 51HD's own Rennie. And a rainbow of brigadiers, CREs, GSOs, ADCs.

'What are all those buggers doing watching us?' mused Tommy Tucker, 'weighing up their chances of using us if von Runstedt breaks through again and we have to do another Dunkirk?'

3 MARCH 1945:

Colonel Doug and Lieutenant Owen became the first Northamptonshire Yeomen to set foot in Germany as they took their new scout car up to the banks of the Rhine for a 'look-see'. The colonel was contentedly smoking his old pipe which George Jelley had miraculously salvaged from the crushed ruins of the old car.

7 MARCH 1945:

Slender John Stenner had found an empty house for the crew. His commander, Captain Humphries came in and said, 'Any chance of a brew, Johnny?' John squatted to pump the Primus stove. Suddenly he was grasped in strong, brutal arms. He struggled, but to no avail. Visions of SS man-hunters crossed his mind. What a fate after surviving so many pitched battles!

Then a woman's voice sounded in his ears. 'Tommy! Lovely Tommy! I am come.' He was swung round to see a huge, sturdy Dutch woman laughing at him. 'This is my house. I go away. From Germans. Now I come back. You stay here, lovely Tommy, so Germans not come back never again no more.'

9 MARCH 1945:

A move nearer to the Rhine. Captain Humphries announced to the lady of the house that they were going. Immediately John Stenner felt those strong female arms clasp him to ample breasts, whilst the voice stated, 'Ah, but you are too young to be in the war. You should be at home with your mama!' Which caused Humphries to blow his nose rather suddenly.

'Some genius at Corps,' Hank Bevan said to Bill Fox, 'has chosen the code word "Splosh" for our full dress rehearsal over the Meuse.'

'I would have thought that "Beecher's" would have been more relevant,' responded Bill. 'Somebody's sure to fall in. Don't they hunt at Corps?'

14 MARCH 1945:

'Splosh' and a vicious-looking river. Boats revving up for launching. Much good-humoured banter. Suddenly a sharp, high voice cut through the hubbub, impressing not by volume but by expectation of obedience. 'No parading, colonel. Just battle stations. Treat me as a fly on the wall.'

'I'd squash a bloody fly on the wall, wouldn't I?' muttered Cliff Cuthbertson to Michael Hunt, who shot back 'You won't squash this one!'

This one was a small, abrupt man who came scuttling along like a beetle, talking as he went. Monty himself. Field Marshal Sir Bernard Montgomery come to look-see. The colonel muttered to David Bevan, 'Who do we have? Reliable people, commander and driver, who won't send Monty to the bottom of the river?'

Still approaching, the field marshal barked, 'I'll take that one', pointing an unerring finger at Sergeant Moralee's Buffalo. Bill Fox, standing close to Moralee, mouthed, 'Bugger this one up and we'll all be a penal battalion serving with the French Foreign Legion.'

Moralee's driver, Litster, happened to be one of the few who had taken happily to the clumsy Buffaloes. He took the field marshal over the rushing, foaming river and back, with hardly a splash of water on the toe-caps of his shining shoes. A relieved corporal on the bank shouted 'Can you swim, sir?'

Montgomery, a fierce smile slitting his face replied, 'I didn't need to. I *am* with the Northants Yeomanry, am I not?'

As cheering sounded along the bank, David Bevan thought, 'Clever! Bull's-eye for morale!'

19 MARCH 1945:

The regiment's final move towards the Rhine ended the day in the German town of Calcar. Shorty Coleman was, he said, 'liberating Germany', having found a large barrel of brandy in a ruined cellar. With others he rolled the barrel down the street but found that, at their allocated billet, the barrel was too big to pass through the door. *Nil desperandum!* They attacked the harmless barrel with machetes, splitting a hole large enough to effect the transfer of the brandy from barrel to mess-tins to bath.

Don Foxley, the strict Baptist, became involved in a more serious incident, after his mates had been experimenting with German wine, beer and Schnapps. Wandering along a row of shops, one said, 'Look at all that bloody wealth. You'd have thought losing the war the Jerries wouldn't have anything left in their ferking shops. Look at that china, like we never had in *our* house. And jewellery there.'

Others agreed. 'We couldn't afford that stuff at home. I'm not bloody well leaving that for some Nazi bugger to enjoy after the war.' Don was worried. 'That'd be looting. A crime. Get shot at dawn.' But months of bitter fighting, frustration, loss of friends, wounding, freezing and now to see exquisite china in an enemy shop?

'Bash up the bloody lot! Show 'em what *kaput* really means. Ferkin' Nazis!' Picking up expensive cups, jugs, plates, crystal glasses, ornaments; smashing them, throwing them against broken walls, treading them into dust. Two troopers used large vases as fencing swords or claymores until the ornaments were worn down to jagged remnants. And soon, nothing left to smash.

Then the beginning of despondency, a sense of failure, shame at their own purposeless fury. Troopers began to apologize to the empty shop. 'Stupid thing to do. As bad as the bloody Nazis. What was in that booze? What if some widow woman owns the shop – all she's got? We're *worse* than bloody Gestapo. Shit! That's the last time ...'

20 MARCH 1945:

Troopers, with sore heads after the late-night china shop rampage, were doubly devastated by the latest news. The colonel! Another scout car turned over. Too badly injured this time. The end of the war for him this time. Our Colonel Doug.

21 MARCH 1945:

In action tank crews cooked their own meals. Here in Calcar the cook's wagon was serving dinner in the main square. Corporal Whittles, ready with his mess tin, saw a large calibre German shell whistle over the crowd and crash into the ruins of the town hall. Another shell came down and exploded short, in a bracketing style. The next shell would be right in the middle. Where the queue stood. Some men ran. Others lay down or crouched. Whittles saw the huge shell hit the church tower, spin through the air. Swoop down. Bounce along the ground with the motion of a rugby ball. Come to rest by Jack Aris's cook's wagon, as though waiting to be served.

Men remained in a motionless tableau, hardly breathing. The shell lay there. Unexploded. Did not explode. Probably was not going to explode. They left it there, like an outcast leper in ancient times.

Michael Hunt had drawn a leave pass in the latest lottery. A week's leave in Britain. Starting 26 March. But the crossing of the Rhine was to start 23 March. Mike must wait patiently and duck frequently. Stan Upstone had gone down with what looked like food poisoning, intolerable stomach gripes. So Rex Jackson, MM, was called to command – the Buffalo driven by Mike.

Major the Lord George Scott returned from his lucky leave in London to find the colonel evacuated and himself now commanding a regiment about to fling itself into one of the greatest and most complicated military operations in history.

In the dusk Major Bevan and Captain Boardman cautiously moved along the high *Bund*, the vast built-up river bank, through which gaps had been blasted to allow the Buffaloes a less steep approach to the river. They inspected the new, incomprehensible, invisible infra-red light signals which would flash to a screen in each Buffalo with a kind of direction signal. Both officers felt exposed as the British artillery bombardment roared overhead like an unceasing multitude of express trains, answered by occasional coughs from the German guns.

22 MARCH 1945:

Kempy was writing home to his dad. The letter would never pass the squadron censor but he could give it to somebody going home on leave.

> I never knew it would come to this. Driving this crazy iron box that's not seaworthy enough to be called a boat, and not battle-worthy enough to call a tank. It simply wallows in the water, yes, just like a great beast, a Buffalo in a mud-bath. A right indignity to put a real Sherman driver in this thing. Couldn't they have used a marine, or a service corps driver, or a pioneer?
>
> Anyway, you need a decent boat to cross this river. Have you seen the Rhine in these parts? It's like a little sea: wide, deep, evil-looking, swept by fast and dangerous currents, not to mention the mortar fire from the German side. You really need a proper boat to do this job.
>
> I suppose you could say that I am still 'up front'. And it's necessary to get the Black Watch and the Gordons and the rest over this river and rush on to Berlin (with us in Shermans to support them, I hope). Perhaps some day historians will write all this up as a heroic deed. But they won't be driving a mechanical monstrosity that is an insult to decent, drooling-at-the-mouth, fly-blown-eyed, shitty-arsed buffaloes!

22–23 MARCH 1945:

On the Allied side of the Rhine massed forces gathered like locusts in a ripe cornfield. Infantry waited like one vast football crowd. Buffaloes waited like one vast boat show. Rank upon rank of trucks continued to arrive with ton upon ton of supplies. Guns, some of them to be fired now, some of them to be ferried, strewed the area like fallen logs in a hurricane-blasted forest. All waiting for the word 'Go!'

Tom Boardman adjusted his special spectacles which would enable him to discern the otherwise invisible infra-red direction signs. His crew checked the screen with its hatching of cross-wires upon which the infra-red directions could be read. Rex Jackson looked up at the artificial moonlight of searchlights playing on clouds to guide them over the pathless river, remembering a similar artificial moonlight near Caen.

Don Foxley stared through the gap in the *Bund* towards the darkly perceived river, wondering if it would be swifter than the Meuse. Brian Carpenter repeated to his driver, Titch Burnand, the magic formula for Buffalo survival, 'UPstream going in, DOWNstream coming out. Third gear IN the water. First gear LEAVING it.'

Zero hour: in the dark Hank Bevan radioed, 'Advance! Good luck!' Buffaloes in bottom gear groaned slowly up the steep slopes of the broken *Bund* and lapsed into giddy slides waterwards as they cleared the top. Tom Boardman monitored the waves of vehicles, loaded mainly with thronged Highlanders this trip, twelve Buffaloes in each wave, but Tom thought they looked most like lines of crabs, pointing squat prows upstream. Fighting the current. Being driven down-river. Aiming sideways always for the far bank.

Michael Hunt drove his Buffalo scrabbling up the slope which was supposed to be a gap, toppling over at the top, then pointing down into the low, obscure waters. Rex Jackson thought it was the Ardennes all over again, tanks sliding down icy slopes, choosing their own route. But, instead of soft snowdrifts, there was an unseen, unknown, hungry, foaming river. Don Foxley, his craft sliding into the waters, thought this was worse than Raamsdonk.

Brian Carpenter's Buffalo had to load a Wasp, a Canadian flame-thrower mounted on a Bren gun carrier, whilst a squad of burly Nova Scotia Higlanders had to squeeze in too. The gap in the *Bund* had collapsed so Titch Burnand had to climb his vehicle nearly 30 feet from ground level. At the summit the overloaded Buffalo poised, then dropped its bows and hurtled like a comet down at the river.

With an explosive splash the vehicles seemed still to be nose-diving to the bottom. Water washed right over the driver's hatch, which Titch frantically wrenched shut, shouting 'We're sinking!' Even the bronzed veterans from Nova Scotia paled perceptibly. 'Rev, Titch, rev!' shouted Carpenter. A tremendous thrust of engine revolutions caused the Buffalo to come surging to surface level like a submarine bursting up, after which it resumed its normal placid turtle waddle through the waves sent up by dozens of other vehicles.

The night was brightened by the artificial moonlight but distorted into alternate dazzle and blindness by flashing shells, the scene reflected and further distorted by glassy, tossing waves and spume trails. In this lurid, crashing, battering confusion, Corporal Whittles's ferry came to shore. The ramp was dropped and Highlanders rushed off towards the mysterious, hidden morasses beyond. Before the tank men could raise the ramp the night was riven by the most brilliant rashes of fire as a Highlander exploded bodily. Others staggered, fell, crawled forward, lay still. Another infantryman stood up and a mine drove fangs of fire into his legs.

'Keep the ramp down!' yelled Whittles, 'and for Christ's sake stay on board all of you.' He himself ran down the ramp, trod in what might be the footmarks of the infantry, caught a fallen man by the collar and, heedless of the man's injuries, dragged him up the ramp. Fetched another. And another. Eight. Blood streamed amid the water splashes on the ramp. Distantly a feeble voice cried, 'Medics! Medics! Help!' But Whittles's orders were clear ('No landing!'). It had to be 'Ramp up! Driver, back off!'

Yorkshireman Wilf Mylan, sometime squadron pianist, unloaded on the far bank. The next sight would be burned on his retinas in the greens and blues from the brightest of explosions. He saw a wounded British soldier hurrying towards him from about 20 yards away. 'Down ramp!' he called to Johnny Taylor, 'I'll go get him if necessary.' But a Schu mine burst under the soldier, wrapping him around with flame, a red flare which showed that his foot had been blown off. He staggered forward. A second mine burst crimson and flailing. He was gashed, and burned, and writhed in his death agonies. A third mine blew him bodily off the ground. The body fell in a wild somersault, landing on a fourth mine, which blew the body to pieces and catapulted the head on to the ramp of Wilf's Buffalo.

Rex and Mike watched their Black Watch platoon double away across the watery wilderness, where land looked only like a calmer river. 'Up ramp! Back off!' As Mike responded deftly, another Buffalo, its driver confused by the traitorous light and whirling currents, crashed into Rex's craft. Mike's engine stalled. The river caught the clumsy iron box and tugged it, spun it, rushed it away downstream. To where the enemy still held the immediate bank. Mike saw his lucky London leave being spent in a German prisoner of war camp.

He forced the engine to start up again, applying dangerous revolutions. But where were they? After spinning violently several times they were both mentally bewildered and physically sick. But their briefing had been precise, illustrated with a scale model, even showing a large crane beside a railway line. Rex gave a shout of gladness to see the large crane in black silhouette against the ruddy sky. Mike might still get his leave. He aimed the Buffalo at the *Bund* but struck it at a place where there was no gap. In something like an apoplexy of despair, he slammed out even more engine revs, driving the Buffalo up a mountainous slope which it had never been designed to attempt.

Stan Hilton's Buffalo, like others, was provided with a Polsten cannon on a mounting, fired by a sensitive trigger cable. River crossed. Load of Argyll and Sutherlands delivered. Sailing home. The gun pointing towards the home bank. And the gun started firing!

Nobody had ordered fire. But, as though handled by some newborn ghost, it was firing at any Yeomanry or staff officers who might be watching Stan's arrival home. A wild rush to the gun, interspersed by two more bursts of spontaneous firing, revealed that the hastily-constructed gun mounting had worked loose, allowing the cannon to swing far enough to put pressure on its own firing cable in a way nobody thought possible. Stan (now a corporal) and crew crept in to the home bank, feeling like dangerous renegades fighting their own regiment. But the sky was still too dark from them to be recognized by some highly indignant staff officer.

Les Carr's ankle still ached and had come up swollen again from his Loon-op-Zand injury. But he was refusing to go back for treatment until this exciting mission had ended. Waiting for Les's Buffalo was a long, seventeen-pounder anti-tank gun. Basically too large for the Buffalo it was accommodated on two large baulks of timber on top of the tank. Wedged with kapok-filled floats the gun rode above the Buffalo like a parasite bird on a real buffalo's back. The enormous weight made the craft wallow even more than normal. Les drove into the water as slowly as possible.

A great cracking sound, like high explosive hitting home, sounded behind Les's ear. One of the timbers had broken. The weight of the gun tilted the Buffalo over, one side shipping water. Les was considering prayer when another crash shook them to the core. A strange Buffalo, also out of control, had rammed them amidships. The river pulled the two vessels apart as angry cries shrilled from the decks.

'Stupid ruddy imbeciles! Mucking oafs! Morons! Couldn't even find your own mother's paps! Try watching with your eyes instead of your arses! Where d'y' think yer ferking are – the dodgems?'

Les did not have time to trade courtesies. The collision had snapped the second timber and righted the Buffalo. But the gun, with its incongruously long muzzle, had settled down like a giant eagle upon the struggling Buffalo in what can aptly be termed the mating position. Beset by visions of imminent drowning, Les carefully nursed more power into the engine. Mercifully the vessel grounded on the far bank. Spurred by the momentum, the great gun considerately rolled on and unloaded itself farther into Germany.

It was still early on the 23rd when RSM George Jelley conducted the Highlanders' general, Rennie, down to a returning Buffalo. The general was no longer the sheepskin-disguised traffic warden of the Ardennes, but paraded in full glory of red trimmings, and surrounded by staff.

'Sail at attention,' smirked a Yeoman from the depths of the landing craft. 'I heard that,' responded the general. 'Never mind the bull! Just you get me over this bloody river safely, and I'll thank you. But good show, Yeomanry, so far! Keep it up.' He sat like an interested tourist, watching the Buffaloes fight back and forth through the currents; refusing to duck when high spouts of water betrayed German shell fire; jaw jutting in the approved manner; eyes swivelling again and again to penetrate the normal fog of battle. 'I have had a peculiar feeling, something between pessimism and dismay, about this plan,' he was heard to say to a major, 'wondering if it was to be another Arnhem. But our Yeomanry friends seem to be delivering.'

He and his retinue disembarked, waved in a friendly fashion to the crew, and ploughed through the mud into the wilds of mist, smoke and continuing explosion flashes. The Buffalo waited for wounded men to be loaded. Usually it was one man carrying a comrade, or two stretcher bearers depositing their burdens – some awake and joking, others already stiffening. Fifteen minutes passed.

The ramp was delayed because this time it was an entire procession escorting a single stretcher. The Highland general lay on that stretcher, his face pallid, his clothes torn, his red trimmings besmirched with brown mire. 'Artillery fire,' whispered the staff captain to a trooper. 'Killed him outright. Go steady. Take him back.' The returning Buffalo resembled, in some watchers' minds, a medieval funeral barge, taking a dead King Arthur away through the mists and home to Camelot.

The SSM on the home bank was not so poetic. He said to the Buffalo commander, 'Ol' Churchill's coming over tomorrow. For Gawd's sake don't bring that bugger back wrapped in a blanket.'

24 MARCH 1945:

Stan Hilton's Buffalo was cautiously loading another Wasp, the Canadian flame-thrower. 'Nasty things these, Watch it,' ordered the infantry sergeant. The Wasp on its carrier base was a fast tractor but difficult to control. It failed to brake, crashed into the Buffalo, rupturing the flame fuel container. Liquid, sticky, warming, smelling of petrol splashed over

Stan's overalls, across his face and into his eyes. He reacted, raising his fists to rub his eyes.

'DON'T!' cried the Nova Scotian sergeant, grabbing Stan's arms. 'Get back to the aid post fast, laddy. And don't light any flaming cigarettes.' Stan felt himself loaded onto a stretcher, although his lower body was unaffected. Strong hands restrained his own hands. He was quickly carried into what sounded like a low cave, echoing with guttural German voices, some in extreme pain.

Firm but kind hands poured a cooling potion over his eyelids, fussed about him, swabbed his face. 'See if you can open up now, corporal.' Reluctantly Stan opened his eyes, half expecting to see the blackness of the permanently blind. A harassed but smiling medical officer, an unfamiliar Highland doctor, pronounced, 'You'll do. You wouldn't have done, if somebody had lit that stuff. Your middle name would have been Guy Fawkes. But you'll need to go down the line for convalescence, sonny.'

'Convalescence?' worried Stan. 'I don't want convalescence. I'm OK. They need me on that silly Buffalo. Not many people can work those awkward boxes. We're still flat out delivering supplies and we've lost casualties.'

'What's the problem? Hilton, isn't it?' This was the more familiar voice of the Northants Yeomanry's own MO, Captain MacIntyre. 'Don't let them send me back, sir. You know how important it is for us to keep those ferries running. Just for a day or two more?' The two doctors conferred. 'Very well, corporal. Off you go if your legs will carry you. But, if your eyes play up, come back here, toot sweet. No heroics! That's an order.' Stan snapped 'Yessir!' and fled – mainly from the gruelling sight of so many wrecked German bodies, bloodily exposed and under grim treatment which, to the layman, was as frightening as the original wounding.

25 MARCH 1945:

'That's two days' successful crossings. We seem to have got this job all neatly worked out and wrapped up. Not much to go wrong, now,' said John Stenner, considered by his huge Dutch hostess to be too young for the war. He was standing with Sergeant Eric King watching the day's second uneventful disembarkation of hurrying Highlanders. There had been only a few flashes and splashes of German response. 'Pooh!' thought Johnny, 'Nothing like St-Aignan.'

Charlie Broadbent stood at the bottom of the ramp, fearful like most tank men of straying too far on strange land which might be liberally sown with anti-personnel mines. Ghastly things, those. Even the frail plates of a crudely swimming Buffalo were a safer haven for tank men. Safety is what you know.

With an almost artistic beauty, in the way these things happen, and with infinite time for appreciation which the watching eye and perceiving mind allow, a sunburst of red glory rose from the ground around Charlie's legs, followed by the rending screech of the speeding shell which had already landed. The sunburst aged into a thunderstorm of billowing black clouds and blinding, spreading light, transforming Charlie into the figure of a glowing messenger from beyond space. He began to rise, disintegrate and topple. The furious blast flung him back up the ramp as though the earth were disowning him. The full ear-shattering rending of explosion, and its grilling blast, tore at Johnny and Eric whilst they were still flinging themselves down on the water-swilled, hard iron plates of the Buffalo.

Eric crawled forward while Johnny waited hesitantly. Eric shook his head. 'Never had a bloody chance, poor sod. Equally, never knew a thing about it.' Still on hands and knees the sergeant said softly, 'Find your own way home, Charlie boy.'

26 MARCH 1945:

Young Stenner was haunted by yesterday's sight. It heightened the natural fear for one's own skin. But no way was he going to show it. Nevertheless, Sergeant King noticed the look of relief on the boy's face when they were given a different job, ferrying out thick steel tow-ropes to sunken Buffaloes on the river-bed, prior to specialist units undertaking recovery work.

Rex and Mike were stranded beyond the *Bund*. Scraping noises from the tracks had alerted them to damage to a number of 'grousers', heavy iron track extensions to cope with soft ground. They crawled around in the mud, cursing their luck. 'What a way to prepare for homeland leave,' grunted Mike. The grousers were rusty and difficult to unbolt. Damaged ones from one track had to be transferred to the other, at least to enable the short journey to the fitters.

They moved to the command post for orders. In the corner of the post the popular squadron captain of C, Ken Todd, was being treated for wounds. Michael Rathbone was also there, standing whilst an orderly bandaged his elbow. Rex heard Ratters ask the MO how Todd was. 'Clean wound on the outside which encourages him, especially as he hasn't felt any great pain yet. But all tangled up inside the stomach and the back. Should survive, but how many years can a body continue to function like that?'

Outside the post Rex was handed a tin. 'What's this?' he asked. 'Self-sealing hot drinks. New idea. Lovely grub,' replied Jack Aris. It was indeed hot but not too lovely. Harry Graham's Buffalo was parked there with a great shell hole bored through it. 'Thank God I wasn't inside that death trap when it happened,' said Harry, also holding a self-sealing hot drink. 'Hey, Mike! Not gone on leave yet? You'll need to duck and weave a bit still before you get there.'

Their Buffalo quickly repaired, Rex and Mike set off on one more journey. There was a general order that Buffaloes should cross the river only in groups under command of an officer. However, Bill Fox was waiting at the *Bund* shouting, 'Don't hang about. Damn the standing orders. You know the way. Have a pleasant cruise.' At the far bank, where they now drove a little way inland to unload, they found little Trooper Jock MacGregor sitting in a quickly dug hole, waving his arms and shouting, 'Mines! Dinna gae tae the reet. Mines! Nae tae the reet.' Jock swore that a German patrol had passed only a few minutes before and that one German had actually trodden on his helmet as he ducked into the hole. 'Psychiatrist's case,' grinned Mike to Rex.

They almost became psychiatrists' cases themselves. As they drove into the river for Mike's last homeward leg (ending London), a batch of Moaning Minnies fell around them. Mike accelerated into deeper waters. More Minnies fell, still at their range. Mike took evasive action like a naval destroyer at speed. Batches of half a dozen Minnies seemed to follow. 'They must have an observer somewhere,' shouted Rex. 'Damn 'em,' Mike shouted back, 'I WILL go on leave', again driving the long-suffering craft beyond regulation revs.

This time they found the gap in the *Bund*. Bill Fox, waiting there, bawled, 'Now shoot off to England, Hunt. What are you damn well loitering about here for?'

27 MARCH 1945:

The days of harrowing crossings, with little or no sleep, found crews with bloodshot eyes, drooping eyelids and bad breath. Given a brief break – because ferrying went on day and night – Johnny Howell's crew thankfully stripped down, out of their oily, sweaty overalls, lay down on the engine covers and instantly fell asleep. Until 'Wake up you silly sods' bawled the irate SSM, banging on the Buffalo's resounding hull with an empty shell case. 'You'll get court-martialled. The squadron is away.'

Johnny Howell took a great leap into the driver's seat wearing only vest and pants. Started the engine. Splashed into the wake of the squadron. The engine stalled. That meant the main pump failed to operate. That meant water began to fill the crude vessel. That meant minutes before the ship went under. Johnny fiddled switches, pedals, gears. Nothing happened.

'Where's the bloody lifebelts?' shouted somebody. 'Back on the bloody *Bund,*' replied another voice.

At the moment of ultimate catastrophe an even more belated Buffalo hove alongside and cast a tow-rope. In the scramble Johnny saw all his clothes going overboard. Still half naked he jumped to reach them, capsized, and went plunging deep into Rhine waters. He surfaced, blowing and spitting petrol- and oil-tainted water.

'Come out of there, Johnny,' yelled his mates. 'You're the ugliest looking mermaid in the whole of Germany.'

Charlie Robertson, now a major, came back from leave to find that his Black Watch company had been ferried across and then disappeared into oblivion. Charlie took a ferry to the edge of oblivion. Within oblivion, at a vital bridge at Empel, massed German counter-attacks had tried to wrest the bridge back again. Lance-Corporal McBride with only five men had held the bridge for twenty-four hours against odds of more than a hundred to one. 'It will be a Distinguished Conduct Medal for McBride,' Charlie thought.

Ratters, one elbow stiff with bandages, was sent with a composite force of Buffaloes and engineers over the Rhine, across the misty ground beyond, to set up another ferrying operation at a stretch of deep flooding which the Highlanders were having difficulty in crossing. The Buffaloes made hard work of it in the floods which hid deep, track-clogging mud.

28 MARCH 1945:

At the far side of the flood Rex Jackson, with an unknown replacement driver from reserve, found himself bogged down with recurring grouser trouble. There was nothing for it but another crawl in the mud, unbolting grousers and swopping them, flattening oneself in the mire as Moaning Minnies responded to the Highlanders' onward advance. The new driver was neither as skilful nor as helpful as Mike.

Moving again, as they approached another stretch of water they passed several grossly bloated bodies of several German soldiers. The driver went beserk. 'You're coming the wrong way. We're in the German lines. You'll get us all killed. I'm not going any farther.'

Rex, the mildest of men, bespectacled and undemonstrative, slowly pulled out his revolver. 'You'll drive this crate. And you'll drive it where I tell you. I've never fired this gun at a German yet. But, so help me God, I'll fire it at you. Advance!' – thinking 'My bluff! He'll never fall for it.' But, just as quickly as he had paled, the driver blushed, became sullen, climbed into his seat and started to cross the water ahead.

Time seemed to have stood still. Nothing in the world was distinct. The rushing, greedy waters were eternal. Rex mused that the shades of Hades itself lay beyond this Stygian river and they were the ferrymen. And who pays the ferryman? Then the *Bund* appeared out of the mists. The gap. Refuge. Reality. A first-gear scramble up over the rubble.

The mists cleared. The sun shone through. The place was empty. Infrared signs still blinked unnoticed. The locust army had gone. All of them. Far away into a land of Lorelei and Erl Kings and Götterdämmerung. And of SS, Gestapo and Hitler.

12 Victor Easy?

10 APRIL 1945:

Buffaloes had been returned to compound and the old Shermans restored to joyful Yeomen. Expecting to bash on to Berlin, or at least to Bremen, they found themselves back in West Holland to guard against rumoured Nazi 'werewolf' raiders over the Maas.

Two Geordies were discussing strategy. 'This bloody war's gaan on for ever. When's it gaan to end?' asked Cliff Cuthbertson. 'Why aye, it's still farther from 'ere to Berlin than awa' from N'castle to Land's End, man,' observed Jimmy Sables. 'Aye, and I'll tell y' what! We'll be fighting the roody Ruskies after we've finished wi' Jerry.'

2 MAY 1945:

The regiment fired another 'all stations Yoke' barrage across the Maas. Then the abhorrent news flashed through: 'Back to Buffaloes for a crossing of the River Ems.'

4 MAY 1945:

Stan Hilton and Sergeant Falconer walked into their billet to find the family seated for a meal but bowed in profound prayers. The Yeomen waited silently in the doorway. Then, as the family sat up, Falconer tried to joke, 'Were you praying for liberation?'

The father laughed and shouted, '*Praying* for, friends? *Thanking* for! Liberation of all Netherlands. The *Boche* has capit ... capul ... *zich overgeven* ... over given! Ask for, you say, armistize? We hear BBC. Thank you God! Thank you friends!'

Meanwhile Captain Rathbone had been summoned for an advance party to Enschede, prior to crossing the River Ems. Then, for the last time in the war, the orders were changed. Destination now: Zwolle by the Zuider Zee.

7 MAY 1945:

Ian Carmichael, actor, now brigade major, 33rd Armoured, signed an order to the 1st Northants Yeomanry: 'Cease fire!'

A new code word: VE Day. Victory in Europe. VE, in wireless speak was Victor Easy. Easy? Right from the Normandy beaches to the Rhine *Bunds* no Yeoman had found himself to be an easy victor. But it *was* Victor Easy. Victory day! Liberation! *Bevrijding* to the Dutch.

Zwolle was a fine city for a final destination. Tank crews were welcomed into Dutch homes. The cheering, honking liberation traffic was held up again and again by smiling policemen so that a Yeoman might cross the street. Girls, elderly women, even normally staid Dutch men, embraced the Liberators and began to dance with them. Dancing erupted into singing as more and more civilians persuaded more and more Yeomen – still bewildered from the mists of Limburg, the snows of the Ardennes, the floods of the Rhine – to join in a wild, joyous ballet that lasted into a torchlight revel, like a pagan rite, which nobody wanted to end.

For Michael Rathbone the special delight was simply eating smoked eel, and being challenged by Dutch enthusiasts to a chess match.

9 MAY 1945 – D + 337:

The final curtain call to this epic pageant of war was to take place, for the 1st Northants Yeomanry, in the vast Grote Kerk, in the presence of civic dignitaries. As RSM George Jelley proudly watched his men march smartly to the church and then modestly shuffle up the aisle, he pondered, 'We wouldn't have saved so many in '14–18!' The regimental padre, released from his routine of hurried burials, announced the hymn, 'Now thank we all our God'. Lessons were said, prayers intoned, feet became restless, coughs were barely suppressed.

Until: 'Regiment and congregation will stand whilst the Regimental Roll of Honour is read.' The list of our dead. Our recently dead. 'We will remember them.'

Trooper Shellam, W. The first: around that cursed corner in Normandy, and into the sights of that waiting Panther.

Lance-Corporal Madelaine, R.H. 'Tommy' ... Sergeant Valentine, G.A. ... Corporal Hickson, F.E. Those lovely people. Great comrades. Always reliable. We do remember ...

Trooper R. ... Trooper R. ... Say those names again, Padre, run into each other, overlying, conjoined, as they died and as their bodies were buried, one charred flesh indivisible.

SSM Turton, S. ... Captain Crofts, R.J. Jimmy Kerr remembering the night march, the tank hit four times, blazing, a funeral pyre, hatches jammed shut, Jimmy and pals inside. THAT, Padre, was a time for prayer!

Sergeant Finney, F.G. ... Sergeant Goosey, J.T. Ray Ager back driving Tom Boardman's tank on that night march. Little Ray, the front man in all that Allied mechanized host, yet surviving. Why? When all these names ... ?

Corporal Stanley, J.W. ... Trooper Wellbelove, E.W. Fred Gibbs remembering his previous regiment, 148 RAC, almost annihilated like the 2nd Northants Yeomanry, firing at a Tiger; our shots bouncing off like tennis balls; his shots turning us into an inferno; me, unheroic Fred leaning back into the turret to pull the blazing gunner out by his epaulets. Did he survive?

Sergeant Bamford, C.T. ... Lieutenant McColl, R.S. Cliff Cuthbertson remembering St-Aignan, and his commander, Mr Brown, being wounded; and Arthur Dwight taking command, calling Cliff up from co-driver to take over as turret operator; and an 88 shot crashing right through the co-driver's seat, past a shocked Michael Hunt, boring through the very seat Cliff had left seconds earlier.

Lance-Corporal Reboles, G. ... Lieutenant Green, E.V. Johnny Byrne remembering a hesitant German surrendering near Vught; an idiot on our side firing, killing the Jerry, causing a further battle; and thirty human beings – be they Germans – killed unnecessarily, almost criminally.

Sergeant Danson, K.T. ... Trooper Blakiston, J.R. Harry Graham wondering 'Will Arthur Dwight make it?'; Ron West worried about Harry Brown, last seen engulfed in flames; Jack Aris pondering, 'How will Eric Good play golf with only one arm?', all of us hoping that they, Eric Marchant, others, will survive, come home.

Sergeant Huitson, R.A. ... Wilf Mylan remembering a Canadian, leg gashed, body shattered beyond belief, still breathing; wasps swarming on the bloody flesh of his leg, maggots already emerging; the medic saying, 'Best chance is bandage the wasps, maggots, all into the leg – provide some leeching'; the mass of wasps crunching into the raw meat under the khaki field dressing; in battle you learned about Nature's realities.

Corporal McGranahan, H.B. ... All of us wondering: in that eternal moment when time stands still, that moment we had all known as, powerless to move within time, we had watched Death hurtle, flaming and black, towards us, in that moment as the spirit plunged into the darkening tunnel, or hovered a moment at the brink of a bedazzling golden sunrise, did they know of our unceasing love for them?

And Trooper Williams, T.H., the youngest of our departed ...

The church parade ends. Blazon their names on wall memorials in school halls. Sculpt their sacrifice on stone monuments in village squares. And may the widows enjoy their meagre pensions.

The church parade ends. War ends. We rush out into the sunshine amid the swarming, cheering crowds of Zwolle. Into a torrent of gaiety and imbecility as powerful as the rushing waters of the Rhine. But already some of us are agitated, dispirited, feverish. Gnawed at by virulent maggots of insanity. Bred by the flies of persisting fear and horror. Hatched in dank and inaccessible recesses of the mind. The festering of invisible wounds.

There will be no first-aid posts for us down the long road back to normality. No psychiatrists for our unburdening. No easy return to the confessional of priests. Only our own ghosts gone on ahead. And waiting for us.

Among our families and friends and workmates maybe we shall bear the ignominy of shuddering with visible fear, throwing ourselves to the floor in an epilepsy of memory, hiding pale-cheeked under some table as the shells of lightning flash and the guns of thunder blast the embattled skies.

There will be no baling out of the entrapping nightmares, perhaps causing the assault upon wives at a frenzied midnight awakening, or the brutality to children after the stress of daily work. And our vain worship in church, and our bungled lovemaking at home, pervaded by the echoes of the obscene songs the old soldiers used to sing: the sodomy with Salome and the lechery with Peggy O'Neill.

And in the renewal of self-seeking, the self-importance, the self-centredness of peacetime, Rex and Mike and Hickie and Hank Bevan will need to be about their own business. They will not be there, with their concern, their forced optimism, their unshirking protection when those new battles commence.

Nor will Tommy Madelaine (lost in those first shots at La Taille): nor will little Wellbelove (smiling in that final sleep beyond St-Aignan): nor will Bobby McColl (sliced to human shambles in Raamsdonk): nor will Hughie McGranahan (cruelly obliterated at the very last under the trees of the Ardennes): nor will Vaughan Green (his last poem encrusted with blood in his pocket).

Or will they come softly out of that wiser darkness, to guide us ways we do not know?